Coming Soon

Coming Soon

*Film Trailers and the Selling
of Hollywood Technology*

KEITH M. JOHNSTON

McFarland & Company, Inc., Publishers
Jefferson, North Carolina, and London

Elements of chapters one and two appeared in the
Journal of Popular Film and Television 36, 3 (Fall 2008).
An earlier version of chapter four appeared in
Convergence 14, 2 (May 2008), pp. 145–160.

LIBRARY OF CONGRESS CATALOGUING-IN-PUBLICATION DATA

Johnston, Keith M., 1973–
　　Coming soon : film trailers and the selling of Hollywood
technology / Keith M. Johnston.
　　　p.　　cm.
　　Includes bibliographical references and index.

　　ISBN 978-0-7864-4432-8
　　softcover : 50# alkaline paper

　　1. Film trailers.　 2. Advertising — Motion pictures.
I. Title.
PN1995.9.T68J64　2009
384'.83 — dc22　　　　　　　　　　　　　　　　2009021312

British Library cataloguing data are available

©2009 Keith M. Johnston. All rights reserved

*No part of this book may be reproduced or transmitted in any form
or by any means, electronic or mechanical, including photocopying
or recording, or by any information storage and retrieval system,
without permission in writing from the publisher.*

Cover image ©2009 RubberBall Productions.

Manufactured in the United States of America

*McFarland & Company, Inc., Publishers
　Box 611, Jefferson, North Carolina 28640
　www.mcfarlandpub.com*

To Beccy, for believing

Acknowledgments

My interest in trailers was first sparked when I spent a year abroad studying film at the University of California, Santa Barbara. In Chuck Wolfe's 101B: History of Cinema class, I saw a print of the first synchronized sound trailer, for *The Jazz Singer* (1927). Although trailers had always been a part of my cinema-going experience, watching that first Vitaphone trailer made me aware of the format as a historical entity in its own right, and one that seemed indivisible from the technologies that informed the production, distribution and exhibition practices of cinema.

Inspired by this to write "something about trailers and film history," I produced a series of undergraduate film history essays, with support from Chuck Wolfe and Mike Cormack at the University of Stirling. After a break from academia I returned to the topic of trailers for my Masters and doctoral research, supervised by Aylish Wood at the University of Kent. A superb sounding board over those four years, Aylish's advice, suggestions, and critical eye never failed to improve my notion of what this book could cover and what I was capable of producing.

I would like to thank the United Kingdom Arts & Humanities Research Council, whose decision to fund a doctoral project on trailers made the subsequent pages possible. I am also grateful to the University of Kent's Colyer-Ferguson fund, which awarded me a foreign travel grant in 2005. Without access to archives in Britain and the U.S. the historical end of this project would be sadly lacking. Special thanks therefore to Barbara Hall (AMPAS Margaret Herrick Library); Hayden Guest (USC/Warner Bros. Archive); Lauren Buisson and Julie Graham (UCLA Arts Library–Special Collections); David F. Miller (20th Century–Fox Legal Files); Mark Quigley (UCLA Film & Television Archive); Kathleen Dickson (NFTVA Viewing Service); and all the staff at the BFI Library.

Bill Seymour, Paul N. Lazarus, John Sittig, and Simon Ashberry all agreed to be interviewed on different aspects of trailer history. Bill and Paul gave me an invaluable insight into National Screen Services, the trailer production company responsible for so many of the classic film trailers, while John and Simon's input clarified central concepts within chapters one and four. Their full interviews are transcribed in the appendices.

This particular "coming attraction" has taken four years to arrive. I want to thank my colleagues, Su Holmes, Andrew Klevan, Alex Clayton, David Turner, Marit Knollmueller and Nigel Mather, along with my friends, Alan Colquhoun, Jennifer Mau and Keri Stevens for sharing a small part of my obsession.

When I was eight, I won a *Jungle Book* coloring competition. Since then, my mom and dad have been convinced I had a future working in film. The older I get, the more I appreciate their constant support.

Finally, my wife has lived the ups and downs of this project for more years than I like to admit. For her patience, encouragement and a seemingly never-ending supply of tequila, this is dedicated to her.

Contents

Acknowledgments	vii
Introduction	1
ONE • "Something BIG Is Coming!"	27
TWO • The Rival Screen	60
THREE • Technology and Genre	91
FOUR • The Mobile Trailer	124
Conclusion	153
Appendix I. Interview with Bill Seymour	163
Appendix II. Interview with John Sittig	168
Appendix III. Interview with Paul N. Lazarus	171
Appendix IV. Interview with Simon Ashberry	174
Chapter Notes	179
Trailer-ography	191
Bibliography	201
Index	211

Introduction

The "coming attraction" trailer offers us a unique window on film history and debates within film studies. Compelling images for stars like Humphrey Bogart were created, expanded and honed for audiences through the trailers for *The Petrified Forest* (1935), *The Maltese Falcon* (1941) and *The Big Sleep* (1946), while genre trailers centered visual and thematic motifs such as the romantic-horrific characters and shadowy Expressionist *mise-en-scène* in Universal horror trailers for *Dracula* (1931), *Frankenstein* (1932) and *The Mummy* (1933). *Becky Sharp*'s 1935 trailer featured an early public demonstration of (and education in) Technicolor's new three-strip color process, and the disparate British and American trailers for *Alfie* (1966) displayed different concepts of British identity. Directors positioned themselves as a central creator in the trailers for *Psycho* (1961), *The Ten Commandments* (1956) and *Quiz Show* (1994), while the appearance of both the female body and the (dominant) disembodied male voiceover raise issues of how previews deal with contemporary cultural and societal shifts in portrayals of gender and sexuality. Stardom, genre, technology, national identity, auteurism and representation: the film trailer is a distinctive source of historical and textual information that allows us to investigate how the Hollywood film industry (or any other national cinema) saw itself, imagined its products, and built up its public persona.

Yet the film trailer remains an overlooked resource within both film history and film analysis.[1] Despite the resonance they offer to key debates, critical and academic opinion on these previews has not developed much from Howard T. Lewis' 1933 definition of them as advertisements that offered a selection of "interesting and colorful" highlights.[2] In more recent years, a negative critical slant has begun to emerge: Andy Medhurst colorfully described trailers as "pumped up bullies, yelling out torrents of absolutes," while BBFC examiner Mike Bor noted they were "manipulative pieces" and,

A typical star image from *The Maltese Falcon* trailer (1941), centering Humphrey Bogart as the main star attraction within the film.

as such, "not a matter of aesthetics or teaching ... a potentially harmful experience."[3]

One of the central aims of this book is to rehabilitate the trailer, to push beyond the relative paucity of academic discourse surrounding these previews and to show how essential the trailer text can be within all avenues of film studies. To accomplish this goal, I will posit that analysis should treat the trailer text as a unique short film, rather than a lesser (abbreviated) form of the feature film. The trailer itself has been historically regarded as a transient element of cinema, defined by particular temporal and spatial conditions—projected in cinemas weeks in advance of the feature—and only considered in relation to the film being advertised. Because of this, trailers have never been seen as unique creations. Until the advent of the Internet, they were not seen after the initial cinema screening, they were not well archived, and they bore no mark of an individual voice or producer. While the feature film has been analyzed and explored as a composed and constructed entity, the trailer is looked upon as a compilation format justified purely by economic results. This limited view of trailers has meant they have rarely been regarded as highly structured, complex films in their own right, with specific conventions and aesthetic qualities that are distinct from the feature film.

This current project advances the argument that trailers are revelatory texts that add to the overall picture of film history. Trailers began to appear around 1912, became the film industry's primary sales technique through the 1920s and 1930s (alongside other studio-controlled publicity materials such as press books, posters and slides), and are a key text in understanding the creation and delineation of distinct sales messages and formats. The parallel narrative trailers offer to film history adds to academic debates around the development of the Hollywood star system, the definition of genre characteristics (particularly the visual iconography of gangster, horror and musical genres), and, a central focus for this book, the introduction of new technology. Although trailers are part of film marketing, they remain the sole audio-visual format within promotional materials and are treated throughout as unique, individual objects of study. Where relevant, the chapters will reflect on the concurrent press books, film websites, newspaper commentaries, and interviews with producers that cross over with, and influence, trailer production. But the primary focus remains the trailer text itself, and what analysis of that text (in its historical context) can add to our understanding of film history. A closer consideration of the process of theorizing and demonstrating such analysis will follow, but I want to begin by addressing other academic opinions on trailers that have preceded and informed my own work.

Trailer study is not a widely recognized field. Only two books and a handful of articles have devoted any time to these unique texts.[4] However, since trailers are part of an organized marketing campaign, the idea of studying trailers sits within the developing work in film marketing. My own interest in trailers was, in part, a response to Janet Staiger's article "Announcing Wares, Winning Patrons, Voicing Ideals: Thinking about the History and Theory of Film Advertising."[5] Staiger's work opened up the possibility of seeing film advertising as more than an adjunct of the feature film, that it was possible to think about, and analyze, these promotional texts in their own right. Her suggestion for possible routes into the study of film advertising and marketing is largely economic, and contains a call for more work on the reception of promotional materials, but it legitimized the notion that such materials were within the purview of film studies. Similar justification came from Barbara Klinger's work on Douglas Sirk, which analyzed recurring traits in marketing and promotional items for films such as *Written on the Wind* (1956) to reveal how they were positioned within the "adult" film genre.[6] By focusing on posters, trailers, lobby cards and media reporting, Klinger explored the social sphere where promotional texts and audiences interact: while my own work on trailers does not cover reception studies, the analysis throughout this book follows the work of Staiger and Klinger, revealing the importance of the trailer as a site of negotiation between the studio and the intended audience.

Previous trailer studies have taken other approaches to trailer analysis than the combination of textual analysis and historical context that this book will develop. One of the first academic articles on trailers, Mary Beth Haralovich and Cathy Root Klaprat's "*Marked Woman* and *Jezebel*: The Spectator in the Trailer," defined the trailer as an adjunct of the feature film being advertised.[7] Their argument was based on the premise that the trailer's structure mirrored the feature narrative, using titles to bridge any spatial and temporal discontinuities, and ultimately punishing the figure of the "dangerous woman." The lack of close analysis of the trailer — and its own unique narrative — limits their work, particularly as the strong star image of Davis as a dangerous woman is central to the trailers for *Marked Woman* (1937) and *Jezebel* (1938), an image that remains open and active at the end of both trailer narratives, not tamed or reintegrated. Haralovich and Klaprat miss the opportunity to investigate the unique trailer narrative being created, and are too quick to assume the trailer will reproduce feature information (and ideology) intact. There is also no acknowledgment of the temporal positioning of their work — they assume that a trailer viewer has already seen the film in question, and can reconstruct the trailer in relation to that viewing. Until the advent of video, audiences would largely view trailers in advance of the feature and would not see them again after they had viewed the film. Part of the historical aspect within this current work is to use the historical network to recreate the feeling of seeing the trailer as a unique text in its own right, advertising something forthcoming (and not already seen).

Lisa Kernan's *Coming Attractions: Reading American Movie Trailers* offers a further step toward the kind of theoretical work I am developing here. The only current book-length study of trailers (in the English language), Kernan's work tries to cover the entire history of sound film, developing a master narrative of trailer history. To cope with the scope of this project, Kernan divides that history into three categories: Classical, Transitional, and Contemporary. Mirroring other master narratives, Kernan's work focuses on various trailers within these periods, identifying them as star-, genre- or narrative-based types. There is a determinism underlying a lot of her work, a suggestion that trailers are moving toward a refinement or evolution, but she never spells out exactly what this development will be. However, she does suggest a critique of film histories that valorize "industrial and institutional historiography while ... minimizing the importance ... of grounding film history within a point of view about our actual historical object, the cinematic text" — as I will demonstrate, this is a view that parallels my own.[8] Unfortunately, Kernan does not pursue this theme, adopting instead a rhetorical analytical approach to trailers, thinking of them largely in linguistic terms rather than visual — she is particularly interested in the appearance of titles and the use of dialogue and voiceover to talk to an imagined spectator. But like Haralovich and Klaprat, the approach taken toward the trailer is temporally disingenuous, never certain whether analysis should consider it as a pre-or post-filmic event. Given the limited temporal position the trailer used to inhabit within the exhibition circuit, this current project argues that the best way to understand such a text is to place it within its historical context. Kernan's call for the film text to be central to film history is one this project echoes, but within a stricter definition of the methodological borders for such analysis.

Defining those borders necessitates a consideration of the relevant academic debates around film history and close analysis, and the place of the film text within historical study. Any discussion of the process of writing film history begins with Robert Allen and Douglas Gomery's *Film History: Theory and Practice*, a pioneering work in film historiography. Allen had separately called for more concerted film history scholarship that explored "economic structures, the relationship between cinema and other forms of popular entertainment, technology, the organization of labor, or what might have gone on the billions of times the texts of film history were "read" by viewers" as areas of investigation.[9] These elements are reiterated in *Film History: Theory and Practice*, which examines four major approaches to film history, examining the case for aesthetic, technological, economic and social film histories. Throughout the book, however, there is little sense of how analysis of the film text might function within these historical frameworks. The case study from technological history, for example, explores Gomery's work on Warner Bros.' conversion to sound. This research represents a landmark piece of film history writing that expands knowledge and challenges existing preconceptions through the use of financial and industrial research. Yet nowhere in the work on this historical moment is there any consideration of how this affected the aesthetic or structural aspects of the film texts produced (or whether such a question remained relevant).

Allen and Gomery convincingly argue their case that film history needs to expand beyond traditional sources, to move beyond production and distribution and consider film exhibition and reception. As Thomas Elsaesser identified, however, this exemplary work did not make "the films themselves ... the object of study," and even when dealing with aesthetic and social history, "where one might expect to find something about the ... quite considerable number of films we do possess, the case studies ... concentrate mainly on the many different discourses that marketing or publicity create."[10] Elsaesser refers to this moment, in the mid–1980s, as the creation of a New Film History: "which has resolutely turned its back on interpretation and on the question of what beliefs or images films shape or transmit."[11] The suggestion here is that despite expanding the range of institutional sources and archives that could be explored, despite increasing the number of questions that film history could ask, *Film History: Theory and Practice* also shut off one of the most potent avenues of exploration: the content of the film text itself.

Since the publication of Allen and Gomery's film historiography, other books and collections have attempted to define the future path of film history. The "History and Analysis" section of David Bordwell and Noel Carroll's *Post-Theory: Reconstructing Film Studies* identifies two essays that "show how particular films can be illuminated by historical research."[12] Donald Crafton's work on *The Jazz Singer* (1927) explores the myth around the film's financial and popular success, but its focus is not on the film as a text, but the film as a historical event, the 1927 reception by critics and audiences.[13] Richard Maltby's work on *Casablanca* (1942) is more promising. It opens with a particular scene from the film, and develops its argument through a particular narrative ellipsis and how that ellipsis can be accounted for through a combination of censorship and the conventions of the classical Hollywood cinema. The essay focuses on multiple interpretations of one (unseen) moment, the construction of different spectator positions, and how these are often prescribed by the work of industry bodies such as the Production Code Administration. Although it offers a range of historical sources—from Joseph Breen's notes on the film to Hal Wallis' thoughts on different endings—the article moves further and further away from its "3½ seconds" of classical Hollywood cinema and any textually specific analysis. Close examination of the sequence could explore performance styles, focusing on how Bogart prowls the room, habitually lighting cigarettes, while Bergman remains relatively static, a pivot within the scene; alternatively, analysis of cinematography or editing technology would examine the series of camera tracking shots that push in on tight close-ups of Bogart and Bergman, or how editing choices initially draw the audience in toward the characters, and then, after the "3½ seconds" Maltby identifies, backs away from them again. Unlike Crafton's essay, Maltby does use historical research to cast light on textual detail, and the possibility of multiple interpretations, but his focus remains historical rather than analytical. This preference for historical work over close analysis reflects the editorial stance of Bordwell and Carroll, who note that the purpose of the collection is to suggest new theories and new approaches to film studies, with "less film interpretation" and a "de-emphasis on dazzling readings of particular films."[14] Although Maltby's work contains useful suggestions, *Post Theory* (like Allen and Gomery before it) offers little sense of how close analysis and film history can work together.

Jeffrey Richards returned to the division between these two fields when, in 2000, he identified the differences between Film Studies and Cinema History:

> Film Studies has been centrally concerned with the text, with minute visual and structural analysis of individual films ... with the eliciting of meanings

that neither the filmmakers or contemporary audiences ... would have recognized. Cinema History has placed its highest priority on context, on the locating of films securely in the setting of their makers' attitudes, constraints and preoccupations, on audience reaction and contemporary understandings.[15]

While both are valuable and needed, he sees a "rewarding convergence" between the two approaches that favors his own concept of empirical cinema history. This convergence is focused on three specific areas: individual film analysis (of *mise-en-scène*, script, performance), an understanding of the social, political and industrial landscape at the time of production, and the contemporary reception of the film through box office figures, critical opinion and audience reaction. Richards' contributions to a book such as *Best of British: Cinema and Society from 1930 to the Present* demonstrate how his idea of convergence would work in practice: chapters on *The Guinea Pig* (1948), *The Blue Lamp* (1950) and *The Ladykillers* (1955) combine narrative detail, information on post-war society, politics and cultural changes, and accounts of critical reception.

Yet the work in *Best of British* underlines B. F. Taylor's criticism of Richards' approach for largely ignoring one element (film analysis) in favor of the other two (historical knowledge and reception). Taylor claims that "context undermines or, in fact, nullifies the importance of the film's specific detail.... If an approach is based upon three central and seemingly equal tenets then why should one of them suffer disproportionately in terms of attention? Would not it be far simpler just to remove the first of these tenets from the approach?"[16] Looking at Richards' work in *Best of British* Taylor's point is clear: despite an astute and comprehensive combination of historical, political and social knowledge, this information swamps close analysis of any textual information. There is little consideration of whether *mise-en-scène* analysis could offer alternative critical positions, and textual detail is largely limited to narrative description and setting. However, Taylor's dismissal of Richards also elides the purpose of his work, to create "empirical cinema history" that reveals evidence about the society when the film was made, to offer contemporary examples of social and cultural issues. The film text becomes another source of evidence, a historical fact, rather than the focus of close analysis. While Taylor's goal is to promote close textual work as the dominant tool of analysis, Richards' is aiming for a larger cultural history.

Taylor's rejection of Richards' convergence theory is tied to his own largely ahistorical approach to film analysis, which locates its meaning in evidence gathered wholly from the textual characteristics of the film. John Gibbs claims that such an approach is able to

> relate our sense of the meanings of a film back to the movement of the camera, a use of color, or the organization of décor and character ... [and] is one

of the reasons why a *mise-en-scène* approach makes for a most satisfying criticism ... it enables you to anchor your understanding of a film, and to support your argument with evidence.[17]

Gibbs and Taylor find meaning located in the film itself, with no recourse to the historical context of production or reception. Taylor's analysis of the British New Wave uses historical detail, but only to challenge critical writings on the New Wave since the 1960s—the work of V. F. Perkins, Jeffrey Richards, and Andrew Higson. Their writings are put in historical critical context, but aspects of the film's style or aesthetics are not analyzed in relation to larger societal or cultural issues, or the workings of the British film industry. Taylor and Gibbs see no need to look beyond the boundaries of the frame for meaning.

In relation to this current study of trailers, elements of these preceding approaches to film marketing, history and analysis remain useful. The expansion of what film history could be about, the move to treating marketing materials as a recognized analytical subject, the possibility of combining historical and analytical methods: these are all key developments that have informed my own work. What I intend to do through this book is push these elements further, to intensify the ideas around film analysis—as presented by Taylor and Gibbs—and to synthesize it with the focus and archival precision of film history as practiced by Allen, Gomery, Maltby and Richards. I support Taylor's desire for more analysis of how film texts work, but I'm equally interested in what they can reveal as historical sources. Consideration of the trailer *mise-en-scène* will remain central throughout the book, but not at the expense of the temporal position that historical knowledge offers. The work of Haralovich, Klaprat and Kernan raises a methodological question when approaching trailer analysis: they offer analysis from a historically informed position, post-trailer and post-film viewing. In this way, they asked questions around whether the trailer accurately reflected the film, rather than what unique qualities the trailer might display. Throughout this book the historical situation of production, distribution and exhibition will be used to explore the range of textual meanings that may have been available in that trailer's temporal and historical moment. This approach synthesizes elements from both Richards' and Taylor's work, emphasizing the close textual analysis of *mise-en-scène* and meaning favored by Taylor, but linking that to the historical moment that Richards is promoting, ultimately pushing toward an integration of text and context that is suggested by Richards' work, where context does not undermine textual information, but repositions and emphasizes the role of textual analysis.

This synthesis of techniques mirrors a more recent congruence of film analysis, history and reception studies, which has been termed a "new" film history. A brief focus on a specific collection of essays that expand this area of film studies, *The New Film History*, will consider their methodological approach and its relation to this current project.[18] The introduction to *The New Film History* delineates how such an approach can function, and what its conventions are. The authors stress that such work represents "historical scholarship that emphasizes the critical analysis of primary sources relating to the production and reception of feature films," but that such historical work also requires skills of "formal and visual analysis" in order to deal with the unique text of the film.[19] This combination of methodologies is developed by a list of three elements that characterize the New Film History. First, the emphasis on uncovering the "cultural dynamics" of film production, and how these are shaped by historical processes and individual agency. Importantly, they state that the New Film History "places the film text at the nexus of a complex and dynamic set of relationships between producers and consumers."[20] This reflects my own concern to situate the trailer text at the center of a network of discursive influences, and how these can often be seen within the trailer itself. But the New Film History also stresses the move toward reception studies as a core element of how current research is moving beyond production studies, with a list of sources for reception studies that includes "publicity materials, audience surveys and online fan communities."[21] Although publicity materials remain central to my own work, my use of them differs from what is suggested here. My concern in using trailers is to treat them as unique short films, not simply as adjuncts that reveal something of the feature film they are advertising (or its reception). As an innovative short film format, trailers are complex layered texts that can be analyzed in themselves, for what they say, for how they communicate and position studio-, star-, technology-, and genre-specific messages. They are more than windows into film reception or to the wider world of feature publicity materials.

The second convention of New Film History is "the central importance of primary sources," something that was also stressed by "old" film history.[22] Allen and Gomery's *Film History: Theory and Practice* was a direct call to action for film researchers to move beyond existing histories, and stressed the importance of primary sources and archival work in revealing and constructing new areas of film historical research. Although there is a suggestion that the New Film History has expanded the range of primary sources, its list— memoirs, personal papers, production files, scripts, censors' reports, publicity materials, reviews, fan magazines and Internet discussion groups—is, bar the Internet, perfectly located within Allen and Gomery's earlier work. Whether a condition of old or new film history, the place of primary materials is not in question, and much of the work contained in this book directly analyses and relies upon primary evidence from sources in the British Film Institute library, the AMPAS Margaret Herrick library, the Warner Bros.

archive and the 20th Century–Fox Legal Files: from original trailers, to press books, script archives, interviews, production reports, and studio memos, they are an essential store of historical and contextual information.

The third criteria for the New Film History is "an understanding that films are cultural artifacts with their own formal properties and aesthetics, including visual style and aural qualities."[23] This seems to reflect Richards' earlier call for cinema historians to study *mise-en-scène* as much as paper sources, but despite claiming that new film historians should look beyond narrative toward the "look and sound" of films, there is little sense of how this work should be undertaken. That is not to say that the essays in *The New Film History* ignore specific films, but their use tends to be limited to historical markers, elements of history rather than the filmic object being analyzed. Mervyn Stokes' essay on *Gone with the Wind* (1939) discusses the film in relation to the historical depiction of the South, and refers to narrative events and dialogue: but there is no close analysis of *Gone with the Wind*'s specific textual qualities (i.e., its use of color within the landscapes of the "South," or whether framing, editing or camerawork might limit or expand its depiction of the "South"); James Chapman's work on *Master and Commander: The Far Side of the World* (2003) talks about narrative and adaptation but there is no sense of the film's specific *mise-en-scène*; Laurie Ede discusses the importance of set designers without illustrating their work with textual examples; and Mark Glancy's essay on the reception of *Blackmail* (1929) offers only a brief textual description of the film's initial silent sequence.[24] Visual detail appears in some essays—Jeffrey Richards' work on swashbucklers mentions the color of costumes; Sue Harper's overview of 1970s British cinema refers to costume and setting in relation to *Ryan's Daughter* (1970)—but only Jonathan Munby and Sarah Street offer any sense of how the film text looks and sounds. Munby's compelling analysis of visual style in *Menace II Society* (1993) examines how the film fluctuates between documentary-style realism and the over-saturated color of 1970s blaxploitation, while Street's analysis of specific sequences from *Black Narcissus* (1947) considers how censorship decisions changed the film's meaning in its original release.[25] These latter examples convincingly demonstrate how close analysis of visual and aural evidence can function "at the nexus of a complex and dynamic set of relationships."[26]

Demonstrating a methodological approach that synthesizes elements from film and historical analysis is something this work will expand upon in more detail later in this chapter, and then apply throughout. Much of this analytical technique, particularly the creation of the historical discursive networks that surround trailer production, can be located in the broad definitions of the New Film History that are defined above, not least the desire to expand "the boundaries of historical knowledge and ... understand films both as texts and context."[27] But equally, my interest in specific analysis of the text places as much emphasis on identifying and examining the complex layers of *mise-en-scène* within trailers (a similar focus as that of Taylor, or Gibbs) as situating that text historically (as in Richards or Crafton). Understanding the visual and aural qualities of the unique film text is a key convention within the New Film History, but based on the evidence of the recent collection, I am moved to repeat Thomas Elsaesser's words on Allen and Gomery's work, twenty years earlier: why aren't "the films themselves ... the object of study"?[28]

This lengthy discussion of one particular book is important because it reflects on many of the issues that are central to my own approach to unifying elements of film analysis and film history. Perhaps it is, again, the tendency within film history (old and new) identified by Elsaesser and Taylor, the privileging of context over text, the focus on analysis of primary archival source material rather than close textual analysis of primary audio-visual texts. All of the references made to *The New Film History* must acknowledge that these are essays, not given the length necessary to move into the kind of textual work I will argue for through this book. This lack of analysis—covering a full film or series of films—is avoided in my own work through the use of short films such as trailers, a choice that allows me to develop and demonstrate my own method using a variety of textual examples. There remains much to admire in the New Film History's focus on text and context, and there are echoes of that approach in my own work, but I want to move further into the notion of close analysis and what that—in synthesis with a network of historical context—can reveal about the construction of meaning in the trailer text.

To create this synthesis, this book combines the strengths of both historical and analytical disciplines, encapsulated in my term "unified analysis"— "unified" because of the unification of text and context at the heart of this endeavor, as well as the attempt to "unify" these different approaches into one theoretical concept. Unlike Jeffrey Richards' idea of "empirical cinema history" (defined as recovering evidence about "contemporary values and attitudes ... entering the mind of the 'silent majority'"[29]), unified analysis is equally concerned with the creation of text-specific meaning as it is with the historical moment of production or reception. Unified analysis marries these concepts, and allows for a deeper understanding of text and history. Close analysis of the text can reveal a historically specific reading, and placing the text within a network of historical information—a web of social, cultural, political, economic and industrial strands—is an aid to discern and identify potential textual meaning. Analyzing text and context together creates a more potent reading and understanding of the different textual strata, while moving from text to context and back to the text means that the historical network continually informs and aids textual analysis. This unity of purpose means that film analysis can reveal important historical information, and film history can be a tool for discerning and identifying textual meaning through contextualization.

This exploration of the historical moment through trailer study will demonstrate the ability to meld historical and close textual work into a coherent analytical technique that attempts to analyze these trailer texts from a contemporary perspective, to try and discern the intent of the producers and, in part (although this project makes no claims to be a reception study), suggest what reactions a contemporary audience may have had. Barbara Klinger has noted that any attempt to create what she refers to as a total history (and which is referred to here as the historical moment) "may well be an impossible enterprise," especially given the work done in post-structuralism and linguistic theory, but that pursuing such a course does not "guarantee truth, but [does] promote rigor in making propositions about the past."[30] This rigor demands that close attention is paid to both sides of the proposal — to attempt to understand the historical processes through an examination of primary evidence (where possible), to recreate a compelling and informed picture of the historical moment, and to use that knowledge to inform textual analysis. At stake within the writing of this new approach to film history is the ability of an historian to open up a period of history, to offer their views on the texts produced in that period and show how such analysis adds to and enriches our knowledge.

Balancing these different techniques, unifying them into a coherent and unified analysis, involves a methodology sensitive to the requirements of each approach. In order both to explore the methodology that underpins such analysis, and to reveal the possibilities and opportunities offered by this approach, the chapter will move on to a specific case study. Arising out of the discussion of related literature, close analysis of a classic trailer text will demonstrate how unified analysis builds on and enhances the work that has gone before, while establishing its own identity. Trailer analysis starts from the principle that each trailer contains compact layers of information: these cue the viewer toward a future film release, promote star images, highlight generic pleasure, position visual spectacle and display technology, all within a potent document that carries traces of its specific historical moment. Trailer analysis must consider the basic structural conventions underpinning these layers: the use of excerpted visual information from the advertised film, the superimposition of inter-titles, the addition of graphic wipes and dissolves, the complicated soundtrack mix of musical cues, dialogue and voiceover address. A unified analysis of these complex texts must investigate each dense layer alongside the network of influences that affected the original production, and uncover the potential meanings contained in the trailer text. The following analysis of the trailer for *Singin' in the Rain* (1952) investigates a range of different readings of the text, before moving on to demonstrate how the construction of a network of resources offers a more complete reading. Dissecting the trailer in this way, examining the variety of opinions and techniques that this makes overt, will reveal not only the unique nature of the trailer's layered text but the prospect of synthesizing theoretical concepts into a new, unified approach to film history and analysis.

From the point of view of film history, the *Singin' in the Rain* trailer could be regarded as an example of advertising for MGM's successful run of musicals in the late 1940s and early 1950s. As a compendium of already popular MGM musical numbers, historical analysis such as that favored by Robert Allen or Donald Crafton could trace the development of these songs, track their original placement and consider them as narrative building blocks for this new product. The trailer promotes a major star — Gene Kelly — and could be used as evidence in a historical narrative based around his star image, showing how this altered over time. The trailer can also be seen as part of a technological history of color filmmaking in the early 1950s. Approaching the trailer from this perspective would consider the dominance of Technicolor's three-strip process; investigate the application of new lighting equipment to increase color depth of field; or examine the aftermath of the 1950 federal decision that forced Technicolor to set aside cameras and personnel for the use of independent producers and minor studios.[31] It would also be possible to specialize purely in trailer history: tracing the development of the departments and companies responsible for these advertisements, focusing on individual techniques—process printing, the use of animation, titles, elaborate graphic wipes and fades—or considering the hybridization of the trailer sales message that appeared in the late 1930s and through the 1940s.

Treating the *Singin' in the Rain* trailer as an analytical subject reveals an equally wide range of perspectives and possible readings. Close analysis of the *mise-en-scène*, similar to John Gibbs or B. F. Taylor's work, reveals a sophisticated editing strategy in the middle of the trailer, where long crossfades link the appeal of the three stars—Gene Kelly, Debbie Reynolds, and Donald O'Connor—through character placements that "merge" the performers into one another, across a range of different songs and routines. This focuses attention onto the named leads, but it also links them to the known pleasures of the film and genre—the musical routines. Equally, close attention to aesthetics reveals a structural conceit that opens and closes the trailer. In the opening sequence, the camera starts on a medium shot of dancers, pulls back and cranes up into an extreme long shot full of neon signs advertising casinos, theatres, cinemas and hotels—a movement that suggests an enlarged perspective on events. This transition, from the personal (the dancers) to the public (the wider world), offers a suggestive link to the traditional structure of a hybrid trailer style, which expands its sales message to encompass as many audience lures as possible, then has to distil those down into a simple, personal message. At the close of the *Singin' in the Rain* trailer, the individual strands (musical numbers, narrative, spectacle, stars) form a hybrid message of new and known pleasures, which then focuses down onto one specific message—the star image. The reverse of the opening camera movement, craning down from extreme long shot to a medium shot on Gene Kelly, reflects the trailer moving from a grander narrative to an individual sales message. The specific aesthetics of the trailer reflect an essential function of the trailer structure.

Close analysis of aesthetics is also central to critics such as Mary Beth Haralovich or Sue Harper, who explore how films and advertising represent dominant ideological concepts of capitalism and patriarchal heterosexuality. The *Singin' in the Rain* trailer can be seen to support such systems, but the textual evidence both proves and challenges such a concept. The trailer's homage to capitalism is evident in the opening sequence—the excess of promotional billboards for casinos and theatres—and it continues to wallow in images of excessive consumption and wealth through its presentation of the 1920s Hollywood studio system, one of the most potent myths of 20th century capitalism. Issues of gender representation include masculinity in the shape of Kelly and O'Connor, while the depictions of Debbie Reynolds and Cyd Charisse appear to fall into traditional good girl/bad girl clichés. Such generalities run counter to a close analysis of the trailer, however, where the images of Reynolds and Charisse appear stronger and more in control than their male co-stars. The trailer problematizes these issues, rather than condensing them into easily identifiable elements. Examining such representations requires teasing apart the intricate layers of information and potential meaning within the trailer, but it also needs some contemporary grounding in order to make sense of what is being depicted. Any attempt to understand the aesthetic or representational content of the trailer, particularly as a 1952 phenomenon, requires a more directed and integrated form of analysis that is open to all the possible influences.

By contrast with these existing approaches, unified analysis of the *Singin' in the Rain* trailer begins by building a network of the historical, industrial, economic, cultural and technological influences that may have informed its production. This discursive network will not only offer a sense of the trailer as a contemporary text, but it will provide any analysis of the trailer with a variety of facts and concepts that could explain structural or aesthetic concerns. A complete reading of the trailer also functions in synthesis with related evidentiary networks based around 1950s trailers, musical trailers, Gene Kelly trailers, Technicolor trailers and MGM trailers. To understand the layers of information present in each trailer produced, it is important to be able to identify and examine each layer individually and as part of the whole. In the case of the *Singin' in the Rain* trailer, close analysis of the trailer text reveals key elements—the depiction of star personalities, color film technology, the dismantling of the studio system, the growth of competitive technology (television), gender roles—but all are contained within a larger concern, harking back to a golden age, a nostalgia-driven sales message that has as much to do with contemporary events of 1952 as the narrative content of the feature itself.

The historical situation of the trailer is intrinsic to understanding its layers of meaning. The opening sequence, with the dancers dwarfed by flashing neon advertisements, is overlaid with the words:

> In the SPIRIT and FUN of AN AMERICAN IN PARIS
> M-G-M NOW BRINGS YOU
> The BIG, BIG Musical Show of the year![32]

The trailer moves on to a long shot of the three stars dancing in the rain, then cuts to a shot of a soundstage, equipment and technicians in the foreground, an ornate Art Deco set with dancers in the background: "This is the story of a great moment in motion picture history ... when the screen learned to talk."[33] As identified earlier, this could be seen as a paean to capitalism, but it's also tinged with nostalgia, looking back to bygone years and glory days. Hollywood in 1952 was at the end of its golden age: tarnished by the 1948 Paramount Decree that demanded the major studios divest themselves of their exhibition arm; challenged by the popularity of the "rival screen," television; and facing a decline in audience numbers. The trailer may hark back to the 1920s, but the problems of the 1950s are implicit in the text—the neon Loew's Theatres signs that are prominent in the opening image offer a reminder of the loss of MGM's exhibition circuit, while the references to "Talkies" highlight the introduction of problematic new technology. Despite referring to the launch of synchronized sound as a "great moment," the trailer's attitude toward technology is ambivalent. In a long excerpted scene, "R. F." (the head of Monumental Pictures) fumes about the success of *The Jazz Singer*, O'Connor offers an Al Jolson parody, and Kelly dismisses sound as "a freak." Although R. F. announces the studio *will* make talking pictures, in this trailer, hardly anyone talks. There is no voiceover, no dialogue — only singing. The songs, all from previous MGM hits, offer another level at which trailer content is looking back, not forward. With its 1920s setting, and its songs from pre-existing 1930s and 1940s MGM properties, the trailer retreats from its contemporary situation to the studio's glory days. The diegetic threat posed by the new technology of sound reflects, in this trailer, the contemporary Hollywood reaction to a contemporary (non-film) technology, television.

Linking *Singin' in the Rain* to these industrial concerns is not a simple matter of constructing a network of convenient dates or events—the evidence comes from the text of the trailer. Placing the trailer within this network enables the text to illuminate historical data, but in turn this data can offer an explanation for textual detail. Although the threat of television could explain the trailer's use of Technicolor, there are other historical and textual forces at work. Color technology is overtly displayed in this trailer, every scene infused with incredibly bright and vibrant colors. As befits musicals (and musical trailers) of this era, the color is used to convey fantasy elements over realism, with the bulk of trailer scenes focusing on more dream-like or imaginary moments. The trailer stresses the expressive opportunities of color through Cyd Charisse's emerald green dress, the blood-red nightclub where Kelly dances, the luminous yellow raincoats: these function, on one level, as a promotion of the feature's spectacle and, more obliquely, target television and rival color film processes. The depth and range of colors shown in the trailer obviously contrast with the new technology of the black-and-white television screen, but the combination of textual and historical analysis suggests a more compelling reason: bolstering the flagging fortunes of Technicolor itself. With color processes such as Anscocolor and Eastmancolor entering the Hollywood production system from the early 1950s, Technicolor's monopoly was under threat for the first time. This could go some way to explain the wealth and range of expressive coloring shown in the *Singin' in the Rain* trailer, where technology is a key narrative and sales concept. MGM, which had financially backed Technicolor and used it frequently for their musical productions, needed to continually promote the spectacular aspects of Technicolor — as the final trailer titles make clear: "The EXCITEMENT you Expect/In Color by TECHNICOLOR."[34]

Unified analysis of this preview also allows us to examine how the use of technology in the trailer can call attention to issues of star image and representation. Debbie Reynolds may be third-billed, but the technologies of sound and color film allow her image to become more dominant throughout the trailer than either of her male co-stars. Although Reynolds' appearance seems to fit within an image of wholesome 1950s womanhood — depicted in the kitchen, in feminine pink outfits, or romantically framed with Kelly — she does control elements of the *mise-en-scène*. In the "Singin' in the Rain" sequence (with the three stars in raincoats), she is in the center of the screen: as the identifying titles zoom on from left and right, they draw the eye back toward the center, and toward Reynolds. In the kitchen scene, she is again with O'Connor and Kelly, but here she initiates the song "Good Morning" and, again, she is centered, facing the camera; they are in profile on the left and right of camera, framing her performance. During the trailer's central montage sequence of song clips, she links the songs "You Were Meant for Me," "Dreaming of You," and "You Are My Lucky Star," with cross-fades that match her on-screen placement from number to number. The basic technology of the trailer — editing, graphic wipes, sound mixing — center her image through the trailer, and the use of color adds to that — her yellow raincoat, pink dress, and light blue dress (in the kitchen scene) are contrasted with the drab gray suits of her co-stars, once again drawing attention onto her. The only visual that displaces Reynolds' dominant image is again cued by color — when Cyd Charisse's character is introduced, a languid camera movement tracks along her legs then lingers on the crotch and breasts of her tight emerald green outfit. The color technology of Technicolor — which the trailer emphasizes because of the historical and industrial situation that has been identified through the network of influences — also positions star and character imagery, and allows the feminine characters a degree of control in the bulk of the trailer. Technology, star, and representation are often highlighted in the same scenes, confirming the complex layering contained within trailer texts.

A thorough examination of these networks of influence and the texts that were produced make it possible to investigate the breadth of contemporary meanings inscribed in the text. This is the goal of a unified textual analysis, which synthesizes the best elements of disciplines based around historical factors, representation or aesthetic patterns. Individually these may reveal an aspect of the trailer text but it is only in combination, in unifying these diverse approaches, that the text can be completely explored. The *Singin' in the Rain* trailer may not be particularly unique — it utilizes many structural concepts and narrative techniques present in trailers from the late 1920s — but its moment of production was, with a specific set of studio-, star-, cultural and technology-centric concerns. What unified analysis offers is the opportunity to understand and explore these layers of meaning, to test historical information against the evidence of the text, to place textual evidence within a network of influences and discourse, and to situate the text in its unique historical moment. In the case of the *Singin' in the Rain* trailer, this analysis reveals the central issue of film technology, contemporary concerns over technological change, and the ability of technology to foreground star images. While technology has not always been regarded as an important factor within trailer study — particularly in relation to concepts such as star, genre and narrative — its centrality to the production process, and the continued development and dissemination of trailer texts, will be explored here, and throughout the book, in order to demonstrate its key role in any complete understanding of trailer history.

TECHNOLOGY AND HISTORY

Trailers are products of technology. Their creation in the early 1910s may have been a result of increased demands for movie- and star-specific publicity but their dominance of movie promotion during the 1920s coincided with concurrent developments in optical printing and editing technology (such as the Moviola) that powered the transformation of the trailer from a short presentation of excerpted scenes to longer, more advanced structures based around a montage of excerpted footage, graphic title work and symbolic screen wipes. While these behind-the-scenes production technologies were not publicized for audiences, their stylistic results were displayed with increasing frequency in contemporary trailer texts. When it was necessary to promote major technological changes to the cinema experience — such as synchronized sound, color or widescreen — the most effective promotional and educational tool was the trailer.

Despite this central role within production and sales message, the concept of a technology trailer whose narrative was structured around new processes or technological developments has never been fully explored.[35] Lisa Kernan's *Coming Attractions: Reading American Movie Trailers* makes little mention of technology, and a recent DVD trailer history (*Coming Attractions: The History of the Movie Trailer*) was more focused on individual excellence as the historical agent of change.[36] Indeed, the grand narrative of trailer history suggested by Kernan and the documentary holds little appeal for me, or the unified analysis contained within this book. Partly this is because it necessarily elides and contradicts those trailer texts that don't fit conveniently into the larger theory, but mainly because insisting on one overarching inclusive narrative inevitably excludes large sections of trailer history in the process of creating a logical cause-and-effect story. Watching the documentary's construction of trailer history brought to mind John Belton's words, from the introduction to *Widescreen Cinema*: "I aim to rewrite the simple, linear technological histories ... [to] provide a fuller scenario which is sensitive to the dead ends and detours which inform the cinema's development."[37] Belton's idea echoes through my own writing, and its emphasis on looking beyond traditional historical narratives informed some of the work on unified analysis contained in these pages. Although the bulk of this book deals with the expansion of technology from the 1950s on, it is worth here introducing an earlier technology-based star image, and one that demonstrates the ability of unified analysis to explore the layered texts of the film trailer.

> Ladies and gentlemen, I am privileged to say a few words to you in this most modern and novel manner ... the first living Vitaphone announcement ever made announcing the coming of one of the year's outstanding pictures.[38]

These are the first words spoken by John Miljan in the 1927 *Jazz Singer* trailer, and they immediately center the notion of technological change and its impact on trailer structure. Prior to *The Jazz Singer*, trailers were generally built up around an edited selection of excerpted scenes, inter-titles and animation that focused attention onto star images and narrative events: star Ivor Novello is central to the British trailer for *Downhill* (1927), but it also conveys the narrative trajectory his character goes through in the feature; the *Bride of the Storm* (1926) trailer builds up story information through editing and animation while titles and images highlight star Dolores Costello. Unlike the polished editing and animation techniques in these examples, *The Jazz Singer* trailer

Actor John Miljan presents the first Vitaphone sound trailer for *The Jazz Singer* (1927).

offers static long shots of an actor (Miljan) talking directly to the viewer, prerecorded footage and excerpted scenes—but the strength of the sales message is a bravura display of the possibilities offered by synchronized sound. It initially appears that *The Jazz Singer* trailer has a dual sales message, selling both Vitaphone and Al Jolson: "you are not only going to have the opportunity of seeing Mr. Jolson but through this marvelous invention Vitaphone you are also going to be able to hear him talk as well as sing."[39] Jolson is centered through a combination of Miljan's words, shots of him at the film's premiere, and excerpted scenes from the film itself. Importantly, Miljan's promise—that audiences will see and hear the star—is not met within the trailer, and Jolson's star image remains silent. In contrast, Miljan's voice dominates all three segments of the trailer, centering the "modern and novel" Vitaphone synchronized sound technology for audiences and creating a nascent technological star.

Unified analysis of the trailer reveals historical, stylistic and technological precedents for the trailer structure and use of sound. Although Jolson had sung in an earlier Vitaphone short (*Al Jolson in the Plantation Act*, 1926), his silent appearance here was due to an edict issued by Sam and Jack Warner that the trailer should not spoil the impact of the synchronized scenes—those scenes were likely unavailable anyway, given that Vitaphone's sound-on-disc technology restricted sound editing techniques.[40] The style of the *Jazz Singer* trailer, with its demonstration of a synchronized direct audience address, had been established in earlier Vitaphone productions: the 1926 *Don Juan* premiere program featured Will Hays' recorded speech on the marvels of sound, and the second collection of Vitaphone shorts showcased a comic monologue by George Jessel. Understanding these historical precedents allows us to see that *The Jazz Singer* trailer was not a unique occurrence. Equally, they show that the trailer does not simply rely on earlier technological experiments, but develops them, demonstrating the continued possibilities offered by synchronized sound.

The trailer is divided into three sections: John Miljan's initial address and comments on Vitaphone; his voiceover commentary on edited footage of the film's New York premiere; and two excerpted scenes from the film. Each of these presents a separate technological advance: in the first, Miljan's speech is perfectly synchronized and demonstrates the Vitaphone process. The premiere sequence features upbeat jazz on the soundtrack, over which Miljan speaks, showing that Warner Bros. have the ability to effectively mix different sound sources as well as combine previously filmed footage and a voiceover. The scenes from the film are technologically the weakest section, rendering Jolson mute and with an instrumental version of "Mother of Mine" playing on the soundtrack (the trailer can be said to be accurately representing the film here, since these scenes were not among *The Jazz Singer*'s singing or talking scenes.) This structure highlights the technology's different strengths and offers little sense of the human star or film narrative — the traditional focus of most 1920s trailer advertising. The trailer confirms the primacy of technological change as a sales device: the first attempt to center and showcase a film technology as an individuated star.

This star image was not confined to one trailer, but developed by Vitaphone (and others, including Fox and Paramount) into the "master of ceremonies" trailer: a direct contradiction of the notion that technology did not have a lasting aesthetic effect on trailer structure. Lasting as long as fifteen minutes, these trailers gradually introduced more editing techniques, cutting away to photographs and silent shots from the movie. Narrative content from the feature was always balanced with the opportunities offered by Vitaphone's sound technology: there are references to "the living voices of Mary McAvoy [and] Lionel Barrymore" or Dolores Costello speaking "for the first time."[41] The presence of a strong technological message did not mean human stars were completely absent — synchronized sound remained an aural technology, and the stars' visual presence did grow stronger as the "master of ceremonies" trailer developed (including Al Jolson introducing the 1928 trailer for his own film, *The Singing Fool*).[42] By 1929–1930, as sound-on-film editing practices became more advanced, and sound films became the dominant production mode, specific references to sound technology disappear from trailers. Sound nevertheless remained an essential ingredient of the structure: the addition of a narrative voiceover, music, sound effects and dialogue changed the way sales messages were constructed. The presence of a strong technological image dissipated as audiences grew to expect it, but its very presence — and the suggestion that such technological change could function as a star image — boosted the overall role of technology within trailer history.

This discussion of synchronized sound technology and its impact on trailer production demonstrates that new technology has always been central to trailer history. This book will explore the role of technological change within trailer production and dissemination since the 1950s, with particular focus on the changes new technology has brought to issues of aesthetics, narrative and structure. The introduction of new screen technologies has an immediate stylistic impact on the most basic of trailer elements: graphic wipes function as eye-catching interruptions or overt transitions within trailers, often shaped as hearts, musical notes, envelopes and silhouettes — doubling the size and shape of the screen they cover, adding color to them, or giving them the illusion of depth inevitably alters the potential use and meaning of the wipe. Titles would have the opportunity to stretch across the wider screens, allowing for more imaginative placement and animation; or they could grow to fill the smaller technological screens of television and the Internet. Narrative in trailer structures is traditionally conveyed in aural and visual terms, but here again the use of excerpted footage emphasizes the wider screen composition, or the use of special effects–created visual spectacle to fill the image. In all three cases, new technology affects the ability to convey themes, moods or narrative information within the larger trailer text. This is not to promote any sense of technological determinism: as Steve Neale has observed, "cinema is not reducible to these technologies."[43] In all the trailer analyses that follow, technology may be a primary topic, but it is always considered within the network of influences that underpins unified analysis, part of a wide range of potential influences and discourses that are brought to bear on trailer production.

Like the unified analysis that underpins it, the project's focus on technology was driven by textual information as much as historical research. An initial viewing sample of 400 trailers (ultimately rising to over a thousand) from 1925 to 2005 demonstrated the range of possibilities listed earlier: a kaleidoscope of stars from Jimmy Stewart to Jim Carrey; genre-defining moments in the Western, science fiction and the modern blockbuster; Biblical, natural, supernatural and extra-terrestrial spectacle; structural conceits of direct address and specially filmed sequences; all contained within a strong narrative structure. Running alongside these options was a larger narrative of trailer history: their birth as silent slide shows between 1912 and 1916 through an alleged "classic" era in the 1930s and 1940s, an artistic expansion in the 1960s, the blockbuster effect of the late 1970s, and the modern consolidation of their role in cross-media film marketing. Analyzing the trailer texts themselves revealed the recurrent phenomenon of new technology, a disruptive force that didn't fit conveniently into established film or trailer histories and which challenged some of the existing historical debates (e.g., the relationship between the film and television industries in the 1950s, the role of visual spectacle in the science fiction genre). The idea of trailers as disruptive texts also consolidated the project's move away from a master narrative and toward the focus on specific historical moments suggested by unified analysis. Rather than seamless evolution, where little diversions are subsumed by larger themes, the areas explored throughout this book point away from macro-narratives toward a conception of history where deviation is valued, and where a specific moment in time is favored ahead of an overarching story. It is impossible to completely escape the master narrative — none of the texts analyzed here exists in a historical vacuum, and the construction of the discursive network occasionally relies on secondary or tertiary (narrativized) reports — but there is an attempt throughout to consider moments of disruption in their historical setting, a basic principle of unified textual analysis.

The evidence of the trailers also sharpened the book's focus on four elements of technology and their impact on the trailer text. Between 1925 and 1950, there are pockets of technological change that disrupt normal trailer structures: synchronized sound in Vitaphone's "master of ceremonies" trailer has already been considered, but the introduction of Technicolor's three-strip process and the use of deep focus cinematography can also be seen as deviations from the hybrid trailer form. While these remain useful case studies, the 1950s presents a more compelling technological disruption within the trailer industry, with widescreen, 3-D, stereophonic sound, television and special effects technologies dominating trailer structure and, in some cases, offering a permanent revolution in trailer style and content. Unified analysis of 1950s trailer texts reveals the decade as a pivotal moment for new technology and its effect on the film industry. Chapters one and two reflect on this disruptive moment from two perspectives — how trailers promoted the development of film technology designed to combat the rival screen of television (Cinerama, CinemaScope, 3-D), and what effect the television screen had when television "film" trailers began to be produced. Through unified analysis of central 1950s trailers, the chapters consider how technological change is positioned as a competitive process, what impact these disparate technologies had on the trailer text itself, and what new facets these trailers reveal about accepted historical views of 3-D, widescreen and the film industry's antagonism toward the television screen.

The primacy of the 1950s is also reflected in its use of special effects technology to produce visual spectacle within trailer texts. Like many of the technologies covered here, special effects techniques were not unique to the 1950s but the decade saw the first flourish of their potential and widespread use. Chapters three and four offer different views on the rise of spectacular visual imagery and its growing centrality within trailer sales messages through analysis of a particular genre of trailer, and a consideration of how the big screen spectacle has been translated onto the new dissemination technologies of home video, the Internet and mobile media players. Unified analysis of trailer texts focuses on specific historical moments and examples, in order to challenge the current debate on spectacle displacing narrative within science fiction films. Trailers for *Destination Moon* (1950), *Star Wars* (1977) and *Terminator 2: Judgment Day* (1991) offer a shifting display of technology-led narratives and effects-based imagery, while video, Internet and videophone trailers show how the increased mobility of trailer dissemination technologies challenges the use of spectacular visual information on smaller media screens.

As this brief summary makes clear, any consideration of the link between technology and the trailer must consider the dual role technology plays in both producing and disseminating the trailer text. Since 1950, the trailer has expanded beyond the cinema screen onto televisions, home video, DVD, computers, mobile videophones, media players and games consoles. Although trailers are still described as "film" trailers, referring to their promotion of a forthcoming film release, the term also suggests that trailers are an inherent part of the theatrical cinema experience.

As Lisa Kernan defines them, trailers are "created for the purpose of projecting in theatres to promote a film's theatrical release."[44] This reduction of the trailer to its theatrical shelf life limits our understanding of the format and its successful expansion across different media. The present book explores this distinction between film and other dissemination media by focusing on the trailer text as it crosses these media boundaries. As pioneers of filmed material on smaller and more mobile visual screens, analysis of trailer texts allows the book to explore debates surrounding the relationship between film and other media screens.

These new screens also complicate the temporal position of trailers. Since the 1910s, trailers have been defined as "coming attractions," a suggestion of pleasures yet to arrive, broad hints as to what audiences could flock to see next. More so than the feature film texts they promote, trailers exist in a very particular temporal window — a week, month or year (in more recent blockbuster marketing) before the debut of the feature film they are advertising. This continual anticipatory sphere suggests trailers are always a coming attraction, always teasing audiences about what is forthcoming. Yet the exhibition status of trailers until the late 1970s contained within them a fundamental opposition: namely, to "trail" and to be "(forth) coming."[45] Trailing involves being behind, following on, while to be forthcoming is to be ahead, not yet arrived. In the U.S. this linguistic and temporal duality was further confused when the same short advertising film could be described as both "trailer" and "preview," functioning in both past and future tenses at the same time. Although there is a historical explanation of the terminology — trailers originally "trailed" the main feature in theatre double bills (alongside newsreels, cartoons, short films) — it does not clear up the complex temporality of trailers.

While this book's focus on new dissemination technology deals broadly with aesthetic and structural issues, it is worth considering here the change in temporal address that such technologies have brought about: from a future temporal event ("Coming Next Week") to a present one ("Now Available").

Trailers that debut on the Internet or in cinemas still promote films as "Coming Soon," "Coming Summer 2008" or list an actual release date; television trailers launched on or after the film's release date promote it as "Now Showing" (if they make any temporal claim at all); the video and/or DVD release trailers state the film is "Now Available'; and classic film releases (either theatrical or on DVD) are based on the premise "Do You Remember?" Recent films such as Steven Soderbergh's *Bubble* (2006) have challenged traditional distribution patterns, with simultaneous cinema, DVD and pay–TV release. *Bubble*'s trailer replaced the classic "Coming Soon" message with "Available January 27"— the move from the future to the present is situated in the changing use of language. "Available" suggests it is obtainable, immediately accessible rather than a future event. In this case at least, the temporal position of the new dissemination technology (DVD) has begun to enter the previously future-event trailer (cinema and Internet).

From widescreen, 3-D and television in the 1950s to CGI, the Internet and the iPod in the 2000s, trailers have remained a key marketing tool for film producers. Yet despite the depth of historical, social, cultural and industrial knowledge contained within these texts, despite the information they offer on stars, genre, national identity, and technology, the trailer remains an unknown resource within film studies. The purpose of this study is not to join the dots of trailer history, to offer a grand narrative that illuminates all these issues. Instead, it will follow the clues and evidence found in a unified textual analysis of specific trailer texts between 1925 and 2005. At stake within the writing of this new approach to film history and analysis is the ability to situate a text in its historical network of discourses and knowledge, and to use that network to deepen our understanding and analysis of the text itself. This is not a work of film history, or film analysis — it is a unified analysis that aims to explore the moments of disruption highlighted by the texts themselves. This approach focuses on the intricate and the complicated over the simple and straightforward; investigates missteps and dead-ends as well as successes and achievements. Through unified analysis, trailers are revealed as complex, layered texts that cross media boundaries, act as a site of historical discourse, challenge existing debates, and foreground the place of technology as a key element of their success.

CHAPTER ONE

"Something BIG Is Coming"[1]

The trailer for *Beneath the 12 Mile Reef* (1953) promotes an exciting new star image from its first frames—but that star is not human. Instead of an actor, the trailer hails 20th Century–Fox's CinemaScope, the technology responsible for the new wider screen dimensions displayed through the trailer text. CinemaScope is "the Greatest Step Forward in the History of Entertainment," a "modern miracle," its "amazing anamorphic lens" engulfing audiences "in the panoramic range of an underwater world."[2] Descriptive titles and voiceover hyperbole have been used in trailers since their inception to promote human star images such as George Raft ("A man's man ... a woman's lover"), Bette Davis ("a great actress draws the scarlet portrait of a gorgeous spitfire") and Humphrey Bogart ("the most dangerous man in the world's most dangerous city").[3] In the *Beneath the 12 Mile Reef* trailer, the star is technological and, instead of close-up shots of actors, visual information is displayed to provide evidence of these claims of stardom. From its opening shot of an orange sunset to the underwater world filled with turtles, sharks and a giant octopus, each image describes and displays the innovative attributes and increased ratio of CinemaScope's wider screen. The evidence of such contemporary trailer texts highlights the presence of a technological star, similar to that identified in the earlier analysis of the 1927 trailer for *The Jazz Singer*. *Beneath the 12 Mile Reef*'s trailer may contain the traditional trailer conventions of wipes, titles and excerpted feature images, but the trailer is dominated by the CinemaScope aesthetic: the balanced composition of fishing boats floating on the ocean; the giant turtle that swims "into" camera; the tiger shark that glides across the width of the image. Each shot emphasizes the importance of the wider screen to convey such sequences. The star of this trailer is not the actors, divers or creatures we see, but the technology that is responsible for capturing them and projecting them onto the cinema screen. Understanding that cinematic technology was presented as a star in this historical moment allows us to explore how these trailer texts created this image for audiences, what contemporary industrial and social concerns are written into these short films, and what long-term effects this moment had on trailer aesthetics and structure.

The 1950s loved technology. From the introduction of credit cards, jukeboxes and automatic doors to computers, space rockets and the atomic bomb, the 1950s saw a major collision between technology and consumer culture. Labor-saving devices were introduced into homes, developments in cars and planes revolutionized travel, and television began to change people's entertainment habits. This technological love affair extended into the film industry — particularly an industry still reeling from the double blow of falling audience levels and the 1948 Supreme Court ruling that forced the studios to sell off their exhibition sectors. Hollywood's attitude toward new technology in the 1950s was invariably reactive. They saw technology as a new (or at least improved) audience lure, coaxing people back into movie theatres and away from new pursuits— the rival technology of television, the move to the suburbs, and the expansion of leisure activities. The new cinema-specific technologies introduced in the 1950s were weapons that attempted to turn the cinema screen itself into a site of difference, not simply film versus television, but studio versus studio and technology versus technology, each process emphasizing new experiential qualities of size, depth, smell, hearing or touch. In order to display the unique attributes of each technology, and to educate and excite audiences over the latest screen "improvement" the studios relied on their favorite method for differentiating competitive products: the film trailer.

The unique perspective offered by trailer study reveals that the relationship between film technologies in the early 1950s is more complex than the standard evolutionary history allows. Unified analyses of key trailer texts from this period allow us to fully explore the more competitive interrelation between these rival technologies and how they were positioned against each other through promotional discourse. Although most were revisions of earlier processes (mainly from the 1920s and 1930s[4]) the 1950s was the first financially successful rollout of both widescreen and 3-D processes. Rather than see the 1950s as an evolutionary progression toward more sophisticated equipment and filmmaking practice, trailer analysis allows us to examine how technological information was conveyed to audiences, how it was related to competing processes, and how the display of individual technology in these trailer texts actually affected 1950s trailer aesthetics and structure. With over 20 different technological processes debuting during the 1950s,[5] the chapter focuses on a key historical moment — the introduction of Cinerama — and investigates the ripple effect this caused in trailers for 3-D and CinemaScope, which used existing knowledge of Cinerama to align themselves with its popular success.

Existing writing on widescreen cinema of the 1950s has tended to focus on the economic and technological history of CinemaScope, with passing reference to both Cinerama and 3-D.[6] The main consideration of analytical or aesthetic issues is contained in classic articles by Charles Barr and André Bazin (from 1963 and 1953, respectively) that investigate the changes this new process suggested for theories around visual composition and montage editing.[7] Barr's essay is interesting because of the stress he puts on close analysis of aesthetic elements in widescreen films such as *The True Story of Jesse James* (1957), *Rebel Without a Cause* (1955), and *River of No Return* (1954). His argument concerns the process by which audience interest can be led across the image, without the use of close-ups: "If a Scope image is decently organized the eyes will not just 'jump around' ... they can be led to focus on detail, and to look from one thing to another within the frame with the emphasis which the director intends."[8] Although focused on individual talent (several directors don't meet Barr's standards of widescreen composition) this idea of a continuous image, and its association with a more realistic portrayal of space, clearly underpins Barr's positive assessment of CinemaScope, and his concurrent rejection of montage editing as a structural device. Bazin's essay goes so far as to proclaim the end of editing: "one can see that the evolution of film in the last fifteen years has tended toward the elimination of editing ... the wide screen will only hasten the adoption of that most modern of tendencies ... the stripping away of everything extrinsic to the quintessential meaning of the image."[9] Although history has proven that editing has, if anything, thrived since the introduction of CinemaScope, this contemporary distinction (or discourse) between widescreen aesthetic and montage editing places the 1950s widescreen trailer in a unique critical no man's land: able to display the wide images that lie at the heart of the film's visual style, but reliant on editing for its coherence and structure. This dichotomy, and the concept of widescreen images leading the eye across the image, will be explored in more detail through the chapter.

John Belton's *Widescreen Cinema*, which offers a history of widescreen production from 1895 through the present day, comments on Bazin's and Barr's approach to CinemaScope, seeing their histories as unable to "capture the complex interplay of ideological, technological, economic, and sociocultural forces that informed the development of widescreen cinema."[10] My own approach to Belton's work combines a critical view on his findings with a desire to extend its scope. I echo his notion of trying to understand the complexities of the process of writing history but his primary concern with "the writing of a history of widescreen cinema rather than with analysis of the visual and aural style of individual widescreen films" is a limitation of his potential findings.[11] Throughout his book, though more markedly in the section on spectatorship, he brings in many examples of print and press book marketing materials, using them to refine the idea of action extending beyond the cinema screen: but nowhere in the book does he consider how the attributes of a system designed to be visually expansive were sold in the film industry's main audio-visual promotional tool. While this is no doubt enhanced by my own interest in the trailer format, the presence of so many print-based promotional texts suggests a hole in the widescreen history Belton builds so successfully elsewhere in his book. A central aim of this chapter is to develop one section of Belton's extensive history — the 1950s — in order to demonstrate that his historical account can be intensified through the addition of textual analysis.

The *Beneath the 12 Mile Reef* trailer that opened this chapter offers a compelling example of how unified analysis can increase our understanding of both the text and the historical moment in which it was produced. Textually, we can see title work that positions it competitively against 3-D, wide images of sunsets and underwater spectacle that links back to Cinerama, and (although a tertiary sales message) a Romeo and Juliet–style narrative. Taken on its own, the trailer offers suggestive aesthetic, structural and thematic motifs: unified analysis can identify whether these are representative to such technological advertising or unique elements to this trailer. Contemporary evidence taken from trade journals, interviews, and studio files allow a deeper consideration of how these trailer texts create meaning: in this case, 20th Century–Fox studio memos confirm that the first set of CinemaScope films were designed to give audiences something bigger than the content of traditional narrative features, hence the reduction of narrative information in the trailer. Analysis of the network of historical and cultural influences also illuminates specific trailer detail: the popularity of underwater explorer Jacques Cousteau in the 1950s is mirrored when the trailer offers to take audiences "down ... into the last unknown ... with intrepid adventurers'; while the claim "The Most Awesome Underwater Climax Ever Filmed ... The Battle with the Giant Octopus" suggests the producers were aware of Walt Disney's rival underwater epic, *20,000 Leagues Under the Sea* (1954), in production at the time and with its own giant octopus finale.[12] By focusing on the specific moment of 1953, and the layered text of the trailer, unified analysis of trailers such as *Beneath the 12 Mile Reef* offers an intervention in, and an interrogation of, traditional film histories and attitudes toward widescreen cinema.

The chapter will use this combination of textual and historical analysis to reveal new perspectives on the aggressive studio posturing of the period, investigate how cultural attitudes toward female sexuality are written into visual texts, and reinterpret the assumptions made over viewer interaction and knowledge of cinema technology. Analyzing these trailer texts offers a new sense of how to describe, talk about and understand the study of widescreen and 3-D technology, and underlines the importance of trailers as historical markers that can be sifted for meaning and information on contemporary concerns. The impetus here is not to try to reclaim the 1950s technology trailer as an important evolutionary marker in trailer history overall, but to consider this unique historical moment in its own right. As we have already seen, *Beneath the 12 Mile Reef*'s trailer casts its proprietary technology as the primary sales message, creating a nascent technological star. Through unified analysis of trailer texts from each process, this chapter will explore how the rival star images of Cinerama, 3-D and CinemaScope were developed and maintained through the 1950s.

Cinerama: A "New Kind of Hero"

> We didn't want to be judged on subject matter.... The logical thing to do was to make Cinerama the hero. And that is what we have tried to do ... introducing our new kind of hero, the Cinerama camera.[13]

Lowell Thomas' words, from the premiere of *This Is Cinerama* (1952), encapsulate the technological impetus that would temporarily dominate the Hollywood industry in 1952–1955. In making their widescreen process the star image, Cinerama differed from earlier cinematic technologies that were positioned as tools to aid or enhance existing stars. Technology trailers for Vitaphone and Technicolor had placed sound synchronization and color film at the heart of the sales message, but the process tended to be linked to a human star. The *Jazz Singer* trailer may have centered "this marvelous invention Vitaphone" but it still linked the technology to an assumed audience desire, "to hear him [Jolson] talk as well as sing."[14] In the first Technicolor trailer, *Becky Sharp* (1935), Miriam Hopkins was "transformed from phantom shadows into the breathless beauty of living color': existing human stars retain a level of dominance in previous technology trailers, enhanced by the technological star but rarely eclipsed by it.[15] Cinerama was different because it was offered to audiences as its own star, a technological hero above and beyond the traditional elements of a Hollywood sales message. The display of this stardom would come through the visual spectacle that the Cinerama camera captured and projected onto its three-screen system: a star image based on panoramic scale, a wider screen aesthetic, and its claim to immerse the audience in the picture. Adverts claimed that with this new technology, "plot is replaced by audience envelopment ... the medium forces you to concentrate on something bigger than people."[16] The emphasis again falls on the process over the individual — immersion over narrative and characters, the Cinerama camera rather than the human actor — and this focus on technology and its visual products echoes through not only Cinerama trailers, but also other technology trailers of the early 1950s. Unified analysis of Cinerama trailers will explore this concept further, and suggest how the technological star image was introduced, developed and ultimately replaced by the human stars it attempted to eclipse.

The concept of the technological star was made overt through Cinerama advertising but, given this chapter's focus on the first iteration of 1950s technology trailers, there is a temporal issue that needs to be addressed. From the launch of Cinerama in 1952, and for the first nine years of its existence, the process was advertised and marketed without the use of trailers. Because of a complex mix of company organization, marketing strategy and technological limitations, the first trailers to be produced in Cinerama did not debut until 1962. So, while Cinerama is the first widescreen technology of the 1950s, in trailer history Cinerama trailers come last, after the main period of 3-D and CinemaScope, and just as Panavision begins to supersede all the preceding technologies. The absence of these trailers' texts problematizes the central concept that Cinerama trailer aesthetics influenced trailer advertising for the competing 3-D and CinemaScope systems. To address this, a unified analysis of Cinerama's 1960s trailers is used to provide evidence of how the Cinerama aesthetic of the 1950s infused both contemporary technology trailer advertising and the later 1960s trailers. Such analysis will demonstrate how Cinerama trailer texts from 1962 (and later) share common aesthetic and structural concerns with the Cinerama star image of the 1950s. Trailers for films such as *How the West Was Won* (1962), *The Wonderful World of the Brothers Grimm* (1962) and *Grand Prix* (1966) cannot be regarded as pure examples of 1950s Cinerama trailer advertising, but they continually refer back to the ideas, conventions and themes of *This Is Cinerama*'s launch advertising: technological widescreen spectacle and audience immersion. These trailers are structurally and aesthetically dissimilar from other "mainstream" previews of the 1960s (which had largely returned to hybrid trailer forms based around human star, genre and narrative), and they offer suggestive traces of what a 1950s Cinerama trailer would have looked like. Analysis of the trailer texts and the network of influences surrounding their production will investigate the Cinerama aesthetic that developed in the 1950s, how the Cinerama trailers of the 1960s distil that aesthetic into a distinctive trailer structure, and how the positioning of Cinerama's technological star is an essential first step in understanding the competitive technology-centered trailers of 1952–1955.

The trailer for *How the West Was Won* opens with the kind of screen-filling visual spectacle that established the Cinerama star: the camera soars above the earth, flying gracefully toward a snow-capped mountain range that stretches across the width of the three-screen image. It holds this shot for several seconds, allowing the grandeur and scope of the image to engulf the viewer, commencing the trailer sales message with the known travelogue content of the five previous Cinerama films. As the trailer continues, however, it becomes clear that the spectacular content of the Cinerama aesthetic is being challenged by the introduction of narrative, mixing the Cinerama star with more traditional sales devices: "The panorama of the West, background for a thrilling story of pioneers forging a nation out of this wild, tractless land."[17] On the word "story," the trailer cuts to an image of two men wrestling, crashing over tables—individuals encroaching on the medium that decreed itself to be bigger than people. This is the central dichotomy of the *How the West Was Won* trailer—although it visually depicts the Cinerama elements of amazing imagery, widescreen wonder and audience immersion, the voice-over suggests that such visuals of mountains, prairies and river rapids are no longer enough to hold an audience's attention. The travelogue element, the "panorama of the West," will now function as background to a thrilling story—the spectacular visuals of Cinerama reduced to a landscape that a story is told on top of. In this trailer narrative, the pioneers forge a nation out of "this wild tractless land."—so, in the trailer structure, will this new Cinerama venture forge a new, narrative-based identity out of the amazing imagery of that same land. The narrator intrudes on each instance of impressive travelogue imagery: over an extreme long shot of a raft spinning down the river rapids, he notes "an epic tale unfolds'; when a wagon train is dwarfed by the wide open prairie, we are reminded that this is a "saga of three generations ... conquering the wilderness."[18] In this trailer, the narrative strand continually tries to conquer Cinerama's presentation of spectacular landscape and wilderness through the repetition of words such as story, plot, saga and tale.

The bulk of the *How the West Was Won* trailer (the first preview produced for Cinerama theatres) represents this tug-of-war, between the demands of a studio narrative and Cinerama's established technological star image of spectacle and audience envelopment. This structural balance was informed and influenced by a production deal between Cinerama and MGM in the early 1960s, but to fully understand how the imposition of narrative elements affected the structure and presentation of the Cinerama star, we can compare the *How the West Was Won* trailer with an earlier preview, produced in 1961, for Cinerama's third travelogue film, *Seven Wonders of the World* (1956). This trailer squeezes the Cinerama image onto 35mm film to promote the feature's forthcoming 35mm release to normal (non–Cinerama) theatres and, like the five Cinerama films produced in the 1950s, taps into the growing U.S. leisure market by presenting a mix of native and foreign locales. Never shown in Cinerama, the 35mm preview remains the first attempt to condense the Cinerama aesthetic into a trailer format and there are clear markers that later trailers attempted to follow. Opening with a sweeping helicopter shot down the East River of Manhattan, the camera tracks along the urban landscape of jagged skyscraper shapes, with the narrator acting as tour guide. The immediate size of the image and the quantity of information packed into the screen tie the trailer into Cinerama's launch statement — to make the technology of the Cinerama camera the hero. With no focus on the individual, and its stress on known and unknown spectacular locations — from Manhattan to the exoticism of the Far East and the Amazon — this 1961 trailer is the closest suggestion to the "absent" Cinerama trailers of the 1950s, resembling a Cinerama film in miniature. However, reducing the picture ratio to fit onto 35mm also accentuates the lack of the original Cinerama star — as John Sittig notes, Cinerama footage didn't always transfer well to theatrical or television showings because shrinking the image size meant "they were trying to sell the name without showing anything different to what people were used to looking at."[19] The trailer still offers a sense of the main attributes of the Cinerama star image — the sense of travel, the point-of-view camera that soars over these amazing sights (offering a sense of the "active" participation such footage was intended to create), and the access the technology offers into previously unseen locations — travelogue imagery offered as audience hook. The most telling moment comes when the Cinerama logo appears, over a shot of the Great Pyramid — the trailer may have wanted to parallel an established wonder with a technological one but, by 1961, Cinerama was also in danger of becoming a relic of an earlier age.

The trailers for *How the West Was Won* and *The Wonderful World of the Brothers Grimm* are best understood as an attempt to relaunch the Cinerama star for the new decade, to reassert its star image qualities alongside (and often ahead of) the new narrative focus. Promotional material for both films distinguish between "Early Cinerama" and "Today's Cinerama,"[20] and the evidence of the trailers supports a continuity with the 1950s aesthetics. To summarize the scale of the production, the *How the West Was Won* trailer uses long shots of wagon trains traveling across the horizontal width of the screen, ramshackle boats being tossed across and around the screen by the rapids, train carriages that stretch across the image, a buffalo stampede that bears down on the camera, the animals filling every inch of the larger screen. Many of these spectacular images also emphasize the second important aspect of the Cinerama aesthetic: enveloping the audience. *How the West Was Won* splits its trailer structure in three, first establishing the opening landscape and narrative, before moving into a lengthy second act, where stars and characters are heralded. After this, however, the shift into an "active" audience section is highlighted by the voiceover that notes that the film will "bring you the glorious frontier as has never before been possible in a motion picture."[21] The images that accompany, and follow, this announcement create a compelling third act to the trailer narrative, one that brings spectacle and point-of-view camerawork to the forefront of the sales message. Starting with an image of soldiers firing at (then charging) the camera, the trailer cuts to the buffalo stampede. This is shown from in front, as the buffalo stream forward; from the side, as they thunder along; and then from physically inside the stampede, legs thudding past and over. The trailer then cuts to a train as it rides across the horizontal frame — then to a shot from in front as the train speeds into camera, and over it. As the train powers over an incredibly thin bridge, the Cinerama camera (riding on the cow catcher) tilts down slightly, to emphasize the drop beneath. Then, the camera (still on the front of the train) barrels headlong toward a blockage in the track — and smashes right through it, planks of wood splitting and spraying across the image. Having put the viewer in the midst of a gun battle, stampede, and on the front of a runaway train, the trailer then cuts to a further "active" sequence. As Indians attack a wagon train, the trailer lingers on a long shot of a wagon as it teeters, then tips over. The trailer cuts inside the rolling wagon as it turns, faster and faster, bodies falling out of the rear, boxes slamming into the canvas sides, the dusty landscape outside revolving at an increasingly frenetic rate. The third act of this trailer ends with the emphasis on the Cinerama camera as hero, capturing these epic landscape images and the active, point-of-view shots.[22]

This three-act structure in the *How the West Was Won* trailer balances technology and narrative, offering the spectacle of Cinerama's travelogue heritage and its concept of audience immersion alongside the Hollywood conventions of star and narrative content. *The Wonderful World of the Brothers Grimm* trailer also features this mix, but its balance favors star identification over the Cinerama-specific traits. The placement of stars in both trailers mirrors the earlier 35mm preview for *Seven Wonders of the World*, where individuals were dwarfed by their surroundings. In the narrative trailers the star images are centered in the middle of the three screens. This ties into the traditional hybrid trailer of Hollywood, where star images and close-ups would dominate the screen, be identified through title work, and often associated with particular hyperbole. The increased screen size of Cinerama reduces the impact of this convention, because the star image can only ever fill a third of the available screen. By attempting to include star trailer conventions in these Cinerama trailers, the star appearance is lessened, swamped by landscape and information on either side of them. The introduction of the star images (seventeen in *How the West Was Won*, twelve in *Brothers Grimm*) is also more restrained than the Hollywood standard. There is little optical work, with only the star names appearing below their images, and the voiceover links each star to a simple narrative characteristic: "James Stewart is the mountain man ... Gregory Peck as Cleve Van Valen, lucky in cards — and in love."[23] Nowhere do the stars truly inhabit the wider screen available to them, or align themselves with the new technology that made the wide screen possible. The image ratio favors Cinerama the hero, with its impressive display of spectacular vistas. The process remains focused on something bigger than people, never allowing the human star to completely occupy the image.

From the evidence of *How the West Was Won*'s trailer, it is clear that "Today's Cinerama" was aesthetically similar to "Early Cinerama," no matter what other publicity material might claim. The introduction of hybrid trailer messages based around genre, star and narrative did cause some structural change, but the main change these trailers wrought was not internal but external — within the Cinerama theatre itself. Trailers for *How the West Was Won* and *The Wonderful World of the Brothers Grimm* launched simultaneously in Cinerama theatres worldwide, advertising the alternate film. As the first trailers to debut in Cinerama, they caused their own unique problems. The Cinerama projection technology required four reels of film — three for picture, one for sound — and the projectors could not run for more than sixty minutes. Every Cinerama installation began its presentation with a musical overture, had a fifteen-minute intermission, and ended with walk out music — each stage built around loading or rethreading the projection equipment. There was no place in this program for projecting trailers. When it came time to produce trailers for the narrative films, Cinerama also decreed that trailers could not run before the feature, because the films "always opened with a big bang, like the rollercoaster at the start of *This Is Cinerama* ... they didn't want to take away from that impact by showing a trailer ahead of the film."[24] Its placement dictated by the very technology it was promoting, the trailer eventually ended up being shown during the fifteen-minute intermission. It would be excessive to blame the failure of these narrative projects on bad trailer positioning, but the potential to effectively market future films was significantly reduced when audiences were not physically in the theatre to watch the preview. Cinerama audiences were used to visiting the snack bar, stretching their legs, smoking or using the toilet during the intermission — the trailers became an interruption, not only of that free time, but also the ongoing narrative of the feature. By allowing the technology to dictate the placement, Cinerama trailers never became a seamless part of the entertainment being presented.

Whether influenced by bad trailer placement or not, the financial success of the two narrative films was less than the company hoped for, and the Cinerama technology ultimately proved too cumbersome for future productions under the MGM deal. *Grand Prix* offered "the most exciting experience of your life," *2001: A Space Odyssey* (1968) promised "the ultimate trip" but those experiences were based around narrative content, not the heroic Cinerama technology, which had been replaced by the 70mm SuperPanavision anamorphic system.[25] Despite this, the *Grand Prix* trailer offers a faux Cin-

Although the Cinerama three-camera system stopped producing films in 1962, high profile films such as 2001 were still released in Cinerama theatres. *2001: A Space Odyssey* trailer (1968).

erama aesthetic through a tripartite split screen that shows different views of the racing cars, pit lane and spectators, a point-of-view camera that races round the track, and an image that stretches out from Academy ratio into full widescreen. By using three screens, the trailer recalls Cinerama's original three-projector system; by literally reducing and expanding the image, it mirrors the presentation of *This Is Cinerama* where the film expanded from a "square" black-and-white screen to its color full widescreen ratio; by highlighting the ability of the wider screen to show the viewer more information, the trailer places Cinerama's widescreen aesthetic at the heart of the sales message; and by centering an extended point-of-view shot, it links back to the concept of enveloping the audience, so crucial to the original Cinerama star image of the 1950s. Despite its 1966 production date, the *Grand Prix* trailer has more in common with *Seven Wonders of the World* and the absent trailer texts of the 1950s than with contemporary widescreen trailers. Cinerama may have been phased out in favor of a cheaper, easier process, but the Cinerama star image, its aesthetic content, was well established and had been hugely influential from *This Is Cinerama* on. Although no Cinerama trailers were produced in the 1950s, the evidence of the films and the 1960s trailers provide strong clues as to what those 1950s absent texts would have contained: stunning travelogue imagery favoring long shots over medium or close-ups, an attempt to immerse the audience, making them active rather than passive, and no attempt to focus in on an individual person, or star image. Cinerama was the star, the camera was the hero, and the trailers reflected that image even after the process itself had been replaced. Cinerama may have failed to revolutionize the Hollywood industry with this approach to filmmaking, but these structural conventions and aesthetics continued to shape and influence other technological developments of the early 1950s. We will return to widescreen technology later through an analysis of the launch of CinemaScope, but first we need to consider Cinerama's main technological rival in 1952: not another attempt to create a wider screen, but a deeper one.

The Third Dimension: "3 Times as Thrilling!"

> *[The] new entertainment miracle, third dimension ... makes the screen absolutely real and alive. People, objects, landscapes take on a depth, dimensions such as they have in real life. And it has an added quality— objects actually seem to come out of the screen. So real, they almost touch you.*[26]

Richard Carlson's words, spoken in the "flat" trailer for *It Came from Outer Space* (1953), encapsulate many of the 3-D attractions that the new technology offered as a lure to audiences. His sentiments—the screen coming alive, reference to depth and reality, objects coming out of the screen— are repeated over and over in the 3-D trailers of 1953 and 1954 and encapsulate what these 3-D previews will offer as a technological free sample. The presentation of these elements create a trailer aesthetic that foregrounds extreme 3-D moments, editing them together to create a narrative where technology is again a central star image. Like Cinerama before it, the 1950s 3-D craze has been largely overlooked, regarded as a "dead end" both aesthetically and technologically—but the trailer evidence offers a compelling link between 3-D and the other contemporary technologies. This section will focus on the visual content and competitive positioning of a series of 3-D trailers, particularly the use of experiential images and subjective point-of-view shots that foreground 3-D's technological aspects and echo technological rival Cinerama. The genesis of a thematic link between 3-D and CinemaScope trailers will also be explored, in particular the use of key footage to showcase the technology's range and the suggestive sexual links that many of these trailers draw between the female form and the technological process. Through this unified analysis it becomes clear that 3-D was not a dead end, but a crucial bridging step in the development of 1950s technology trailer conventions.

Trailer production to promote 3-D went through three distinct stages between 1952 and 1955: from "flat" trailers to promote 3-D films ("flat" here refers to standard film projection, with no 3-D element), to full 3-D trailer advertising (where 3-D glasses would be required to view the trailer), then back to "flat" trailers that offer little or no technological sales message, focusing attention onto more generic or star-based sales messages. The historical and technological grounds for the rise and fall of 3-D trailers are explored below, but unified analysis of the 3-D trailer aesthetic involves returning to the concept of the absent text. Unlike Cinerama, trailers for 3-D films were produced from the very beginning, but there is an important visual absence that complicates any modern attempt to view and understand them: only two trailers are currently available in their full three-dimensional format, with many others only surviving in their "flat" versions. The absence in the majority of these trailer texts is the 3-D image itself, the visual display of the technology. The following analyses will offer a series of ways to deal with this absence: those 3-D trailers that exist in their entirety (and which can be viewed in three dimensions) will be regarded as potential templates for the placement of 3-D imagery; these aesthetic conventions will be defined and applied to other "flat" trailers for signs of absent 3-D footage; original trailer scripts will be used to differentiate between flat and 3-D previews; and the network of influences that surround and infuse the trailer texts will be interrogated for additional historical or industrial information. This unified analysis will demonstrate the place of 3-D footage in the contemporary trailer texts, explore its attempt to create an active audience, and consider how the technology was positioned against competing processes.

One of the few original trailers to survive in its full 3-D form is *It Came from Outer Space*. After a short series of titles, the trailer opens with a "Master of Ceremonies" segment that features actor Richard Carlson, set against a shadowy desert landscape. The camera tracks forward, framing him in a medium shot, and allowing his 3-D image to loom out of the screen, the desert receding into the background: "Ladies and gentlemen, the events that I'm about to describe may sound incredible to most people — but I know they happened. I saw them happen."[27] Carlson (in character) controls the first half of the trailer, narrating over a series of 3-D images that showcase the technology and that, after his narration ends, then continue his story of alien invasion through excerpted scenes and title work. The Master of Ceremonies functions as part of the story: the trailer narrative is included within the film's diegesis, and the main character offers the audience access to the story world, "including" them through his address and use of 3-D. The trailer makes no specific mention of the technology that is making Carlson's 3-D appearance possible but the footage showcases the additional depth given to the screen. By comparison, the surviving "flat" trailer for the same film has Carlson in the same location, but as "himself" and offering audiences an explanation of 3 Dimension. Rather than placing them "inside" the story (as the 3-D trailer promises to do) the "flat" trailer excludes audiences, offering a non-diegetic

Master of Ceremonies who offers production knowledge, rather than access to the story world. Unlike Cinerama, whose technological star was based around replacing narrative with spectacle, this 3-D trailer combines narrative and technology within its star image. The technology available for each trailer creates two distinct sales messages: a 3-D one around narrative and envelopment, and a "flat" one around a lack of 3-D, using technology as a lure for audiences to search out their local 3-D theatre so that they too can be "active," included within the story world.

The use of 3-D footage in the *It Came from Outer Space* trailer offers a further comparison with the film's "flat" trailer: the latter is hyperbolic while the 3-D version is restrained, using its display of 3-D technology to sell the process and its effectiveness. The trailer offers a synthesis of 3-D imagery: gimmick-laden moments of objects being thrown at the screen alongside a more subtle demonstration of the possibilities offered by depth photography — illustrating Carlson's comment that the film shows people, landscapes and objects in dimensions similar to real life. This strand of the trailer is established early on: after Carlson's introduction, the trailer cuts to a fireball streaking right to left across the sky, placed above a set of trees, which are distinct (and on a different "level") from the desert and mountains beyond. Later, Carlson is shown peering through a hexagonal hole in the side of the ship. Shot from inside, with the interior of the ship in the foreground, Carlson hovering in a mid-ground, and the landscape far back in the distance, the scene offers different levels within the image. We then get Carlson's POV into the ship — a long cavernous space, a distant room full of stars and planets — the camera tracks toward this, so that this room looms toward the camera, becomes clearer, a more defined and rounded image. At the end of Carlson's narration, there is an effective sense of depth in a point-of-view shot of the alien walking behind Carlson and Barbara Rush. As Carlson and Rush walk by two large

Richard Carlson stands in the desert landscape in the flat *It Came from Outer Space* trailer (1953), unable to demonstrate the 3-D footage.

rocks, the rocks extend out of screen then pass off-camera — Carlson moves forward, so that he recedes a little, and Rush becomes the main focus of the image — just as a wispy hand reaches out to touch her shoulder. Here, as well as emphasizing depth, the spatial dimensions of the screen also allow the trailer to reinforce character and narrative information — Rush's position, literally hovering between the human Carlton and the unseen alien presence, caught between them, presages the later takeover of her body by the aliens (seen briefly in the trailer). Layering 3-D images in this way can also be seen in *The Maze* (1953), the other full 3-D trailer. Actress Veronica Hurst claws her way through a series of huge cobwebs, each set at a different depth to the others. The use of 3-D makes her passage through the webs (and toward camera) elongated and suspenseful — here, the 3-D footage offers genre information by combining technologically innovative visuals with a classic horror image. In both trailers, these images structure the display of 3-D, giving the illusion of a real space on screen.

Such scenes work to place characters and locations in their own 3-D "space," stressing Carlson's "real life" dimensions — but the 3-D trailer aesthetic also features a more overt demonstration: the "coming out of the screen" strand of 3-D trailer content. Early in the *It Came from Outer Space* trailer, as the fireball falls to earth, there are two quick images: the fireball rushing into camera, and a piece of rock thrown into camera after the explosion. Both occasions are about shock and surprise, things literally coming "at" the viewer. Two later images continue this part of the sales message — Rush (controlled by an alien) fires two ray blasts from a long wand "at" the audience, and rocks tumble down a cliff-face straight "into" the camera (in which several "fake" or special effects rocks appear to have been added — the ones that literally bounce "into" camera). These represent the strongest use of visual spectacle in the trailer, offering the gimmick of 3-D filmmaking rather than the more composed sense of depth and character placement that the earlier scenes focused on. *The Maze* trailer also uses its presentation of things coming out of the screen for shock value — Richard Carlson jabs his hand forward toward the viewer (noting, and illustrating, that "something from the great beyond reaches right out of the screen at you,"[28]) — but also to reinforce generic staples, with various shots of vampire bats flying "into" the camera punctuating the trailer.

Apart from the use of existing 3-D visuals excerpted from the feature, or specially filmed for the trailer, these 3-D previews also use graphic titles to stress the new depth of the screen. *It Came from Outer Space*'s trailer lacks the frequency of screen-filling titles found in other 3-D trailers, but the quality and use of 3-D footage sells the process more effectively through demonstration.[29] The use of the graphic title work enables a further emphasis on the display of 3-D technology. In Cinerama and CinemaScope, titles literally stretch across screen, underlining the widescreen by filling it. In the case of 3-D, the words seem to float above the screen, distinct from the scenes they overlay, as though the viewer could look "around" and behind them to see the image they were superimposed above. The words themselves may be exclamatory but their use of 3-D imagery relates more to the subtle use of depth photography than the shock "coming at you" examples.

The visual evidence of these two trailer texts shows that a strong 3-D aesthetic was promoted through trailer advertising. The test of the hypothesis presented here — that the three elements of an active screen, objects being thrust at the viewer and an attempt to create a more realistic image formed the basic conventions of the 3-D trailer — would be to apply such criteria to other trailers from the 1953–1954 3-D boom. Although the absence of other full 3-D trailers makes this project difficult, a unified analysis of the remaining flat trailers (particularly the placement of potential 3-D imagery) and their network of influences may offer a partial solution. The ability to identify and distinguish between 3-D and flat trailers is aided by historical information from trailer scripts and the early trailer texts. As with Cinerama, the first 3-D feature to debut in the 1950s was produced outside the Hollywood studio system. *Bwana Devil* (1952) was described as "a feature picture ... that any exhibitor with two machines in his booth can exhibit in full three-dimen-

A strong 3-D sales message lies at the heart of the *It Came from Outer Space* trailer (1953).

Graphic title work suggests the three-dimensional effect in the flat trailer for *It Came from Outer Space* (1953).

sion."[30] The key phrase is "any exhibitor with two machines"—like its widescreen rival, 3-D used multiple projectors to create its on-screen image. The dual success of Cinerama and 3-D—parallel attempts to expand the appeal of the cinema screen through technology that changed the dimensions of the screen—convinced the Hollywood studios to jump onto the 3-D bandwagon while it was still financially successful. Existing projects were transformed into 3-D films in the race to be first onto cinema screens—and it is this rush to be first that lies behind the initial phase of flat trailers. The trailer for *Bwana Devil* did not contain any 3-D footage, no free sample of the technology—and the studio's initial response was the same: desperate to sell the technology as a star but unable to demonstrate the appeal of that star.

The set-up of the projection system created the initial problems—3-D projection required two projectors, running simultaneously, showing two strips of film (left and right eye images) that had to be completely synchronized to create the 3-D effect. Intermissions were needed to change reels (since most theatres only had two projectors, which would normally run in succession, not simultaneously), increasing the length of the screening. In early to mid–1953, theatres displayed slides informing audiences of intermissions to change projectors, or to warn them when in the program to put their glasses on. Like Cinerama, the effect of the wider or deeper screen was considered paramount, and 3-D trailers ran the risk of lessening the impact of the technology. Flat trailers from this time period can be identified by the level of rhetoric in titles and voiceover, centering the 3-D technology in the sales message, but unable to display it. The *House of Wax* (1953) trailer exclaims it is the "first feature production by a major studio in 3 DIMENSION" but despite titles that exclaim "Every THRILL of Its Story Comes OFF the Screen RIGHT AT YOU" the trailer remains a two-dimensional experience. The use of exaggerated language suggests the trailer's status as an early flat trailer, but it also creates strong links between the nascent technology and its Cinerama rival. Titles such as "YOU probe into the screaming terror/ YOU are engulfed in its mysteries/YOU actually sense its chilling menace ... its evil touches YOU!" are reminiscent of Cinerama's claims of envelopment and the active audience.[31] The repetition of "YOU" in such trailers places interaction at the core of this technological sales message — and recalls the promotion of Cinerama: "you won't be gazing at a movie screen — you'll find yourself swept right into the picture."[32]

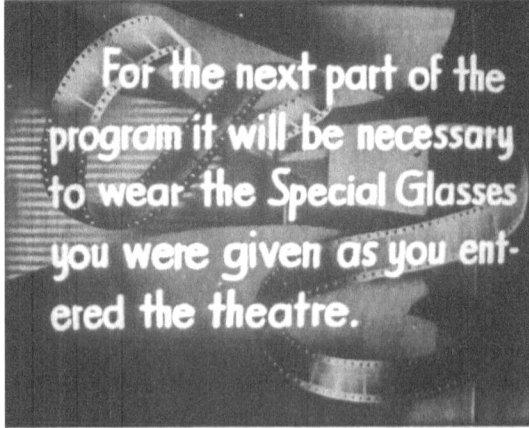

Top: 3-D technology could cause problems for theatres showing flat and 3-D elements within the same program. *Bottom:* Theatres often used slides to warn audiences when to put on their 3-D glasses.

The move from flat to full 3-D trailers can be traced to the middle of 1953 and lasts until 1954, when studios began to phase out their 3-D projects. Although a firm timeline cannot be established for the beginning of 3-D trailer production, the existence of *The*

ONE • "Something BIG Is Coming!" 45

Almost all elements of the theatrical program were 3-D during late 1953, including newsreels, short films and cartoons.

Maze trailer (released in July 1953), original trailer scripts, and the network of other three-dimensional elements of the theatrical program suggest a mid–1953 date. Newsreels, short subjects, cartoons (including animated stars Popeye, Tom and Jerry and Bugs Bunny), and advertising films were all being shown in 3-D by the second half of the year.[33] Even theatre lobbies entered the third dimension — trailer company National Screen and toy manufacturer ViewMaster® issued "movie preview reels ... to promote the release of several 3-D and 'flat' movies" that were shown in special lobby display units to allow "movie-goers to preview the film with realistic 3-D pictures."[34] With the entire theatrical experience becoming 3-D, we can speculate that most trailers for 3-D films from mid–1953 on were produced in 3-D — alongside flat versions that were produced in order to promote the technology in cinemas that had yet to convert. Proof of this last point comes from the Universal and MGM trailer script archives, with annotations that note "3-D version" or "flat version"— often using the same script and imagery in both. This, of course, only confuses the issue of which trailer has survived, but given that 3-D and flat versions used the same imagery, it is possible to evoke the absent 3-D aesthetic even when only the flat version remains.

Of the remaining 30 or so trailers that fit into this dating schema, some broad conclusions can be drawn from their structure and apparent use of faux 3-D imagery. Certain structural and stylistic patterns do recur. The Master of Ceremonies figure features in several trailers, but the general resurgence of this trailer style in movie and television promotion in the 1950s alongside its use in distinctly different flat and 3-D trailers for the same project (such as the *It Came from Outer Space* example, above) reduce the likelihood that this was a specific 3-D convention. However, at least two of the elements identified earlier — a sense of "real" dimensions on screen, and objects thrusting into camera — are all potentially visible in the other trailer texts.[35] The use of layered depth photography is difficult to judge based on the trailers and scripts available — the nuances of character placement within landscape are often too subtle to spot in the flat versions. It seems likely that an ambush scene in the trailer for *Taza, Son of Cochise* (1954) would have allowed the 3-D photography to isolate and accentuate the Indian figures in fore and background, and create tension around the soldiers caught between them; equally, in the *Jesse James vs. the Daltons* (1954) trailer a long shot, through a noose (foreground), as a lynching party approaches (background), offers a sense that 3-D composition was still central to sales messages. The idea of objects being rammed toward camera is a more fertile ground when attempting to fill in these absent texts — from flaming torches in *Drums of Tahiti* (1954), spears in *Jivaro* (1954), harpoon guns firing in *Creature from the Black Lagoon* (1954), or people being thrown over the camera in *Hondo* (1953), the 3-D trailers are full of potential examples. Trailer scripts make clear that these elements are important structural cues: scripts for *Creature from the Black Lagoon* and *Revenge of the Creature* (1955) reiterate scene choices that focus on 3-D visuals: "monster swimming toward camera," "swimmer shooting harpoon into camera," "crowd running toward camera," and "monster walking forward with girl."[36] Although much of this must remain conjecture, what is clear is the important role that the technology played in these trailers — the display of the 3-D footage was central to the sales message, creating a star image around the technology itself.

There is another specific (and highly suggestive) absence that this list of potential 3-D images does not contain: the link between the technology and its presentation of the female body. This association appears in 3-D poster and trailer advertising, but the surviving 3-D trailer texts cannot fully illuminate the extent to which this relationship was visually expressed through a 3-D aesthetic. During 1954, as studios shifted production away from 3-D toward the increasingly dominant CinemaScope process (which, as we shall see later, also pursues this technology/female form association), advertising for films such as *Kiss Me Kate* (1953) and *Dial M for Murder* (1954) became flat again, reverting to genre- and star-based trailer narratives rather than technology. One of the last studio features to be released in 3-D was the Jane Russell vehicle, *The French Line* (1954). Its trailer (produced originally in 3-D) only exists in a flat version, but poster advertising makes clear what the film's important 3-D attributes are: "J.R. in 3D.... It'll knock *both* your eyes out!" Indeed, the flat trailer showcases several scenes with Russell dancing, strutting and jiggling: a suggestion that she was the object that would thrust its way off the screen. Looking back through the available trailers, the link between 3-D technology and sexuality is overt even from the earliest examples: from the abstract images of sensuous female lips and feminine shadows in the flat trailer for *House of Wax* to a fascinating display of masculine and feminine roles in the flat trailer for *Sangaree* (1953).

After some introductory titles the *Sangaree* trailer cuts to a long shot of a screen-filling red curtain. The male voiceover repeats the film's name, then announces that "beautiful Arlene Dahl ... [will] tell you all about it." Female voiceovers were almost unheard of in trailers and the female presence was most often reduced to glamorous images in excerpted scenes or close-ups — so the appearance of Dahl, and her apparent control of the sales message, feels revolutionary. That feeling does not last. Dahl appears and talks about how exciting it was making the film, but says the story is so big, she will have to ask her (male) co-star, Fernando Lamas, to help explain 3-D. As Lamas appears, Dahl turns to him: "Fernando, we have quite a problem. Just how are we going to show these people how wonderful *Sangaree* looks in third dimension?" The suggestion here is that the actress cannot explain anything technologically advanced, but that the actor will be able to through his mastery of technological expertise. However, the following exchange, as Dahl stands demurely to one side while her male co-star tries to explain 3-D, foregrounds 3-D's potential for displaying sexuality, particularly the 3-D glory of the female form. Given this flat trailer is unable to physically exhibit 3-D visuals, Lamas attempts to demonstrate the point by describing a flat screen — he waves his hand horizontally in front of him; for length, he pulls his hands apart horizontally; height — he raises his hand vertically, palm down; and then, "the most interesting thing ... depth." At this point, he makes a circular motion with his hands, as though describing the shape of a sphere. "Now, let me tell you about depth ... depth is ... uh ... well ... eh." The reason he is having so much trouble is that he can't take his eyes off Arlene Dahl's breasts, which his hands, still attempting to demonstrate "depth," are emulating the shape of. Rather than one sphere, his hands momentarily cup two imaginary globes before sliding down in an imitation of an idealized female shape. Uncertain, he takes one last (long) look at Dahl, drops his hands to his sides and says "uh ... it's depth.... I think you have to go and see it to understand." A reassuring smile from Dahl allows them to move on to talk about safer things, such as how epic a story it is. But that moment remains. Not only has Lamas failed in his masculine role (since *The Jazz Singer* trailer, men have always been the ones to educate and inform audiences of new developments) but he has linked 3-D to Arlene Dahl's chest, suggesting that this new technology is only useful because it will allow breasts to thrust their way off the screen.[37]

This link of technology with the female form can be seen in other trailers, both flat and 3-D — Randolph Scott describes his *The Stranger Wore a Gun* (1953) co-star Claire Trevor as "three-d in any language"; *Those Redheads from Seattle*'s (1953) trailer opens with the three red-heads in question high-kicking their way off the screen, petticoats flying around, with superimposed 3-D titles that exclaim "THREE REDHEADS ... IN THREE (WOW) DIMENSIONS"[38]; a female trapeze artist in a low-cut outfit lunges into camera in *Gorilla at Large*'s (1954) trailer; while the positioning of Rita Hayworth in the *Miss Sadie Thompson* (1953) trailer suggest that she was also 3-D in any language. It is difficult to state definitively how explicit this sexual link was, but the most common elements within the available trailers (beyond the generic "something is thrown at the camera") are the presentation of 3-D bodies, with the most common examples being either feminine — or alien. Jane Russell, Rita Hayworth, Claire Trevor and Arlene Dahl might have knocked both your eyes out, but their 3-D counterparts are not masculine heroes, but the Creature From the Black Lagoon, Robot Monster, and the aliens who Came From Outer Space. This use of titillation through technology suggests a contemporary (masculine) uncertainty over the female body — at once desirable and sexual but also alien and unknowable. Fernando Lamas' insecurity over how to talk about the mystery represented by a woman's body, and his need to fall back on the most basic visual cue, represents both the fear and excitement of such imagery. Yet the frustrating absence of full 3-D trailer texts means this imagery remains a potential aesthetic and thematic component, suggestive rather than definitive. Even in the trailer for *Cat Women of the Moon* (1953) — where alien monster and sexually charged female form are combined in the same "body" — the absence of a complete 3-D text means the only absent 3-D image that can be fully identified is a giant spider that lunges at the camera.

In the *Sangaree* trailer (1954), Fernando Lamas fails in his attempt to explain 3-D to audiences, because he can't keep his eyes off Arlene Dahl's chest.

What then can the 3-D trailers tell us

about the display of technology in this short historical moment? 3-D itself has been dismissed as a technology because of its 1950s failure to secure a steady audience, and the subsequent attempts to revive it (3-D pornography in the 1970s, *Jaws 3-D* (1983) and *Friday the 13th Part III* (1982) in the 1980s, IMAX and James Cameron in the 2000s) have met with little success. It is possible to see 3-D as a passing fad, a post–Cinerama attempt to engulf the audience that failed to see the future was wider screens, not deeper ones. What a unified analysis of these trailer visuals has revealed is that 3-D trailers attempted to create their own technological star. Taking the concept of spectacle and audience envelopment from Cinerama, these 3-D trailers emphasize the strongest visual cues, the most prominent displays of the technology's attributes (most often the shock of an object breaking free of the screen) and reassert the need to use key technologically created imagery at the heart of a trailer sales message. Unlike hybrid trailers of the 1930s and 1940s, which were often produced from production off-cuts or without access to a completed cut of the film, analysis of these 3-D trailers shows the necessity of using actual finished footage. In flat trailers such as *House of Wax* or *Sangaree* the absence of 3-D imagery forces the trailer to rely on colorful language and hybrid conventions based around genre and star image; with the introduction of 3-D footage in *The Maze* and *It Came from Outer Space* the emphasis shifts to a trailer structure dependent on important visual spectacle from the film. 3-D trailers may not have created this trailer convention — Biblical epic *Noah's Ark* (1929) used key special effects sequences to structure its trailer — but taking their cue from Cinerama, they redefined the use of technology in such structures. 3-D trailers may not be an essential evolutionary step in trailer history, but their focus on compelling visual information and the display of the technological process makes them a crucial bridge between the technologies of Cinerama and CinemaScope.

CinemaScope: "The Modern Miracle"

> For years producers, distributors and theatre men have been looking for a Moses to lead them out of a film wilderness ... in CinemaScope they have found that Moses.[39]

As the trailer for *How to Marry a Millionaire* (1953) opens, we hear the first bars of a piece of lush orchestral music and see the image of a dark blue curtain. The curtains part, inching sedately across the width of the wide screen, and the source of the music is revealed to be a full orchestra, stretched across the image, filling it from left to right. The titles superimposed over this shot exclaim that CinemaScope is "The Modern Miracle You See With-

The curtains pull back to reveal the full width of the CinemaScope screen in the *How to Marry a Millionaire* trailer (1953).

out Special Glasses."[40] In these opening seconds, the trailer has positioned itself as a free sample of the wide screen technology of CinemaScope with its languid curtain-parting revelation of the orchestra, at once teasing the viewer and emphasizing the width of the screen (the curtains open further and further, wider and wider). The trailer has drawn upon contemporary knowledge of rival widescreen technology with a deliberate echo of *This Is Cinerama*'s own screen-filling orchestra. At the same time, the trailer devalues the other technological competitor — 3-D film technology — with its barbed commentary on the special Polaroid glasses that audiences had to wear. Finally, the shot of the orchestra suggests a link with the legitimate theatrical and concert tradition, and the classical music underscores an association between technology and cultural values. If CinemaScope was Hollywood's Moses, then the early CinemaScope trailers were the heralds that trumpeted its arrival in cinemas throughout the U.S. and around the world. This combination of anti-competitive messages, widescreen aesthetics, social positioning and visual spectacle fuelled the early CinemaScope trailers but these previews are also unique texts that visually document the growth of the technological star in the Hollywood industry.

From the opening shot of the orchestra, the *How to Marry a Millionaire* trailer moves on to strengthen the link between CinemaScope and the competing technology of Cinerama, focusing audience attention onto travelogue imagery. As noted earlier, Cinerama films (and eventually trailers) built spectacular landscapes and scenic images into their sales messages, structuring these elements as a unique part of its brand identity. The CinemaScope trailers — of which *How to Marry a Millionaire* is an exemplary illustration — take this basic structural principle and make it a central tenet of their sales message. This was not an accident — 20th Century–Fox memos make it clear that

CinemaScope had been devised, tested, and marketed with "a definite objective ... to compete with Cinerama."[41] While trailers have always stressed the impressive nature of domestic and foreign locations (even when most were shot on the studio back lot) this tended to have a narrative purpose: the opening of the *Casablanca* (1942) trailer, for instance, quickly establishes a locale for the story but it does not linger on images of the Moroccan city or landscape. The *How to Marry a Millionaire* trailer emphasizes spectacle with recurring views of the Brooklyn Bridge, the Maine ski-slopes, and the New York skyline: travelogue for travelogue's sake. These images have little or no narrative purpose in the trailer's sales message (beyond suggesting a variety of locations within the film) but the trailer returns time and again to similar images, lingering on them, the travel guide structure supported by title work: "Only CINEMASCOPE could bring you the GLAMOUR of the World's greatest city—the THRILL of Maine's ski slopes."[42] The suggested ability of the CinemaScope camera to reveal more of the world to the viewer is a key visual convention within CinemaScope trailers, and the known content of the Cinerama films was used to attract audiences into local CinemaScope theatres.

The repetition of travelogue imagery has deeper connotations than simply recalling technological knowledge. These trailers tie contemporary social trends to the promised CinemaScope experience. The emphasis within the *How to Marry a Millionaire* trailer on the east coast of America, and particularly New York, reflects the post-war optimism of the late 1940s and early 1950s, when Manhattan was a center of art and fashion. The trailer links its views of the city with its status as the gateway to America, showing cruise ships docking at the port. Those cruise liners and the cross-country train trips that are pictured within the trailer narrative show the modern travel options open to the new American consumer-led society. Leisure pursuits such as skiing, previously regarded as part of the upper-class lifestyle, were now seen as possible holiday activities for all. *How to Marry a Millionaire*'s trailer taps into this new desire to get away more, take more holidays, see more of the country and (by extension) the world. John Sittig has dismissed CinemaScope as "Cinerama for the masses," because most CinemaScope films were shot in Hollywood (with some second unit location shooting) rather than produced entirely on location (as was the case with Cinerama).[43] Despite this, these CinemaScope trailers blatantly invite the viewer into this travelogue world, encouraging them to visit these locations through their trip to the cinema. Subtle references to Cinerama continued through the next wave of CinemaScope previews, with the *Three Coins in the Fountain* (1954) trailer mimicking the aerial views of Rome, including languid pans across the Trevi Fountain and the Vatican, seen in *Seven Wonders of the World*. The content of the Cinerama films—in terms of both subject matter and aesthetic—had become a central audience lure for CinemaScope productions.

The *How to Marry a Millionaire* trailer moves away from overt competitive messages after these opening statements and images in order to stress the power of its own technological process. A voiceover comment does refer to the "eye filling" dimensions of Cinemascope but this functions to promote the positive aspects of CinemaScope rather than reiterate anti–3-D rhetoric. Many of the strongest examples of visual information and widescreen aesthetics used as free samples of the process inevitably link the trailer to competing technologies, but the trailer conventions move on to stress what CinemaScope — and the films produced in it — can offer an audience. There was a pressing need for this trailer to establish a strong identity for CinemaScope. Daryl Zanuck, vice-president in charge of production at 20th Century–Fox, described the central tenets of the CinemaScope sales message as the ability to show new horizons, new locations, to balance scale and story, and to provide both entertainment and showmanship.[44] Overall, he was conscious that CinemaScope should be positioned as the biggest and best technology available — having developed CinemaScope from Henri Chretien's anamorphic lens technology (allowing a wider image to be squeezed onto 35mm film stock), in February 1953 Fox announced that all studio productions would be filmed in CinemaScope.[45] Fox, aware that they could neither convert enough movie theatres nor produce enough films in this new process on their own, moved quickly to demonstrate the technology to exhibitors and other studios (some of whom were already attempting to create ersatz widescreen films by cropping existing films into a 1.85:1 ratio). A CinemaScope publicity trailer, *Stereophonic Sound and Picture Test*, had been shown to exhibitors worldwide in March and April 1953, featuring "footage designed to show what the system can do."[46] The trailer helped convince exhibitors to spend money renovating their theatres, and secured licensing agreements with MGM, Disney, UA, Columbia and Warner Bros., ensuring that the process had almost full industry support by autumn 1953. The *How to Marry a Millionaire* trailer, produced and released in CinemaScope approximately six months after this publicity film, had a very precise purpose: to fulfill the promise of this technology by enticing audiences back into the theatre.

The first CinemaScope trailer was for *The Robe* (1953), but analysis of it reveals a lack of conviction. The trailer is uncertain in its use of technology, falling back on more traditional hybrid trailer conventions: the star image (Richard Burton), romance (Burton and Jean Simmons: "The love that defied an empire"), the historical epic genre ("The glory that was Rome") and the literature adaptation ("one of the greatest novels of all time").[47] These are placed alongside the widescreen spectacle provided by the vistas and landscape shots of palaces and the Roman legions, but the technology does not dominate, and the footage does not contain the showmanship and entertainment so important to Zanuck. If CinemaScope was truly Hollywood's Moses, this first attempt to create a trailer in the process lacked faith in its abilities—mirrored by the studio's decision to film the feature in Academy ratio as well as CinemaScope.[48] Like many high-profile launch vehicles, *The Robe* could rely on more than a trailer to inform a wide audience: 20th Century–Fox ensured a high level of national press and publicity for the Hollywood and New York premieres, and followed that with regional hyperbole as the film traveled the U.S. The second release, *How to Marry a Millionaire*, wasn't a traditional Biblical spectacle, and couldn't rely on generating the same level of publicity. The trailer needed to take the CinemaScope brand to new heights, to display this new technology at its best and biggest. Analyzing the *How to Marry a Millionaire* trailer in light of this network of information allows us to focus on its complex layering of visual information, and understand its overriding need to push two key messages: first, that audiences wanted their cinema screens wider, not just for one film, but for every film from then on; and second, that CinemaScope was the only technology that could provide those films.

How to Marry a Millionaire's trailer demonstrates that the first step toward those goals was to fulfill Darryl Zanuck's edict that CinemaScope productions must "give full effect to the large scale and scope of the new medium."[49] To achieve this, the bulk of the trailer's structure is built around the most spectacular widescreen imagery from the feature. 3-D trailers were built around those moments that best defined the dimensionality of the process, so the CinemaScope trailers place particular emphasis on stressing the width of the screen, and what is filling it. The *How to Marry a Millionaire* trailer is formed around the strongest of these big screen images: from the curtain that inches across the screen; the size of the orchestra; the span of the Brooklyn Bridge that stretches across the image; a luxury ocean liner that steams along the horizontal frame; and a fashion show photo shoot that sprawls across the view of the camera. All of these big wide images sell what the titles describe as the "miracle" of CinemaScope, and the trailer focuses on these free samples to sell the process to the audience, but they are not the only things filling the screen in CinemaScope trailers. Graphic title work and star images are also used to define the new screen size and promote the CinemaScope brand.

Inter-titles in the hybrid trailers of the 1940s were not restricted to the center of the screen (titles could appear in different areas, building up a sales message, flashing an actor's name under their image), but there was a tendency to focus on a central image position, particularly for star names, the film's title and any major hyperbole connected to the narrative or genre. With the advent of CinemaScope, there are obvious changes in the use of graphic inter-titles, particularly screen placement: while the titles still inform audiences, they offer a further stress on the new, wider screen. In the *How to Marry*

CinemaScope trailers use graphic title work to lead the eye across the screen. *How to Marry a Millionaire* trailer (1953).

a Millionaire trailer, identifying titles work with excerpted visual information to stress the width and size of the screen, as well as guide audience attention. In one sequence, which shows Marilyn Monroe, Betty Grable and Lauren Bacall sitting on a rooftop balcony, the titles don't simply overlay a close-up image of the star (as would be expected in a pre-widescreen hybrid trailer). Instead, the titles and visuals lead the eye as the identifying names of Monroe, Grable and Bacall appear left, center, and right of screen, below the actress in question. As the titles appear, each actress stands up behind her name, leading the eye across all three, and across the width of the wider screen. Although the scene is excerpted from the film, the trailer uses it to introduce each actress, directing audience attention horizontally across the screen through a combination of image and title work that emphasizes the width of the image, and thus, the process: the full title claims "Only CinemaScope Can Do Justice to Marilyn Monroe—Betty Grable—Lauren Bacall." Later trailers continue this stress on widescreen conventions through graphic title work: in the *Three Coins in the Fountain* trailer the letters of the title "WIDER" gradually move apart, stretching the word across the horizontal image. In the *Knights of the Round Table* (1953) trailer, graphic banners on the left and right of frame confine the excerpted image into a faux Academy ratio. As they raise up, they reveal and accentuate the wider image beneath.

How to Marry a Millionaire's widescreen trailer aesthetics are strengthened through the combination of image and graphic title work, but the sequence arguably advances star trailer conventions as well — rather than one star, and one identifying title filling the screen, the widescreen image presents three stars at once, each in their own space and with their own title. The trailer states that "Only CinemaScope Can Do Justice to Monroe, Grable [and] Bacall," a suggestion that the screen had to get bigger simply to accommodate these big stars. But an earlier title claimed the film features "An Array of Stars as Wonderful and Exciting as This Great New Motion Picture Miracle," suggesting "Scope was already on a higher plateau that the stars had to strive to reach."[50] The titles also make it clear that these stars are there to "Fill the Screen"—further emphasis on the importance of the new, bigger screen over what is shown on it. In the *How to Marry a Millionaire* trailer (as in many of these CinemaScope previews), the technological star threatens to overpower (human) star imagery, reducing them to a secondary sales device, in the shadow of the technological miracle of CinemaScope. Part of the reason for this was the footage available from the first CinemaScope features. Fulfilling Zanuck's belief that CinemaScope films must be epic, these initial productions were dominated by CinemaScope's shot scale, which was better suited to extreme long, long and medium shots rather than intimate, close-ups (which tended to warp when projected). Images had to be composed horizontally, or in depth, and often used longer takes. Given that trailers traditionally used close-up images or excerpted close-ups to highlight star personas, this footage presented some difficulties. The *How to Marry a Millionaire* trailer attempts to use the closest images it can — the three lead actresses are all shown in separate medium shots, posing for the camera — but their central image is swamped by extraneous detail on left and right, threatening to distract attention from their image. Compared to Lauren Bacall's presentation in the trailer for *Key Largo* (1950) which uses four close-up shots of the actress, as well as other excerpted moments that focus attention onto her, in the *How to Marry a Millionaire* trailer she is never shown in anything closer than a medium shot, and often shares long shots with the other actresses, rather than being separate from them.

Despite this difficulty with star images and close-ups, one human star does stand out in *How to Marry a Millionaire*'s trailer, by embodying (or temporarily sharing) the characteristics of the process. As we have seen in some

Marilyn Monroe lounges across the new wider screen dimensions of CinemaScope in the *How to Marry a Millionaire* trailer (1953).

3-D trailers, there is a suggestive link between the female body (or, at least, certain female bodies) and the technology that is presenting them to an audience, in this case CinemaScope. While the *How to Marry A Millionaire* trailer appears to offer a democratization of star trailer conventions — all three female stars have their own introduction, with identifying titles, they share several scenes together, and their main introduction comes in the balcony scene analyzed above — the trailer singles out one star from the other through its choice of wide screen imagery. Marilyn Monroe is first among these female equals in this trailer: our first image of her shows her full length, languidly reposed on a chair, legs stretching out almost all the way across the screen; later, in the dressing room scene with all three actresses, again Monroe is seated, in the far left of screen, stretching her legs toward the center, body barely wrapped in a tight-fitting red bathing suit — despite the presence of her co-stars in the center and right of screen, her costume, and her movement from horizontal to vertical when she stands up to join them, keeps the audience attention on her. Grable and Bacall get their own moments to shine, and take center stage, but they are in medium shots, cut off at the waist, or shown in long shot. The widescreen trailer has already visually positioned Monroe ahead of their star images. Her female body, presented horizontally, takes on the dimensions of CinemaScope, aligning her with the process. In this trailer, it is Monroe and CinemaScope who do justice to each other, not the other performers.

Star images remained key to these initial CinemaScope trailer aesthetics, although they are not as explicit as the links with competitive technology or graphic title work. Very few star images took on the attributes of CinemaScope in the way Monroe did in the *How to Marry a Millionaire* trailer. The opening shots of *The Opposite Sex* (1956) trailer show views of the film's feminine stars before cutting to an image of long, stockinged female legs. A woman's hands reach down and stroke the legs from ankle to thigh — but like the legs, the owner of these hands remains unseen, off-screen. There is a suggestion that the legs belong to Joan Collins, who is pictured immediately after them, but like the other female stars (Ann Sheridan, June Allyson and Dolores Gray) she remains centered in the picture, never mirroring the aesthetics of the wider screen. As with Monroe and Arlene Dahl, however, the link between technology and the female form remains a strong message. *The Opposite Sex* trailer also demonstrates the move away from star images that sprawled across the frame to the placement of numerous stars in one image: in *How to Marry a Millionaire* the three actresses shared the screen; here, up to six actresses are pictured at any one time, with none of them dominating. The reintroduction of medium shots and close-ups (rarer in early CinemaScope projects because of studio uncertainty over how composition should be handled on the wider screen) also reduced the link between star and screen width.

The wider screen could still be used to suggest star persona — in the trailer for *The Great American Past-time* (1956) star Tom Ewell is positioned centrally, but at one point the trailer pulls back to place him between images of two girls, "always in the middle."[51] The use of both wide and split screen aesthetics builds up Ewell's playboy image as well as providing some feature narrative detail.

The use of the technological star of CinemaScope as a central sales message starts to diminish in 1955, as genres and new technology begin to dominate the industry. The ascendancy of genre, narrative, and stars in increasingly hybridized trailer narratives can be linked to CinemaScope adaptations of established literary or Broadway properties, where the technology was reduced to a secondary role within sales messages dominated by songs, dancing and hyperbole based on theatrical or best-seller success. Then, in 1955, the CinemaScope star was further tarnished when 20th Century–Fox, worried about the competitive widescreen system Todd-AO, announced a new widescreen process, CinemaScope 55. CinemaScope was no longer the studio's biggest or best widescreen process, relegated to the "normal" process they produced films in. Its star image on the wane, Fox came to the conclusion that CinemaScope had lost "much of its novelty ... customers were no longer drawn to theatres solely because the picture was in the CinemaScope process."[52] CinemaScope may have seen off the competition from 3-D and Cinerama, but its own success at promoting the wider screen had led to the debut of new, cheaper processes.

The loss of CinemaScope as a strong technological star did not, however, dilute the conventions that had developed through Cinerama and 3-D and that now underpinned the CinemaScope aesthetic. The wider screen was now an established part of the Hollywood industry, and trailers still relied on a widescreen aesthetic — the stars that dominate *The Barretts of Wimpole Street*'s (1957) trailer are all pictured within the borders of a photo album, the pages of which match the dimensions of the wider screen; travelogue images dominate the *It Started with a Kiss* (1959) trailer, as a long red convertible ("just the thing to go CinemaScoping across the Spanish countryside"[53]) drives through the various locations. The CinemaScope trailer may have lost its technological position, but its ability to show epic landscapes, stunning travelogue imagery and to position both stars and graphic titles in new places relied on the wider screen visuals. Even with the decline of CinemaScope's technological status, widescreen trailer conventions echo through VistaVision, Todd-AO and Panavision. The technology may not have forever altered trailer evolution, but vestiges of the 1950s widescreen aesthetic remain.

Conclusion

Trailer texts for Cinerama, 3-D and CinemaScope all begin by displaying an aspect, a free sample, of its central technological star: the *How the West Was Won* trailer opened with an uninterrupted view of a spectacular mountain landscape draped across its three screens; *It Came from Outer Space*'s preview offered a display of depth photography, placing Richard Carlson in a three-dimensional desert setting; and the *How to Marry a Millionaire* trailer emphasized the width of its image with a slowly parting curtain and screen-filling orchestra. The introduction of these three processes between 1952 and 1955 encapsulates the Hollywood studios' attempts to introduce screen-specific innovations in the face of competition from alternative media or leisure interests, not to mention other competing cinema technologies. These trailers enticed audiences with cinematic lures, offering visual spectacle in place of (or in addition to) the traditional title cards that exclaimed "SEE!" "WATCH!" or "IMAGINE!" In these trailer texts little is left to the imagination: they center visual evidence in order to establish the credentials of their disparate technological stars.

The lifespan of these screen stars was short-lived: by 1955 3-D had faded from cinema screens and the dominance of CinemaScope had been reduced by the introduction of new widescreen processes, causing 20th Century–Fox to note that "theatergoers do not know the difference between Panavision and CinemaScope. Seventy mm Todd-AO is an excellent box-office 'name.'... [but] most people think it is actually Cinerama. I do not think the name Todd-AO sells tickets."[54] From Cinerama "the hero" to the Todd-AO "name," the technological star image was reduced as a potent sales message through the 1950s. The decline in star status can be seen in original trailer scripts from the mid to late 1950s that reveal many widescreen and 3-D trailers were produced in different formats with detachable title "tags" that could limit the technological sales message. CinemaScope trailers could be produced in four separate versions: a CinemaScope trailer selling CinemaScope and stereophonic sound, a CinemaScope trailer selling only CinemaScope, a flat trailer (featuring cropped widescreen footage) selling CinemaScope, and a flat trailer selling only the film, with no mention of the technology involved in production.[55] Although the scripts suggest that stereophonic sound was the main loser in the use of these detachable tags, 3-D and CinemaScope (along with other processes, such as VistaVision) could be excised completely from the sales message. The technological star, which had burned so brightly in early Cinerama, 3-D and CinemaScope trailers, had burned itself out by the end of the decade.

Throughout this chapter, unified analysis of the trailer texts has revealed the importance of the technological star in this period, explored the influence of cultural and industrial forces on trailer production, and belied the idea that these technologies had no impact on trailer structure beyond this moment of dominance. 3-D and CinemaScope may have lost their potential for useful exploitation as a star image, but these technologies forever altered the size, shape and dimensions of the cinema screen, and visibly expanded basic trailer techniques. Star, genre and narrative may have reclaimed their place at the heart of trailer structure by the mid–1950s, but the concepts of travelogue, screen-filling spectacular imagery, titles and voiceover that focus on scale, panorama and grandeur, the attempt to immerse the viewer through technological virtuosity — these aesthetic choices echo through trailers as diverse as *Lawrence of Arabia* (1962), *Star Wars* (1977), *Titanic* (1997) and *Pirates of the Caribbean* (2003). Equally, the reliance on finished film footage appearing within the trailer text — rather than the standard practice of using B-roll camera negative or unused takes—focused attention onto visual spectacle that displayed the best attributes of the technology. The innovative nature of 1950s cinema technology may have diminished, but the conventions that the technology trailers established did not disappear when the technologies did.

Analysis of the trailers for *How the West Was Won*, *It Came from Outer Space* and *How to Marry a Millionaire* has explored how a unique historical moment in the film industry was displayed visually through the industry's trailer advertising. Unified analysis allowed us to understand the contemporary meaning of these trailers by considering their textual content alongside the historical network of influences that surrounded their production — from cultural changes toward technology and American leisure activities, to sexual attitudes within 1950s society and the competitive nature of the Hollywood studios. Combining this textual and contextual knowledge reveals a unique perspective on Hollywood's attempt to revise the size, composition and scope of the cinema screen. This revision attempted to use the screen itself as a site of difference, to create a series of technological stars, all in the hope of reconnecting with a lost audience. Contemporary reports from the film industry (and subsequent commentary) blame this audience drain on the bête-noir of television, the rival screen technology that many of these cinema technologies were designed to combat. Adapting the new approach offered by unified analysis, the next chapter will examine the television trailer, a concurrent creation of the 1950s. As the first non-theatrical preview, these unique texts allow us to investigate the true relationship between the film industry and its nascent rival.

CHAPTER TWO

The Rival Screen

> *SEE motion pictures as you've never seen them before — on the new Giant WIDE VISION SCREEN ... with the sensational new dimension! HEAR motion pictures as you've never heard them before — through the miracle of directional STEREOPHONIC SOUND ... three times more realistic than ever before!*[1]

The trailer that this narration comes from, entitled "Wide Vision and Stereophonic Sound," was produced for Universal-International in late 1953. Alongside its descriptive narrator, the trailer featured animation that visually demonstrated the advances of the new technologies: a cinema screen growing wider, and a series of horns (speakers) positioned around the theatre. As we have seen, such technology-specific messages were rife in the 1950s, positioning the cinema screen as a site of difference, offering something bigger and better than the rival screen of television. The "Wide Vision and Stereophonic Sound" trailer seems to fit firmly in this camp, extolling the dimensions of the wider screen and the realism of stereophonic sound — except that this trailer was designed for broadcast on television. The full title of the script is "TV ... Wide Vision and Stereophonic Sound" and throughout there are references to "TV full screen layout" for the animation. Written and produced for the rival screen its products were designed to combat, the trailer contains a dichotomy that raises questions about the true relationship between the film and television industries of the 1950s. If the film industry closed ranks against television, then why were television trailers being produced as early as 1950? If the technological innovations of CinemaScope, 3-D and color were designed to combat the television screen, why use that small, flat, black-and-white screen to publicize them? This chapter explores the creation and establishment of the television trailer, a unique cross-media text that occurs at a crucial intersection of film and television history. Unified analysis of contemporary trailers from three time periods, 1950–1952, 1953–

1956 and 1960–1964, allows us to examine this confluence of media technology through original texts and discourse, considering television as a dissemination technology, a challenge to established cinema trailer aesthetics and an agent of change within the trailer industry.

Lisa Kernan has claimed movie trailers are "created for the purpose of *projecting in theatres* to promote a film's theatrical release,"[2] (my italics) but this chapter will argue that television trailers are an integral part of trailer history and study. As a mirror to the developments of the previous chapter, where trailers were stretched and changed by widescreen, this chapter continues to explore the flexibility of the trailer format. Unified analysis reveals that the mood of experimentation visible in the CinemaScope and 3-D trailers is discernible in the initial television spots: from the different creative approaches of the 1950s to the more structurally homogenous spots of the 1960s, these television experiments do not represent a smooth chronological development or a natural evolution. Rather, they depict a period of trial-and-error where missteps and mistakes reveal more about the time and the available aesthetic options than signs of a growing maturity. Analysis of this move from panoramic Technicolor vistas to small black-and-white announcements should not regard it as a retrograde evolutionary step. The textual and historical synthesis at the heart of unified analysis suggests instead that these TV spots are a revival of silent and early-sound era trailer formats, as well as an echo of contemporary television programming and advertising aesthetics. Alongside these aesthetic influences, television trailers demonstrate unique structural conventions that are imposed and inspired by the technology that underpins them. In the process, television trailers create new rules that are at once similar, yet distinct, from the cinema preview. These stylistic changes can be traced through analysis of early examples of television spots on American and British television. Although relatively scarce, the small sample of commercials that are available allow us to extrapolate a series of standard traits and beliefs that fuel the development of television trailers.

Focusing on these trailers also allows the book to engage in the ongoing debate about the relationship between film and television industries in the 1950s. Trailer statements that present the CinemaScope screen as a site of difference would seem to reflect the traditional understanding of media relations that Ed Buscombe once described as offering "whatever the public could not get from television": wider, deeper, louder and more colorful screens.[3] This notion of a battle between Hollywood and the new television companies has since been complicated by other authors, but as Su Holmes notes (in relation to the British experience), there is still a desire to challenge "the negative accounts of the relations between ... film culture and television."[4] Christopher Anderson has pursued this challenge through extensive historical analysis of industrial and economic sources from American television and film companies in the 1950s.[5] Although largely focused on institutional frameworks over analysis—never making the step into textual study that this current project is developing—his accounts of how David O. Selznick, Walt Disney and Warner Bros. attempted to make television work for them is a compelling deconstruction of the myth of the alleged antagonistic relationship. In particular, the development of the television show *Warner Bros. Presents* as a site for feature film publicity emphasizes how interrelated the industries were becoming, and how promotional interests appear to have fuelled this move.

Karel Ann Marling's work on the television show *Disneyland* mirrors some of Anderson's work, discussing how the Hollywood majors initially regarded television programs as a new site for movie marketing. Again, there is little sense of textual detail, or aesthetics, but Marling references behind-the-scenes features for *20,000 Leagues Under the Sea* that advertised elements of that film (particularly the special effects and underwater photography). Like Anderson's work on *Warner Bros. Presents*, the historical detail is fascinating, and explodes the myth of Hollywood and television as arch rivals, but there is no sense of how *Disneyland*, created to promote both the theme park and new Disney films, featured advertising for releases such as *Peter Pan* (1953) or *Lady and the Tramp* (1955).[6] Marling and Anderson both challenge the myth of the antagonistic relationship, but the absence of textual analysis means there is no detailed exploration of the content of the programs being produced, beyond their dual role as entertainment and publicity.

Su Holmes' recent work on 1950s British television offers an alternative model, analyzing both visual detail and discourse in a detailed study of a specific programming genre, the British film program. Like television trailers, programs such as *Current Release* and *Picture Parade* functioned as key sites of interaction between the film and television industries, and Holmes' analysis considers the visual elements of the shows alongside their production and industrial background.[7] Holmes traces the evolution of the cinema program from BBC radio to television, and then considers the different aesthetic options that commercial television brought in, as well as the continual struggle between film distributors who wanted to "sell" their film and film programs that wanted to show longer clips. Throughout the book, Holmes is conscious of analyzing the "visual texture" of these programs, regarding set design, camera movement, and performance style on the same level as industrial information or cultural influence. Much of Holmes' work on television genre, or the depiction of film premieres, departs from the scope of this current project, but there are two crucial areas of overlap. The first relates to the problem of showing widescreen excerpts on the smaller television screen. Holmes discusses film industry concerns over the incompatibility of the televised film program in showing color, then widescreen, excerpts, and the need for presenters to reassert the technological difference between the media.[8] As will be explored later in the chapter, this debate extends into the production of television trailers for 3-D and CinemaScope productions, and may have influenced the adoption of pan-and-scan technology. Unified analysis of both American and British trailer production will expand on Holmes' work in this area, in order to develop an understanding of 1950s cross-media textual development.

The second area of overlap with Holmes regards the availability of source material for this time period, and topic. With only a few surviving audio-visual elements of the *Picture Parade* film program, Holmes relied on paper records and scripts to recreate the visual texture and structure of these programs: this chapter's exploration of television trailers is informed by this innovative work. In chapter one, trailer scripts for 3-D and CinemaScope previews were used to create a network of contemporary information and discourse. Reconstructing the absent texts provided essential background to surviving texts (be they television programs or trailers), and suggested larger thematic traits that could otherwise have been overlooked or lost. The ability of unified analysis to piece together these absent texts, and to use them to explain or illuminate textual detail, is central to analyzing the early television trailers in this chapter. With few television trailers (or "spots") archived in any audio-visual format, unified analysis offers a similar approach to Jason Jacobs' work on early television drama. Jacobs suggested that when the lack of visual evidence frustrated attempts to make claims about textual or aesthetic content, it was possible to create what he termed "ghost texts." These texts exist "as shadows, dispersed and refracted amongst buried files, bad memories, a flotsam of fragments"[9]: a similar concept to the absent texts that never existed, were never properly archived, or which exist only in document form. With no audio-visual record of 1950s television trailers, no literature on their structure or format, and only a small selection of archived TV spots from the 1960s, any unified analysis of these trailers must rely on contextual evidence of production and reception to provide a sense of what they contained, and what they looked and sounded like. Only though analysis of these absent texts can we come closer to a full picture of how the film industry used television for promotional purposes, and what the texts can reveal about cross-media aesthetic influences.

Jacobs makes a further assumption, that the "absence of the epistemological guarantee of the audio-visual record is a limitation for any historical analysis that seeks to understand visual aesthetics and style."[10] However, this is a limitation on the scope of the enquiry, and assumes that close textual analysis is the primary goal of such reconstruction work. Unified analysis expands that goal by moving beyond visual aesthetics, illuminating structural, thematic and culturally specific elements of the text through analysis of the various discourses that surround it. Through this chapter, the audiovisual gap will not be regarded as a limitation or a lack, but as an opportunity to scrutinize contextual sources in order to perform the task of textual reconstruction. Synthesizing content and context gives us a deeper understanding of the potential contemporary meaning of the text, as well as the visual aesthetics it contains. In the case of "TV ... Wide Vision and Stereophonic Sound," reconstructing just the visual aesthetics of the television trailer would restrict us to comments on the style of animation, or the placement of words on the screen. By expanding the scope beyond aesthetic concerns, unified analysis considers the television trailer within its specific network of influences: including, but not restricted to, industrial (television production practices of the early 1950s), cultural (the widescreen as a reflection of audience demand), and historical (a return to silent cinema trailer styles). Only the synthesis at the heart of unified analysis allows these television trailers to be reconstructed and understood in their historical context. Unified analysis sets out to explore a historical moment through the interrogation of both text and discourse, not simply the evolution of audiovisual traits. Rather than reject Jacobs's approach the chapter aims to utilize it in order to add to our understanding of a unique time period and set of texts. Ultimately, the following study accepts that archival written fragments cannot capture every visual element of the trailer text, but it believes that the analysis of such contemporary fragments, information and attitude remains the only way to explore and open out this lost era of inter-industry cooperation and cross-media aesthetic influences.

The chapter begins in the 1950s, with an investigation of the experimental nature of the first American and British television trailers, with particular focus on how such early advertising was shaped by the restrictions of television technology and the dominant production practices of radio and film. The role of excerpted film footage is key in these experiments, but the introduction of CinemaScope and 3-D only serves to fuel the debates on whether television trailers can fully display elements of the cinema experience. The rival screen of television became a prominent visual billboard for widescreen despite the necessary reduction and repositioning that took place in the transition between the big screen and the small. The disparity of technological display will be reconstructed and analyzed to consider how the television trailer was able to promote products that were designed to combat the medium of television, and what form such advertising took. From these reconstructed 1950s texts, the chapter shifts to the early 1960s to consider the available archival television trailers: an investigation of their aesthetic similarities and differences allows us to track the status of the early structural and stylistic conventions. Key questions in this examination of the trailer's transition onto the rival screen concern the underlying confusion and uncertainty over how trailer aesthetics should be adapted for television, and how they were shaped by the restrictions of the new screen. What should TV trailers do, what length should they be, who should they target, and, most importantly, what should they look like? From the absent trailer texts of the 1950s to surviving television trailers of the early 1960s, this chapter will explore the different approaches to these questions on both sides of the Atlantic.

1950–1956: "A Potent Advertising Media"[11]

> I watched sad radiomen trying to turn it into illustrated radio ... disappointed men from films despairing at limitations of time and space.... The favorite bet was on Intimacy. "It's a small screen, so it stands to reason you have to get in close."[12]

The film industry did not have an overnight epiphany regarding television advertising (in trailer or other formats). The 1950–1956 period explored in the first two sections is more accurately seen as a moment of trial-and-error, an era of experimentation that led down numerous aesthetic cul-de-sacs and structural dead ends. Nigel Kneale's comment may describe his experience of early television drama production, but it also echoes the transition trailers made in this time period, as they moved from the cinema to the television screen. Nascent television trailer aesthetics adapted certain cinema trailer conventions, but they also borrowed extensively from other commercial formats: filmed press advertisements with still images and voiceover; personal appearances from celebrity figures and established presenters (from radio and television); basic animation featuring lettering or cartoon characters; and long dialogue scenes with no editing. The basic technology of broadcast transmission and reception also introduced aesthetic and structural constraints: initially, cathode-ray tubes could only be manufactured to a certain size, limiting the dimensions of the television set's viewing screen and increasing the preference for close-up images; the television signal was black-and-white, at a time when color film production was growing; and mono sound transmissions were often clearer than the visuals they accompanied, amplifying the reliance on voice and music over visual information. This first section will explore the ways in which the television trailer relied on and developed these approaches, before we move on to consider how the structure and format of these early TV spots adjusted to technological change in both industries. From the intimate address of the television screen to the spectacular narratives of CinemaScope theatrical trailers, unified analysis of these texts will reveal the different approaches taken in this period, and what effect they had on long-term interaction between the film and television industries.

1950–1952: Early Experiments

Born Yesterday (1950), one of the first television trailer campaigns, demonstrates the impact of pre-existing radio and film attitudes as well as a burgeoning sense of the limitations (and opportunities) of the rival screen. The film's cinema trailer features drawn titles, still images and excerpted scenes of Judy Holliday, Broderick Crawford and William Holden alongside music and a male voiceover that heralds Crawford and Holliday's screen pairing as well as Holliday's theatrical success in the role. Most of the excerpted scenes focus on dialogue exchanges and are shot in medium or long shot (most likely from camera outtakes not used in the final edit).[13] The *Born Yesterday* TV spots retain the focus on dialogue, but represent a different structural and aesthetic approach. Instead of one trailer, *Born Yesterday* has eleven: the five "one minute" and six "20-second" options are "based on hilarious highlights from the film"[14]; rather than a montage of edited excerpts, the spots focus on one dialogue exchange per trailer; according to Alan Ames, each scene contains "only one or two characters in close-ups"[15]; special sepia-tinted film is used instead of excerpted black-and-white footage from the negative; and the press book description of these spots suggests a chatty, relaxed style, referring to the actors in person not character ("Judy Holliday discusses her career on the stage and Broderick Crawford's reactions to that career").[16] The focus on individual scenes suggests Kneale's description of "illustrated radio," playing out in real time with no editing or title work added to the screen (bar a title slide over the final few seconds of footage, left silent for local announcers). The lack of editing implies an early attitude toward television's presentation of space and time, an uncertainty over how to cut between scenes when the preference was for close images, not long or establishing shots. By specially filming scenes in close-up, the *Born Yesterday* TV spots sideline editing techniques—a key production tool in structuring cinema trailers—and replace them with this notion of an intimate address. The success of the television trailer sales message is linked to its ability to create intimacy between the screen and the audience. Not only does this represent a significant shift from the bombastic address of many cinema trailers but it shows the necessity of finding medium- (and technology-) specific solutions for the television trailer to succeed.

The aesthetic limitations highlighted by the *Born Yesterday* television trailers—the sense of the smaller screen, the reliance on simple audio (particularly dialogue) and visual information—combine both technological and cultural concerns. Like the contemporary film technologies of CinemaScope and 3-D, television was not a creation of the 1950s. The technology to record and transmit picture and sound at high frequencies in basic mechanical form had been developed by the 1920s, but electronic systems (which offered better picture and sound quality) were not publicly available until the BBC's first television broadcasts in 1936. American company NBC mirrored the BBC's combination of live events and studio shows when they began transmission in 1939, but with an additional element: commercial messages. The first experimental commercials were live announcements (for soap and breakfast cereal) read out by NBC announcer Red Barber during a baseball game and an advert for Bulova watches "in which the face of a Bulova watch appeared on screen, it's second hand ticking, while an off-camera announcer told viewers what time it was."[17] The technology of the new medium had already created restrictions as to the aesthetic form of these commercials—live messages read by a known presenter (an intimate presence with whom the audience is already acquainted) and the watch face filling the small screen, in close-up—but they legitimized the notion of buying advertising time on commercial television channels. World War II held back television's growth, but by 1950 (and the trial efforts at television trailers such as *Born Yesterday*) there were almost 4 million TV sets in the United States—representing 9 percent of the population.[18] The physical aspect of the technology present in these television sets exacerbated the idea of the medium's small inferior screen. With a maximum screen size of 12 inches in diameter (and an average of between 5 inches and 9 inches), commentators noted that television had "a long way to go to equal the movies in clarity or size."[19] Television set screens would grow larger as the decade progressed (by 1958 UK television catalogues were advertising 17 inch and 21 inch models[20]) but these initial sets underlined the perceived weaknesses of the medium. The first television trailers of the 1950s (like many contemporary television commercials and programs) attempted to address these limitations by reducing the size of the trailer message.

Born Yesterday's TV trailers demonstrate an early understanding of the technological margins represented by the television screen: close-ups to combat the smaller screen, and dialogue exchanges that make use of the strong audio transmission. The studio producing the film, Columbia, most likely gained this knowledge from their subsidiary Screen Gems, which was established in 1949 to produce television programs and commercials. Screen Gem produced over 200 commercials in 1949–1951, and their expertise is likely to have helped Columbia make the transition between spectacular cinema trailer and subtler television spot.[21] This notion of intimacy versus panorama paints the television trailer as a close acquaintance: as Maurice Gorham noted, the home television audience would "demand a different tempo and a different feeling ... it is hard to imagine the typical film trailer, all explosions and superlatives, raising anything but a laugh in the home."[22] The notion of intimacy present in the *Born Yesterday* TV trailers can also be seen in other 1950 trailer scripts. A TV spot for *Bedtime for Bonzo* (1951) features a celebrity endorsement from cinema actor Percy Kilbride. Although the script does not specifically call for a close-up, its format (a simple audience address where Kilbride talks about seeing the film — "I can't remember when I laughed so much") suggests a similar format.[23]

Both of these early television trailers appear to rely heavily on audio information to support the (simple) visual images. With no surviving trailer available to watch it is difficult to build a complete picture of the visual aesthetics, but Alan Ames' comment on the *Born Yesterday* trailers requires further consideration. We have already established that close images were considered necessary in order to fill the television screen, but the decision to use special sepia-tinted film to "get the best reproduction on video screens" is not so easily explained.[24] Sepia-tinted film was used in the silent era, and then in Westerns of the 1930s and 1940s, to give a "dusty tone" that evoked the look of old photographs. Used primarily for dramatic or pictorial reasons, the film stock also provided low interference for soundtrack recording and playback.[25] Yet none of those reasons explains its use in early television commercials. *Born Yesterday* did not have a historical setting so there was no visual effect to be gained from the sepia tint (the film's cinema trailer also uses no such effect), and the issues with the smaller screen size would seem to argue against using a "dusty tone" that might dull the clarity of the image. The possibility of a clearer audio track is suggestive — the trailers were prepared as 16mm prints and made available to exhibitors through local exchanges — although this print would be converted into electronic signals for transmission, the sepia film stock's low interference levels could have helped the audio clarity. However, Ames' phrase ("the best reproduction on video screens") suggests a visual component has been added by using sepia-tinted film, not an audio one. Without the trailer, or additional information on its production, the use of this particular film remains uncertain. Because of the variety of tests and trial options during this period, it is possible the *Born Yesterday* sepia-tinted television spots were simply another experiment (there is no other mention of sepia tinting in any television trailer script or report). But there remains Columbia's commercial expertise (through Screen Gems) and Ames' promotion of the technique: it may be more useful to see this detail as a visual clue to the early structure of the transitional trailer than to reject it as an aberration.

Alan Ames' discussion of *Born Yesterday* is one of very few contemporary reports on early television trailers, and it provides a sense of the prevailing structural approaches used in these initial campaigns. He describes the different formats as "trailers — sequences of scenes from a particular picture similar to the familiar 'coming attractions' shown in theatres: personal appearances on regular TV programs, and spot commercials like those used for other types of merchandise."[26] Although he does not clarify or further differentiate these types of television usage it seems clear from the network of information surrounding this period that all three options were used within television trailers. Ames' notion of "personal appearances" is the easiest to define — he relates it to television programs such as Ed Sullivan's *Toast of the Town*, a chat show that movie stars appeared on to promote themselves and their new film. As *Bedtime for Bonzo*'s TV trailer has shown, the personal appearance could also be reworked within a more concerted sales message — a concept that recurs throughout the 1950s with stars appearing in TV trailers for *The Benny Goodman Story* (1955), *The Man in the Grey Flannel Suit* (1956) and *Away All Boats* (1956). Ames' distinction between spot commercials and "trailers" is less clear, although the use of feature excerpts ("sequences of scenes from a particular picture") may be the defining factor. The *Born Yesterday* television trailers serve a dual purpose: they are an overt sales message for a forthcoming release, but they are also specially filmed excerpts that could also be "worked into regular television programs."[27] Because the "trailers" described by Ames lack other dominant elements of the classic cinema trailer — graphic wipes, identifying titles, hyperbolic voiceover and narrative structure — it is possible that these were present in the alternative spot commercials.

Early British television trailers may help clarify the distinction between "trailers" and "spot commercials." While the BBC had been broadcasting since 1936 (with a break during the war), British commercial television did not start until 1955 when London received the first commercial transmissions, split between the weekday (Associated Rediffusion) and weekend (ATV) services. Tim Bell claims that the aesthetics of early British television advertising were not visually inventive, "had a reputation for being boring and irritating, for shouting at you ... [and resembling] press ads merely 'done again' for television"; while David Bernstein describes the first Gibbs SR and Crosse & Blackwell adverts as commercials adapted straight from written images and still photographs.[28] Given the initial debt British television advertising owed to commercial templates from the (more established) U.S. market, the first British television film advertisements furnish further clues to other creative roads taken in the earliest television trailers, and illuminate the stylistic traits of the "spot commercial."

The first film to be advertised on British television was *Jacqueline* (1956), a family film from the Rank Organization. *The Daily Film Renter* reported the campaign would begin on July 16, 1956, and use "a series of six 15-second peak hour spots." The trailer was described as mostly "letterpress supported by a spoken commentary" and "simple printed messages announcing the title of the film, its stars and the fact that it would be in Odeon and other theatres this week."[29] This aesthetic choice has two distinct ancestral roots: early British television advertisements (as described by Bell and Bernstein, above) and silent film promotion in the form of cinema slides and early trailers.

Cinema slides were a pre-trailer technique used in theatres where individual lantern slides would "build up" into a basic narrative sales message for a forthcoming feature. Trailer company National Screen Services later adopted this concept for their "Short" trailer, where simple messages were built up using animation, images and inter-titles with little or no use of excerpted film footage. One such silent trailer, for *Orphan of Paris* (1925), was twenty seconds long, and used three slides to convey star and narrative information through title work: a not entirely dissimilar description to the 1956 *Jacqueline* TV spot. Aesthetically, the *Jacqueline* TV trailer seems to have been limited to the barest of all cinematic or televisual devices — words appearing on screen accompanied by a voiceover. There is no apparent use of star imagery, editing techniques or animation to add visual flair to the advertisement, and the exact composition of the soundtrack remains vague. In Kneale's terms, the trailer is illustrated radio, while in relation to Ames' categories, the *Jacqueline* trailer would be classified as the kind of spot commercial used for other products, somehow reducing its status as a film-specific form of advertising.

The reason for this aesthetic simplicity was Rank's desire to beat 20th Century–Fox to be the first film company to advertise on British commercial television. Fox was the first to plan and buy time on ATV, for their CinemaScope picture *Smiley* (1956), but Rank produced a commercial and bought time the weekend before *Smiley*'s campaign debuted. Lionel Barrett, head of Rank publicity, later described the *Jacqueline* TV spot as a "hastily produced trailer," designed to get Rank's name in the trade press.[30] This rush to production explains the simpler, declamatory style of words and narration in the *Jacqueline* trailer, but what about the campaign it was designed to beat? With more time to plan and produce a television trailer, 20th Century–Fox's approach to spot advertising was, according to the *Daily Film Renter*, a very different style from *Jacqueline*:

> The *Smiley* campaign took a more visual form, injecting an entertainment note by using that talented young Australian performer Shirley Abicair. The latter was particularly attractive because the message was purely aural, with never a word appearing on the screen. Instead, the zither-playing star charmingly called attention to the appeal of the youngster in the film.[31]

Kinematograph Weekly also described the ad as "intelligent and effective use of the rival screen. Abicair's [sentences] are refreshingly free of ballyhoo, but clearly make the point that the film is on general release."[32] The report notes that the advert uses the film's zither theme tune over the "already famous" photograph of the film's child star, Colin Petersen — an image that was familiar from the film's poster and on bus advertising. On closer consideration, though, this contemporary praise seems to strike the same note of "illustrated radio" that *Jacqueline* was chastised for. The *Daily Film Renter* heralds the *Smiley* ad as a "first class TV commercial,"[33] but the only evidence of its supposedly "more visual form" is the reference to "pictures" of Colin Peterson. The use of the plural here suggests more than one still image was used — yet *Kinematograph Weekly* refers only to an image of the poster, singular. This is key to discerning the aesthetics on display in this trailer — it may be as visually simple as the *Jacqueline* advert, or the *Smiley* commercial may construct a visual montage around multiple images of the child star. The paucity of information — and the conflicting statements — makes the reconstruction of these absent trailers even more difficult, often unable to explain or illuminate the inconsistencies.

This poster for the 20th Century–Fox film *Smiley* (1956) may also have provided the content for their first television trailer.

The soundtrack in the *Smiley* TV spot is considered more advanced because of its "purely aural" mix of sound elements: but from the reports it is simply balancing the theme tune and Abicair's voiceover. This suggests the audio fulfils the same function as the *Jacqueline* voiceover: listing film, star and cinema play dates. The difference between the two trailers may be concerned with visual information, but for us to consider the *Smiley* TV trailer more stylistically advanced than *Jacqueline* then there must have been more than the mixing of music and voiceover, an absence of titles and one image of the star. Some assumptions can be made based on the available evidence. The *Smiley* TV spot was four times the length of that for *Jacqueline* (sixty seconds rather than fifteen) — it would seem likely that more than one shot of the child star was used, no matter how well known the poster image was. Also, if Abicair called attention to the appeal of Petersen, or offered a sense of narrative detail, it would make sense for the visuals to try and illuminate her words with supporting pictures or images. Without these speculative visual additions, the *Smiley* TV spot could resemble the filmed press ads that Bell and Bernstein describe above. The only aspect we can be certain about is the trailer's aural aesthetics, mixing the theme tune, and the narration from Shirley Abicair. These may have fulfilled the same function as the voiceover in the *Jacqueline* trailer, but the choice to impart all such information on the soundtrack returns us once again to the alleged intimacy of the television screen, allowing Abicair to talk to the audience, rather than at them.

One way that the *Smiley* television trailer is unique is its use of a female voiceover. An unusual choice in the traditional cinema trailer, the use of female announcers was more prevalent (though far from being dominant) in contemporary television commercials. Many of the existing television trailer scripts make no specific notes as to what gender the voiceover or announcer should be, but Abicair's appearance was not unheralded. The *Jeopardy* (1953) TV spots note that the script requires male and female voices as well as an announcer. The first TV spot opens with a woman's voice: "For them, it was the high-road to adventure, but I found terror all along the way." At the same time, the visuals show Barbara Stanwyck, Barry Sullivan and a young boy riding in the car. The link between female voice and image is complex: the voice could represent Stanwyck, another female character or an omniscient narrator. An excerpted scene with Stanwyck makes it clear that the female voice isn't hers, but the introduction of a narrator (not specified, but more likely male than female) suggests it is not omniscient either. The female voice only appears once more: after the narrator says "*Jeopardy*— the thrill picture of the year" a male voice adds "for action" and the female "for suspense."[34] It is possible the female voice was intended to represent a "normal" viewer, a cinemagoer (or "vox pop" as it became known) whose "natural" voice offered another attempt to create an intimate relationship between voiceover and viewer. Until *Smiley*, this remained the only extant example of a female voiceover — although actresses Donna Reed and Julie Adams make personal appearances in trailers for, respectively, *The Benny Goodman Story* and the *Away All Boats* TV spots. Whether this aural element helped the *Smiley* television trailer to stand out from its competitors is unknown.

The network of available information on the *Jacqueline* and *Smiley* trailers reveals as much as it obscures— there is, for example, no strong sense of what the *Jacqueline* trailer looked or sounded like beyond the description of "simple letterpress"— but the reconstruction offered through this unified analysis does help illuminate another creative strand within early trailer advertising. These examples help clarify what Ames meant when he distinguished between a "spot" and a "trailer"— with neither British example using excerpted scenes, either on their own (as in *Born Yesterday*) or as part of a more elaborate montage (as in theatrical trailers), they can be classified as "spot advertisements," a basic television commercial structure based on radio and newspaper advertising techniques. The cinema trailer conventions of star image, graphic titles, music and a narrative voiceover were carried over into this variety of TV trailer. The basic difference in Ames' view between these and a "trailer" was the use of excerpted scenes. It appears that, initially at least, feature excerpts were used separately, specially recorded to function on their own, or in pre-existing television programs. The use of multiple extracts (in one campaign) suggests that these producers understood the repetitive nature of the television commercial world — rather than repeat the same message over and over, the exhibitors could play all eleven commercials, thus allowing viewers to build up an image of the film from these disparate parts. As we shall see in the discussion of the 1961–1964 trailers, the idea of using multiple spot lengths and distinct visual cues would be used in an attempt to target TV spots toward specific demographics—*Born Yesterday*'s TV trailers can be seen as an early move in that direction.

The first flush of television trailers, with their emphasis on personal address, re-shot feature excerpts, and narrative announcers have left very little trace of their existence beyond the examples discussed here. *711 Ocean Drive* (1950) was promoted in Los Angeles using TV trailers in 1951, and in the same year national TV audiences were shown underwater sequences from *The Frogmen* (1951).[35] If we follow Ames' definition of the three television trailer types then it seems likely they would have featured either specially shot close images, a personal appearance promoting the picture, or direct address through graphic title work. With no surviving trailer scripts, or more detailed information on their production, visual aesthetic or reception, it is difficult to make any further claims about the period. The lack of big name releases may be relevant, with studios still unwilling to gamble too much on a medium that had yet to attain mass popularity. In 1952, while there were over 15 million television sets in the United States they accounted for only a third of the population, and there was little or no research on advertising effectiveness. Television trailers may not have been an overnight success, but they represent a significant strand of the Hollywood studios' attempt to colonize the television screen. Feature excerpts were used on regular television programs and stars appeared on chat shows to publicize their new films. Some studios followed Columbia into the production business: Universal-International produced the gossipy *Hollywood Flashes*, while Disney mixed stars, behind-the-scenes information and feature publicity in two Christmas specials.[36] These calculated experiments in the television medium show the studios' uncertainty, but the trailer scripts also reveal a grasp of the boundaries imposed by television technology and advertising aesthetics. The use of screen-filling titles, structuring sales narratives around audio information, and using specially filmed close-up extracts (whether from the feature or a special appearance) suggest that this trial period had already established basic conventions from which new experiments could spring. As cinema brought in new technological marvels, the television trailer would have to find a way to synthesize these initial findings with more established cinema trailer conventions.

1953–1956: New Technology

As TV Trailer #1 for *Abbott and Costello Go to Mars* (1953) opens, it is clear that the TV trailer structure, and the role of feature excerpts within them, has changed significantly since *Born Yesterday*. From long shots of rockets taking off and flying in space to an excerpted dialogue clip of Bud Abbott, the script for this television spot offers a mix of titles, a narrator, quickly edited images from the film and excerpted scenes. The trailer script lists seventeen shots in its sixty-second length: a dramatic difference from the *Born Yesterday* minute-long spots, which were composed of one scene (and shot). Alongside *Abbot and Costello Go to Mars*, television trailer scripts for *Jeopardy, The All American* (1953) and *All I Desire* (1953) mix traditional cinema trailer aesthetics with newer television trailer conventions: there is still a preference for close images of stars and major action beats (Costello falling into a pool, Abbott kissing a female alien), title work is described as "full screen" or "full title" to ensure it fills the smaller screen, and despite the wealth of visual information, most of the sixty seconds are covered by the announcer, or clips of dialogue — audio remained an important element of the television trailer. Other television conventions are absent. These scripts feature no direct address from a star figure, the footage is not specially shot but lifted from the film (the scripts list shot locations from the feature negative) and the intimate narrator has taken on more hyperbolic characteristics. This return to theatrical trailer models—a dominant and popular form with studios and trailer producers—seems to have been driven by several contemporary factors: television production (both programs and commercial) relied less on close-ups and regularly used longer shots for dramatic or comedic purposes; television screens were growing larger; and the growth (and development) of television transmitters meant better and clearer images being broadcast. Equally, 1953 feature production initially presented few technology-specific reasons not to use a montage of feature excerpts: cinema and television screens both showed Academy ratio images and the majority of films were in black and white (252 Hollywood films were in black and white in 1953, as opposed to 163 in color).[37] However, having reclaimed and adapted some film trailer aesthetics, the television trailer faced a new challenge in 1953–1956: the introduction of 3-D, widescreen, stereophonic sound and increased color production. Allegedly designed to combat the rival screen of television, this section will explore how key television trailers for 3-D and CinemaScope films actively position technology as a central sales message. Despite lacking the ability to present a free sample of the film-specific technology, the section will consider how, counter to the established historical view of this period, the television trailer flourished because of its relationship with the new film technologies.

The growth in television spots promoting cinema technology suggests a gap in our understanding of inter-industry relations at this point in time. Taken at its most basic, the television screen was small, black-and-white and flat, while the cinema screen from 1953 on was enormous, color and in 3-D or widescreen. Why then did these cinema technologies become so central to television sales messages? Television commercials could not show color excerpts, play stereo sound, demonstrate the depth photography of 3-D or fit the 2.55:1 CinemaScope image onto a 1.33:1 screen. The issue of feature excerpts dominated trailer production in this era: whether to acknowledge the television trailer's lack of technological display (thus positioning the cinema screen as a superior visual venue) or to ignore the lack and use existing TV spot conventions (audio address, screen-filling titles) to structure the technology-centric sales messages. Unified analysis of key trailer scripts and trade press commentary will explore the role of excerpted footage within television trailer texts, allowing us to consider what restrictions the new technology imposed, the solutions created within these TV spots, and the subsequent rise in television trailer usage through the time period.

The *Wings of the Hawk* (1953) TV trailer scripts position their 3-D visuals in the foreground of the sales message. Visual instructions include "horses thundering towards camera ... biggest explosion ... machine-gun into camera."[38] One of the strongest 3-D cinema trailer aesthetics—items coming out of the screen, aimed at the audience—is mirrored here, a reiteration of the 3-D image as the trailer's core visual appeal. Yet these "3-D" television trailers are flat; they offer no free sample of the 3-D visuals that enhance the thundering horses or machine gun fire. Given the prevalence of flat theatrical 3-D trailers, the presence of faux 3-D footage is not surprising, but its use suggests the TV spots were doing more than simply highlighting the most exciting images. This returns us to the *Born Yesterday* TV trailers, where eleven separate scenes were used to build up a sense of the film's content and humor. *Wings of the Hawk* uses two 60-second and four 20-second TV spots, but instead of offering different angles on the film (that, if the viewer sees all six, add up to a more complete picture), these six commercials repeat the same visual information — the horses, the machine gun, explosions, and shots of stars Van Heflin and Julia Adams (spot #2 "Sex," which partially alters this structure, is discussed later). Instead of building a larger framework for the feature, the television trailers work to remind audiences of the central 3-D visuals—visuals that suggest the action and faux 3-D effects, and which encourage cinemagoers to recall the same images from the full 3-D theatrical trailer.

By centering these visual cues, the television trailer highlights its own lack, unable to offer a free sample of the 3-D technology at the center of its sales message. Without such striking images, the TV trailers rely instead on the narrative voiceover to sell the technology. The written language of the trailer scripts show that these announcers foreground exaggeration over the intimacy of earlier TV spots: "A thousand new thrills in three dimension" or "a thrilling love-story bristling with explosive action — amazingly alive in the magic of spectacular 3-dimension!"[39] There appears to be a dual purpose to these exclamations: without access to the technological imagery, the scripts increase the volume and exaggerated claims of the 3-D-based sales message but they also allow the film studios to differentiate the cinema screen from the television one, mocking the small screen at the same time as relying on it to promote their products. This can be seen as early as the *Abbott and Costello Go to Mars* script, where the narrator states: "Life at home was *never* like this. The laughs at the movies were *never* so wild!"[40] Although there is a narrative purpose to these words (Abbott and Costello are literally away from home, on Mars) the underlying suggestion is that home life (watching television) is dull or unexciting, while the movies are even more wild and entertaining. The subtlety of such messages was reduced with the introduction of new technology and the insistence on the screen as a site of difference — the *Wings of the Hawk* script states that the only place to see this "3-dimension Technicolor triumph" is "on the full-sized theatre screen!"[41] Not necessary for promotional purposes — the final few seconds of all television trailers were left silent for a local announcer to include what cinema was playing the film and when — such inclusions allowed the studios to differentiate the cinema screen from the television one. The nature of such messages appears to support the view of the film industry competing with television, but again, these statements are contained within potent television trailers designed to utilize the broadcast technology and target the new mass audience of television. This contradiction points up one of the key issues of this period: the uncertainty of the studio response to television and their growing (though reluctant) reliance on the medium for box office success.

Promoting 3-D films in television trailers without access to 3-D footage was not a major technological hurdle in 1953–1954. Audiences were used to faux 3-D effects through their use in "flat" cinema trailers (see previous chapter), all 3-D films were in Academy ratio and many were in black and white. Excerpts could still focus attention onto faux 3-D moments, and the voiceover's 3-D-specific messages reminded viewers of the technology. The lack of 3-D display may actually have worked in favor of the television trailer, particularly when the popularity of 3-D began to fade. 1954 TV spots for *Creature from the Black Lagoon* reduce the emphasis on the 3-D process, using the strong visual excerpts to focus on genre characteristics over technological ones. Many of the main technology-centric images are obscured with screen-filling titles that sell star and narrative action, reducing the impact of the faux 3-D shots. The sense that technology has been replaced by genre spectacle is made clear in one of the *Creature* TV spots, where there is a clear option to drop the technology message completely. A notation states that the title "the screen's first underwater three-d thrill" could be changed to "the most terrifying of all underwater adventures."[42] The option to alter the sales message suggests producers were aware of the fading appeal of 3-D, but it also highlights the ability of television trailers to respond to such changes. By not offering a free sample of the technology, the content of the TV spot is more fluid, able to adapt to changing circumstance, and to be replaceable on television screens at short notice. With some American and British theatres reluctant to change or adapt their cinemas to the new technologies, the flexibility of the television trailer may have added to its longevity in the publicity field.

The relative ease with which television trailers could use excerpts to promote 3-D features was not replicated with the introduction of CinemaScope. The first television trailer for *The Black Shield of Falworth* (1954) foregrounds the issue with an echo of Universal's "Wide Vision and Stereophonic Sound" commercial. The *Falworth* TV trailer opens with an animated CinemaScope logo that "zooms up very fast ... When full up, title widens out to edge of field for CinemaScope effect."[43] By opening with this faux CinemaScope effect, the widescreen technology appears to be central, both in voiceover and visuals. The script continues in more traditional style, with its voiceover and title work reiterating messages of panorama and wonder. What the script lacks is any sense of how it will present the excerpted scenes of spectacle and pageantry that make up the bulk of the trailer — there is no statement as to whether the footage was shown in the full CinemaScope ratio of 2.55:1. Given the renewed importance of feature excerpts to television trailer structure, the introduction of the widescreen image entailed further experimentation. Concepts such as pan-and-scan and "letterboxing," which come to prominence in the 1960s and beyond, appear to have their roots in the debates surrounding the use of feature extracts in these television trailers. To reproduce feature visuals in full, black masking was required above and below the thin CinemaScope image, reducing the available television screen area by almost half — what would later be described as "letterboxing." The alternative was to crop the image, to optically reduce the CinemaScope visuals to the size of the television screen, panning and scanning the image so that it would fill that screen. With CinemaScope publicity emphasizing the gulf between the huge cinema and small television screens, the choice of how to represent that gulf, how to stress the bigger and better elements of the new technology, led to further problems for television trailer production.

20th Century–Fox were aware of this as early as 1954. The press book for their production *Black Widow* (1954) devotes a page to television advertising, espousing it as "the greatest modern pre-selling medium ... your own private means of entering the home of every potential customer."[44] While confirming the enhanced status of television advertising within the film industry, the press book is useful for its insight into how CinemaScope footage could be effectively utilized on television. The film's sixty-second TV spot "uses actual film from '*Black Widow*' compressed by the new reduction method. It adds tremendous stature and excitement to the trailer presentation."[45] The prominent placement of this message suggests this was a unique new solution to an ongoing problem — and that the "reduced" footage was different to that offered in the other *Black Widow* TV trailers, which use "actual film showing the stars moving in close-up" (potentially similar to specially shot trailers such as *Born Yesterday*). What then is the reduction method? The use of the word "reduction" gives two options: the aforementioned decrease of the complete widescreen ratio so that it fits onto the television screen (with black masking), or shrinking the widescreen image by cropping the 2.55:1 ratio down to the 1.33:1 of the television screen. The evidence of other television trailers suggests that a display of technological visuals was secondary to using the screen to promulgate awareness of the forthcoming film, its stars and, if possible, its technological process. No possible free sample could be offered of color, stereophonic sound or 3-D and 20th Century–Fox followed a similar path, opting to promote CinemaScope without being able to fully display the CinemaScope image. Fox confirmed that their favored method for televising excerpts involved "cutting off the sides of the picture ... [both] top and bottom reach the frame without any distortion."[46]

The use of optical reduction or cropping in these CinemaScope trailers of the mid–1950s raises the possibility that television trailers were the first iteration of what would become known as "pan-and-scan": the process by which widescreen films are optically reframed and scanned to fit the smaller television screen image. Critics of this process, such as John Belton, believe this desire for the smaller television image killed the widescreen revolution of the 1950s:

> Films which exploited widescreen technology in an attempt to provide an experience attainable only in a theatre were now suddenly asked to adapt themselves to the demands not just of a different but of an opposed technology — narrow-screen television.... [This was] another stage in the dismantling of the widescreen revolution and the demise of widescreen cinema.[47]

Belton links panning and scanning to the first television screening of *How to Marry a Millionaire* in 1961, but it seems certain the process was tested as early as 1954, on feature excerpts for television trailers and programs. But rather than dismantling the widescreen revolution, these TV spots specifically sell the wider screen. *The Black Shield of Falworth* is "even more spectacular in the wonder of CinemaScope at your theatre!" *Captain Lightfoot* (1955) is "even GREATER in CINEMASCOPE," and *Sign of the Pagan* (1954) is "CinemaScope's greatest excitement."[48] These television trailers are caught in the same dichotomy as the 3-D spots for *Wings of the Hawk*— the spots use television to sell cinema-specific technologies, but they cannot offer any proof of those technological marvels; and while dismissing the television screen as inadequate, inferior to the products they are extolling, the trailers rely on that screen to get their message across. Unlike Belton's dismissal of television, it is important to see the television trailer as bridging the gap between the film and television industries — offering strong compelling sales messages while being unable to display the spectacle of the cinema screen image. The television trailer did not dismantle the widescreen revolution of the 1950s: rather, it attempted to propagate it.

The impact of new technologies on the content of the television trailer pushed it further toward the excerpted scene dynamic of the cinema trailer aesthetic, but the nascent conventions of television trailers remained. Despite being unable to show the visuals created by 3-D, CinemaScope or color, almost all TV spots from the 1953–1956 period showcase excerpts within their structure. These excerpts do not feature the technological star image of the cinema trailer, but instead are used to balance star, genre and narrative alongside technological messages. Although the television trailers of 1956 seem distinct from *Born Yesterday* in 1950, the use of optically reduced (or pan-and-scanned) CinemaScope images is not that far removed from specially filming images in close-up in order to make best use of the television's smaller screen (reducing the 'Scope image could transform it into a medium or close shot). The sense of experimentation, of synthesizing elements from cinema, television and newspaper advertising still remains: the basic letterpress experiment of *Jacqueline* may have gone, but screen-filling lettering remains a key element in *Wings of the Hawk* and *Creature from the Black Lagoon*'s TV commercials, superimposed over long shots that emphasize genre or narrative. The experimentation of early CinemaScope television trailers also returns to the personal appearance style first seen in *Bedtime for Bonzo*: Hollywood columnist Erskine Johnston appeared in *Captain Lightfoot*'s TV spot to talk about Rock Hudson and present some cropped 'Scope images.

By 1956 it remains impossible to discern a dominant TV trailer aesthetic. But then, such an all-encompassing aesthetic would be necessarily reductive, and is not desirable. Certain traits dominate — the importance of audio, particularly voiceover; standard time lengths (twenty and sixty seconds in the U.S., fifteen, thirty and sixty seconds in the UK); the continued use of close images to fill the screen; the use of long shots as background for large graphic titles; a reliance on visuals to suggest genre; specific references that direct the television viewer "back" to the cinema screen and insist on the screen itself as a site of difference — but listing these elements does not allow us access to the full range of aesthetic options that these early television trailer texts represent.

Reducing these texts to the components they share ignores what makes these TV spots unique, as does reducing them to a macro-narrative of TV trailer history. While the 1950–1956 period has been described here chronologically, these texts are better understood as a moment of overlap where the film and television industries attempt to grapple with each other. It is possible to see these TV spots as a progression from *Jacqueline*'s simplicity to the more complex montage of information in *The Black Shield of Falworth*, but focusing on that evolution blinds us to what makes each trailer a unique experiment in an uncertain time period for both media. The television trailers analyzed here are not just a list of visual starting points, a cue for what would come next. Reconstructing the visual information of these texts is an important step, but it needs to be considered and weighed alongside the discourse that surrounds them: the synthesis of text and context, visual information and archival data that underpins unified analysis adds to our knowledge of what the trailer might mean, or what its purpose was in the historical moment.

The American and British trailers reconstructed here remain experiments, disparate answers to the same questions— what does a television trailer look like, what does it do, what can it say? The reception of these experiments (and how each was reported) reveals that the film industry was uncertain and uncomfortable over the move from the cinema to the television screen. While embracing the television screen they were eager to reject it; use it as a sales tool in order to sell a competitive visual product; pay the price of advertising so they could promote their latest attempt to bankrupt it. Six years of experimentation had made the U.S. film industry more certain of the value of television trailers, but equally certain that television was an enemy. This enmity may have made it even more difficult to decide how to best use television trailers as a sales tool, or what form the trailer should take: the different options they had tried all came back to the problem of feature extracts and how to use them on the rival screen. The remainder of the 1950s would see further attempts to define what a television trailer was, and what it could do, but the chapter will now shift to the early 1960s in order to analyze the first surviving television trailers. In light of our knowledge of this early period, what aesthetic and structural traits survive into the next decade, how has the antagonistic relationship between media altered over time, and what differences can we see in these later examples?

1960–1964: A Return to Cinema

> Share if you dare the unbearable suspense of the entire human race. Men and women awaiting the end of the world.... What would you do if the world was to end in four months? Lose yourself in love? Hide in fear? Or run amok in wild hysterical madness?[49]

The sixty-second television trailer for *The Day the Earth Caught Fire* (1961) opens with shocking and compelling images: overturned cars and discarded papers litter a deserted Piccadilly Circus; the arc of Tower Bridge stretches over the dried-up river bed of the Thames; under-nourished men and women queue up to fill water jugs; people run over Chelsea Bridge in panic. Each image is presented in long or medium shot, the only graphic title work lists the film's title and production company (Universal-International), and the voiceover gives similar narrative information to the film's theatrical trailer. The trailer aesthetic and structure, based around a montage of excerpted scenes, shows little sign of the nascent television trailer conventions identified in previous sections. As one of the key surviving texts from the early 1960s, *The Day the Earth Caught Fire* TV spots initially suggest an alignment of television and theatrical trailer structure even more complete than the technology trailers of the mid–1950s. Unified analysis of this trailer campaign, the *Spartacus* (1960) trailer scripts, as well as a TV spot for *Dr. Strangelove: or, How I Learned to Stop Worrying and Love the Bomb* (1964), conclude the chapter's exploration of the early years of the television trailer by considering what effect a more settled period of television advertising had on these TV commercials. Specifically, we will examine whether the extant aesthetic conventions are still present — intimate voiceover, reliance on close-ups, full-screen titles and images, and the visual and aural repetition of information. Beyond aesthetics lie structural issues—*The Day the Earth Caught Fire*'s campaign features four separate trailer iterations (a sixty-, two twenty- and a ten-second version), while only one commercial was apparently produced for *Dr. Strangelove*. Investigating the use of multiple commercials allows us to consider the rise (and effectiveness) of demographic targeting within television trailer advertising, the historical situation that underlies these texts, and the larger question of whether these television trailers retain any unique qualities from the period of experimentation.

The Day the Earth Caught Fire's television spots do suggest that the earlier notion of television trailers as a venue for close, intimate images had been abandoned in favor of bigger screen spectacle. Characters are shown in medium or long shot, with two or four characters grouped within a scene, while the trailer lingers on its establishing shots, rather than obscuring them with titles or graphics: this wider shot scale creates a sense of panorama, larger than anything in the television trailers for *Born Yesterday* or *Black Widow*. Basing trailer structure around excerpted scenes appears to come from a late-1950s debate over the use of film extracts on television film programs. The 1956 Universal-International campaign for *Away All Boats* comprised two "specially-prepared trailer-type films" shown on British commercial television.[50] Next to the simpler television trailer aesthetic seen in *Jacqueline* and *Smiley*, the *Away All Boats* spots are a loud assertion of the cinema trailer conventions beginning to dominate film advertising on American television. Although they feature some television trailer aspects—the scripts specify close images ("close angle [on] boats ... montage of close shots of men on deck ... beach assault, close"[51]) and there is a repetition of title and voiceover information—the *Away All Boats* scripts concentrate on quickly edited excerpted scenes that stress narrative and action. The montage of short excerpts was a deliberate break from the film industry's policy of allowing longer extracts to be televised on film programs.[52] In 1956, Al Duff, President of Universal-International, dismissed televised extracts as "three or four minutes of disjointed scenes" whereas a trailer-type film would "sell it to them. We would rather pay for time on TV and do the job our way than get it for nothing and do it their way!"[53] Duff acknowledges that television trailers have an important role within film publicity, and his distinction between the media—between selling and showing—is a condemnation of the televised film program, not television itself. Five years later, the evidence of *The Day the Earth Caught Fire* spots (also from Universal-International) shows that Duff's belief in "trailer-type" TV spots remained influential.

Despite the strong theatrical trailer elements and the new emphasis on selling the film through montage, analysis of *The Day the Earth Caught Fire* TV trailers reveal that earlier conventions still exist, but have adapted to work with this new approach. The soundtrack, for example, so important to earlier television spots, remains central. There is a sense that the visuals, no matter how strong, are unable to sell themselves—they are accompanied by an aural countdown, dialogue and/or the announcer, explained or justified in relation to the trailer narrative. This is clearest in the sixty-second spot, which conveys narrative knowledge through two excerpted lines—"They've shifted the tilt of the Earth ... the stupid, crazy, irresponsible bunglers" and the toast "To the luck of the human race."[54] The soundtrack remains dominant in the ten-second spot, where the announcer and music completely fill the time length. The style of the announcer also strikes an intimate note, with less stridency in his tone. The language is rooted in questions and statements that are directed at an individual viewer rather than a mass audience: "What would you do?" is asked conversationally, not shouted, offering a degree of intimacy between trailer and television viewer.[55] This echo of the intimate screen fluctuates across the four different television trailers, varying on the disparate time lengths. TV spot #1 (sixty seconds) and #2 (one of the twenty-second commercials) promote this angle, but #3 (ten seconds) necessarily uses a more exaggerated style given its brevity.[56] TV spot #4 (the second twenty-second commercial) is much more direct and less intimate, highlighting action and romance above suspense or impressive visuals. Opening with a screen-filling title that exclaims "EARTH'S AXIS TILTS" it moves quickly through a montage of disaster images (cars being blown over, advertising hoardings collapsing, a skyscraper skyline with sirens blaring) before ending on a bedroom clinch between stars Janet Munro and Edward Judd. The change in visual emphasis is matched by the voiceover, in both language and delivery: "Hurricane. Flood. Catastrophe. Can the world survive? See the incredible become real. The impossible become fact." The first-person intimacy of "What would you do?" has become the distant third-person "Can the world survive?"[57]

The difference in tone, structure and sales technique across the range of television trailers for *The Day the Earth Caught Fire* suggests that a complete understanding of the trailers is only possible when they are analyzed in tandem. This allows us to explore the use of recurring visual cues and narrative language, as well as appreciate the simplifying or streamlining of the message in shorter spots or different iterations. In the case of TV spots #1 through #3, the repetition of images becomes important: the long matte shot down to Tower Bridge; a medium shot of four actors in a pub; and a montage of streets scenes where an advertising hoarding collapses and a car is blown into a building (in the ten-second spot, the Thames and pub images comprise the entire visual display). Returning to these images allows the trailer to link the disaster and chaos of the vanished Thames and the street scenes with the intimacy of the pub scene. The spectacle and shock of the Tower Bridge scene is obvious, but the pub scene is less so: while it features lead actors Munro, Judd, and McKern they are not identified or named by title work or voiceover. The moment can be seen as a reflection of contemporary uncertainty over

Images of a deserted London form the backdrop for *The Day the Earth Caught Fire*'s television trailers (1960).

Screen-filling graphic titles became a common feature of early television trailers. *The Day the Earth Caught Fire* U.S. TV spot #4 (1960).

the Cold War, and the omnipresent threat of nuclear war, but it also centers an intimate moment alongside the large-scale catastrophe, the men and women "awaiting the end of the world."[58] The absence of this sequence in TV spot #4 underlines the emphasis on the spectacular over the intimate, or individual, in that commercial.

These four separate (but linked) television trailers represent a growing awareness and application of demographic targeting in the late 1950s. The textual evidence of *The Day the Earth Caught Fire* spots suggests a split between intimacy (spots #1 and #2, possibly #3) and spectacle (spot #4). This division potentially reflects different audience strategies: U.S. television advertising had become more adept at highlighting audience groups through time bands and programming schedules. This complicated the notion of television as a mass audience provider, but made it more attractive to advertisers who wanted to shape their messages toward distinct consumers. Precedent for providing different content across a range of television trailers can be seen as early as the *Born Yesterday* TV campaign, with its eleven separate dialogue-driven commercials. This technique developed through trailers that were written and produced to target specific audiences. The main television trailer scripts produced in 1953 for *Wings of the Hawk* included a TV spot called "Sex." The script repeats the campaign's central message (a 3-D action film) but adds in blatant sexual imagery. Excerpted visuals ("Jail bar kiss ... Lane-Dolenz clinch showing bosom") appear between the action-based images, and the voiceover links action, sex and technology: "The 3-Dimension Theatre–

screen pulses with danger — and desire ... seductive Abbe Lane whose kisses branded her an outcast."[59] As well as extending the earlier link between female sexuality and 3-D (there is no television trailer to emphasize male star Van Heflin's 3-D appearance) the trailer demonstrates an understanding of how trailer sales messages can be tailored for different audiences.

While the *Wings of the Hawk* "Sex" TV spot placed a new sales message within the existing structure of 3-D action, a Universal-International campaign from 1960–1961 shows a more advanced division of sales messages. The titles of the sixty-second *Spartacus* TV trailers state their demographic intentions: "Women appeal spot for daytime use," "Teenage appeal," and "Action." Unlike *Wings of the Hawk* these trailer scripts offer little repetition of imagery. The "Action" spots are dominated with gladiator and battle scenes; the "Women appeal" spot presents love scenes between Spartacus and Variana (an embrace, Spartacus touches her face, the "love scene on grass"); while the Teenage appeal spot replicates some battle imagery (particularly the shot of Spartacus on horseback), but focuses mainly on dramatic scenes of Spartacus "rebelling against authority ... smashing the baton, the symbol of the Senate."[60] The visual differences are matched by changes in voiceover language: the "Action" script roars about "the fierce excitement of men in battle," the "Teenage" script echoes its youthful credentials with "the dynamic young rebel ... young in spirit, young in desire ... young in revolt," while the "Women appeal" script talks about "the rebel who worshipped her ... the general who desired her — even more than he wanted to possess Rome."[61] The demarcation of target audiences with these television scripts distances them from cinema trailers. Both trailer formats rely on montage editing as a central structuring device, but the cinema trailer of the 1960s remained a mass device, aimed at everyone in the audience. These television trailers suggest an awareness of audience profiling not only at a demographic level (between sexes and age groups) but also scheduling — planning to run the "Women appeal" spot in daytime (regarded as a slot for housewives) and the others, presumably, in prime time evening slots.

The Day the Earth Caught Fire TV spots and the *Spartacus* scripts suggest a further purpose behind the split of trailer messages into particular categories. The division of television trailer lengths into sixty, twenty and ten seconds necessarily reduces the information that can be conveyed. *The Day the Earth Caught Fire* TV Spot #3 contains only the most basic audio-visual facts in its ten seconds, and its narrative only becomes clear when compared with spots #1 and #2. There are two possible implications here. First, that the ten-and twenty-second spots were designed to play after the sixty-second trailer, in order to serve as a reminder of the aural and visual stimuli that the longer commercial (or potentially, the cinema trailer) had already introduced. Second, by extension, that the different iterations (or targeted commercials) were designed to break up the longer cinema trailer into manageable (and affordable) lengths for the television screen. From this perspective, the cinema trailer remains a key promotional text, with the television trailers separating out different strands of its mass market message and presenting them in individual spots. That concept may have some validity in certain cases, but it inevitably reduces the power of the television trailer to create its own conventions and effect change — within its own industry and, potentially, back on the cinema trailer. In the case of *Spartacus*, it would be more accurate to describe the television trailers as variations on the film's sales message, rather than echoes. The *Spartacus* theatrical trailer does feature elements of the rebellious lover from the "Women" and "Teenage" spots but they are secondary concerns next to the elements of widescreen spectacle, historical epic and star identification. The "Action" TV spots most accurately mirror the cinema trailer, while the others reduce the spectacle in favor of "a magnificent human drama ... a tender and beautiful love story" — offering a suggestion of intimacy and reasserting a quality unique to the television trailer.[62] These TV spots may replicate elements of the cinema trailer narrative, but they are not simply the reduced echoes of a dominant promotional text.

If the *Spartacus* TV trailers modify the film's sales messages through a series of targeted spots, a more direct replication of an existing trailer aesthetic can be seen in the 1964 cinema and television trailers for *Dr. Strangelove: or, How I Learned to Stop Worrying and Love the Bomb*. However, the influence here does not flow from the cinema trailer to the television spot, but in reverse — the television aesthetic can be clearly seen at work in the theatrical trailer. The *Dr. Strangelove* example is unique in this time period for having the same creative team working on both advertisements at the same time — but the result remains a prime example of the extant television conventions we have identified in the preceding analysis. The trailer opens with a visual assault — a quick-fire montage of titles, excerpted footage and sound effects. In the first forty seconds over a hundred edits flash past, cutting between stark white titles on a black screen and quarter-second bursts of Peter Sellers, George C. Scott and Stanley Kubrick. Existing television conventions can be seen in the use of close images, the screen-filling lettering, and the rapid montage. The trailer uses these aesthetic devices to invoke a dark humor (suitable for the film it is promoting) and introduce a playful relationship between image and dialogue more advanced than existing trailers on either medium. A series of one-word titles — "Why/Did/U.S./Bombers" (intercut with an image of a bomber) — cuts to a woman in a bikini who says "attack," then the general snarls "Russia."[63] The viewer is left to piece together these disparate elements, which promote the film's narrative but also question the very process of trailer construction — making audiences aware of the techniques being used. Over the frenetic montage of titles and excerpted scenes, the soundtrack is equally diverse: a xylophone music track in counterpoint with a deep, percussive theme; and three different voiceovers read out different parts of the film's title (the only announcer portion in either trailer).

The complexity of the trailer can be partly explained by the growth in television trailer production. Both *The Day the Earth Caught Fire* and *Spartacus* (as well as other late 1950s examples such as *Pillow Talk* [1959]) offer short, direct sales messages through quick montage editing, title work and direct voiceover address. Yet there remains a gulf between the existing scripts and trailers and the *Dr. Strangelove* TV spot. The answer lies partly with the trailer producer, Pablo Ferro, and his expertise in the world of television advertising. A Cuban animator based in New York, Ferro made his name through a particular style of animation, a "kinetic quick-cut method of editing whereby static images (including engravings, photographs, and pen and ink drawings) were infused with speed, motion, and sound."[64] Chosen by Kubrick to work on the trailers and titles for *Dr. Strangelove*, Ferro's style infuses the existing television trailer aesthetics with a new energy: drawing on those conventions, but adding in elements from cinema trailers as well as contemporary advertising and modern art. The trailer remains most fascinating because of Ferro's decision to use exactly the same footage and style across the two media—and the TV spot aesthetics only work to extend the cinema trailer style. Long shots are kept to a minimum but close-up images work to promote star names and push the trailer's anarchic structure. The three voiceovers also move between exaggerated and intimate announcement styles—the deep, masculine "Dr. Strangelove," the younger, chattier male "Or, how I learned to stop worrying," and the sultry feminine whisper "and love the bomb"—shifting from cinema to television address.[65] While the trailer does tend toward parody (a final sequence: "SEE/IT/MON./OR:/A/WEEK/FROM/THURS/OR:/SUN./WED./FRI./TUES./SAT./OR:/MON" mocks the more traditional cinema playdate announcement at the end of television spots[66]) it represents the first moment where television trailer aesthetics begin to encroach on the cinema screen that first inspired them.

The *Dr. Strangelove* TV spot should not be seen as the beginning of a revolution in television trailer advertising. Similar techniques can be found throughout the mid–1960s, particularly in film and television advertising for the James Bond series: quick-editing, slick inter-titles that foreground particular visual motifs (multi-colored circles and guns frequently recur) and a repetition of generic imagery structure the cinema and TV spots for *Goldfinger* (1964) and *Thunderball* (1965). However, while these examples show Hollywood studios had grown less wary of the rival screen — and were more aware of its potential for publicity — aesthetic and structural change did not happen overnight. What the Ferro-produced TV spot (and the later Bond examples) show is the range of untapped possibilities still inherent in the television trailer format. The basic techniques seen in *The Day the Earth Caught Fire* (and suggested by the *Spartacus* scripts) — the fast-paced editing, the swift progression through imagery, repetition of aural and visual information — remain central in television spots in subsequent years, but gain in prominence in the cinema trailer aesthetic. Some aspects are less prevalent: the intimate voiceover work tends more toward its cinema trailer roots than the casual delivery suggested in these trailers; while medium and long shots become more central, reducing the reliance on close-ups, which largely return to the pre-television option of providing star images. Beyond aesthetic factors, these 1960s television trailers remain influential. Cinema trailers of the early 1960s were still huge, three- to five-minute epics with hybrid sales messages that included star, genre, narrative, spectacle, and technology elements. When the shorter television trailers began to target specific demographic groups, cinema trailers followed suit — exploitation companies such as American International Pictures started running trailers that appealed directly to teenage and drive-in audiences rather than the inclusive audience of standard cinema trailers. The quick pace of the shorter TV spots may also have led to an increase in the use of teaser trailers — short, advance trailers that, in decades past, were designed to run two or three weeks ahead of the feature film arriving in theatres. By the late 1960s teasers for films such as *Chitty Chitty Bang Bang* (1968) were debuting as much as eight months ahead of the theatrical release.[67] It may not have been an immediate success, but by 1964, the television trailer had begun to exert both aesthetic and structural influence over the older, theatrical model.

Conclusion

By 1963, over fifty million homes in America had a television (just over 91 percent of the population). In many ways, that is the easiest answer to the question posed at the beginning of this chapter: why use the small, flat, black-and-white television screen to publicize feature films (and technological processes) designed to combat that rival screen? Television had become the mass medium that cinema used to be, and buying time on that medium, connecting with that (potentially) huge audience, was simply good business sense. If the period 1950–1964 truly represented a battle between these rival screens, then the evidence of the trailer texts suggests a stalemate rather than an outright victor. Television trailers relied on previous incarnations of the cinema trailer aesthetic, but the unique adaptation of trailer-specific structural and stylistic conventions (alongside influences from press advertising and television production) allowed the TV spot to impact back on the cinema trailer.

The competitive messages found in television trailers for 3-D and CinemaScope ("made to be seen on the full-sized theatre screen"[68]) are absent in the TV spots for *Dr. Strangelove* and *The Day the Earth Caught Fire*, with no reference to the screen as a site of difference, or the perceived inferiority of television technology. This change is reflected in larger cross-media cooperation. By 1964, feature extracts regularly featured on television programs, Hollywood stars were frequent guests on television chat shows, broadcast rights to studio film libraries had been sold, and CinemaScope films such as *How to Marry a Millionaire* had been broadcast on NBC, albeit pan-and-scanned for the smaller screen.

The television trailer remains at the center of this confluence of the film and television industries between 1950 and 1964, a textual no man's land where the aesthetics of both industries merged and combined in new and unique ways. What emerged from this synthesis was more than simply a new dissemination channel for cinema publicity. This period of experimentation reflects the flexibility of the trailer, able to move into a new visual medium and demonstrate that the gap between the media was not as wide as it appeared. By crossing that divide, the trailer enables a dialogue between film and television trailer aesthetics and structure, and suggests that the rival screens have more in common than contemporary commentators would admit. The television screen, and the period of trial-and-error that it represents, offers a new way of looking at trailer structure, a fresh perspective on what a trailer can do, what it can say, and how it can create meaning. Unified analysis of the 1950s television spots reveal that they are fertile texts that were able to champion, challenge, and change cinema trailer conventions. Rather than a reduction of the cinema trailer aesthetic, the television trailer became a new form that extended the trailer's power to channel compelling visual and aural information into short advertising messages. While they share elements (voiceover, excerpted footage, title work) the technological features of the medium they were broadcast in and the products they were advertising necessitated a shift in production style: a shift that we can see through unified analysis of the available archival sources. The experimentation in TV trailer style of 1950–1956 had become more stable and defined by 1960–1964, but its range encompassed the specially filmed extracts of *Born Yesterday*, the personal address of *Bedtime for Bonzo*, the animation of *TV ... Wide Vision and Stereophonic Sound*, the still images of *Smiley*, the title-heavy *Jacqueline*, the cropped imagery of *Black Widow* and the increasingly quick montage-style of *Wings of the Hawk, The Day the Earth Caught Fire* and *Spartacus*. The plurality of styles does not negate the recurrence of aesthetic threads: the preference for close-ups, the repetition of key visual moments, the aural dominance of music and voiceover. There is as much that connects these experiments as separates them.

Although this reference to aesthetic similarity returns us to Jason Jacobs and his belief in the importance of the "visual constitution" of ghost texts, the unified analyses performed on these texts have moved beyond reconstruction and have attempted to understand each text in its historically specific moment. In isolation, these television trailers reveal only details of their construction, their reliance on title work or star images, but considered within the larger discursive network of influences they reveal a wider relationship with silent cinema, press, television production and advertising. By expanding our conception of analysis beyond the simple fact of the text, unified analysis allows us to ask more detailed questions of both the text and the network that surrounds it. Rather than the "approximation" of the text, unified analysis strives for a more complete understanding of it. Central to any understanding of TV trailer texts is our ability to differentiate them from accepted narratives of film, television and trailer history. By seeing them within their own historical moment, we are able to understand the central role these television trailers played in developing new aesthetic and structural models for trailer production, models that were as important for the TV spots of the future as they were for the theatrical trailers in the cinema.

CHAPTER THREE

Technology and Genre

> *Technology is a basic component of cinema, a condition of its existence, and a continuing factor in its development ... witness, for instance, the importance of special effects technology in the recent and hugely successful wave of science fiction films.*[1]

The preceding analysis of widescreen, 3-D and television trailers has confirmed the first half of Steve Neale's observation about the technological basis of cinema, with individual previews presenting free samples of their audio-visual processes. This chapter will move on to examine the second half of Neale's comment, using unified analysis of key science fiction trailers from three commercially successful iterations of the genre (the 1950s, the late 1970s, and the 1990s) to consider how these innovative technologies are displayed, and dispute the recent critical concept that visual spectacle has dominated or displaced narrative in modern blockbusters. Through these three disparate time periods, the trailer has remained at the forefront of film promotion: even with the advent of television trailers, the cinema preview remained the prime audio-visual format for offering free samples of future film blockbusters. As such, it would be the likely venue for any spectacle-based sales message, the logical vehicle to display such visuals to future audiences. Instead, unified analysis of these trailers reveals a complex and shifting interrelation between narrative, character and generic elements, with underlying production limitations often restricting the dominance of the effects spectacle. This analysis demonstrates that the genre trailer — and by extension, the feature film it advertises—cannot be reduced to a single element of visual spectacle, but must examine how such spectacle functions within the larger text.

The science fiction film has often been seen as a traditional site for spectacular visual display. In a discussion that links the rise of effects spectacle to the "New Hollywood" of the 1970s, Kristin Thompson and David Bordwell state that science fiction films "showcase innovations in production design and special effects."[2] Functioning as part of a larger historical narrative, they identify key films that conform to this ideal: a list that includes *2001: A Space Odyssey*, *Star Wars*, and *Close Encounters of the Third Kind*. As this chapter will demonstrate, the association of these three films with the purported revolution in special effects is problematic. The belief that these films exist to showcase special effects for an audience can be examined through close analysis of promotional materials for each film. This work is not limited to the 1970s: Vivian Sobchack's work on science fiction film from the 1950s to the 1980s also identified special effects as "grand displays of 'industrial light and magic.'"[3] This emphasis on display (or a showcase, to use Thompson and Bordwell's term) suggests the ability of effects work to stand outside the narrative, to create spectacle within these generic products.

Miranda J. Banks has noted that the science fiction genre "has always been at the forefront of using cutting-edge technology."[4] The technological nature of this investigation remains key in interrogating the existing critical attitude toward special effects spectacle. Geoff King's work on Hollywood blockbusters explores the impact of new technology on both spectacle and narrative, considering how films like *Jurassic Park* use spectacular sequences (like the herds of dinosaurs flocking around and past the characters) to offer resonance to the narrative. However, although he states that most blockbusters tell "reasonably coherent stories" and that narrative and spectacle "can work together" his work tends toward spectacle dominating, or at least overshadowing, narrative event.[5] He also makes the claim that films such as *Jurassic Park* and *Titanic* are sold "on the basis of spectacular attraction. The scale and quality of spectacle is a major factor in the advertising, promotion and journalistic discourses surrounding their release."[6] Although newspaper articles and reviews lie outside the remit of this current study, film and television trailers function as a major visual component of advertising and promotional discourses. This chapter will challenge the concept that an effects-based spectacle has been used as the dominant attraction within the science fiction genre (and beyond, in the case of the 1990s) by analyzing the trailers (and other relevant promotional material) used to lure audiences back into cinemas to see these genre films.

Choosing three distinct periods in the history of the science fiction genre also allows us to expand the scope of unified analysis from one key innovatory moment (such as Cinerama or television) to consider traits, structural conventions and technological positions that recur across several decades. Covering such a wide selection of trailers and their networks of contemporary concerns and influences should not be seen as a return to an evolutionary schema: unified analysis of these trailers and their respective historical networks reveals no such simplistic pattern at work. The chapter may follow a more chronological path in its investigation of visual spectacle as a central structural concern, but the trailer texts reveal no cause-and-effect development, or the passing of a technological torch. As in previous chapters, the strength of unified analysis lies in its ability to focus on textual complexity rather than simple evolution, allowing us to see a shifting scale of technology, narrative and contemporary influence. Unified analysis of these three periods sees echoes not evolution, no linear narrative but a technological chronology that pays homage as often as it innovates.

While each time period (and trailer) contains unique structural issues, the chapter relies on contextual information to understand the place of visual effects in the sales message, identifying industrial and cultural influences that have affected trailer production. 1950–1956 represents the commercialization and expansion of the genre through a series of films based around fantastic stories of science, interplanetary travel and alien invasion.[7] Because of the importance of this period in establishing generic images and conventions, detailed analysis of the trailers for *Destination Moon*, *Earth vs. the Flying Saucers* (1956) and *Forbidden Planet* (1956) delineates important traits that recur in later periods. Tracing the growth of special effects in trailer narratives, unified analysis considers how visual spectacle relates to contemporary concerns around technology, both realistic and fantastic. After the genre's decline in the late 1950s, the rebirth of special effects technology and science fiction is considered to take place in 1977–1983, when the success of *Star Wars* fuelled the summer blockbuster mentality within the Hollywood industry. The importance of effects within this period is challenged by trailer analysis that reveals a lack of effects-driven images and visual spectacle. Relating this lack to production limitations and the growth of boutique visual effects companies, unified analysis investigates the contemporary shift toward trailers dominated by narrative and character tropes. The final period, 1991–1999, reveals how the recent introduction and expansion of computer-generated imagery (CGI) has allowed visual effects to create realistic, historic and fantastic images: from the digitally animated destruction of *Independence Day* (1996) to the CGI reconstruction of Rome in *Gladiator* (1999). While these trailers contain echoes of the 1950s previews, unified analysis examines whether the recent emphasis on genre spectacle is linked to the selection and repetition of specific CGI sequences within promotional materials.

Throughout, it is important to identify the dual role played by technology in these genre trailers. Basic visual effects technology has been part of trailer production since the 1920s, but it traditionally remained unheralded: a matte painting of the deserted London cityscape in TV spots for *The Day the Earth Caught Fire*, or the rear projection of white water rapids in the preview for *How the West Was Won*. In place of these hidden effects, the science fiction film has offered a more overt display of technology, both within the textual narrative and as a spectacular visual image. While effects shots struc-

A faux newsreel style opens the *Destination Moon* trailer (1950).

tured trailers for *The Lost World* (1925), *Noah's Ark* (1929), and *King Kong* (1933), science fiction trailers from the 1950s on make technology a key narrative and spectacular device: *King Kong* was the eighth wonder of the world, but he represented a (fantastic) threat from within nature; the flying saucers that attack earth in *Earth vs. the Flying Saucers* or *Independence Day* are technological threats, sleek and sinister ships with electronic death rays, a narrative menace and a technological spectacle contained in the same image. This explicit demonstration of special effects is an underlying reason why visual spectacle is traditionally identified as a key generic element. However, rather than dismiss the use of effects only as spectacle, unified analysis offers the chance to consider its purpose within the trailer narrative, and to understand how such spectacle has historically been positioned for audiences.

1950–1956: The Special Effects "Star"

> George Pal ... claims that "special effects" are the stars of his picture....
> Now, "special effects" does not read well on theatre marquees ... yet it is
> unmistakably true. The stars of George Pal's pictures **are** special effects.[8]

As the trailer for George Pal's *Destination Moon* opens, the center of the screen is filled with a silver-gray rocket on the launch pad. A newsreel-style title flashes over the top: "TECHNICOLOR CAMERA REVEALS SECRET ROCKETSHIP TAKEOFF TO THE MOON."[9] One of the astronauts starts the countdown, we see the model gantry inch away from the rocket, before sparks and smoke shoot from its base as the countdown reaches zero. One of the first science fiction trailers of the 1950s, the first minute of the *Destination Moon* preview establishes key special effects trailer conventions that recur through the decade, and beyond — but it also contains any claims of spectacle within a strong trailer narrative. The initial image of the rocket technology focuses attention onto three separate aspects — the rocket launch is at once a key effects spectacle, a central narrative event, and a claim to represent the reality of contemporary rocket technology. The fantastic depiction of space travel and moon exploration the trailer moves on to is rooted in this complex first image of fantasy, technology and reality. Unified analysis of this trailer, along with previews for two other successful science fiction films of the 1950–1956 period (*Earth vs. the Flying Saucers* and *Forbidden Planet*), allows us to explore how genre trailers situated their visual effects in these formative years. Examining the contemporary interest in scientific technology and the industrial concerns over special effects production will reveal that spectacle is rarely the primary element in trailer narratives, more often balanced with competing elements of story, attempts at verisimilitude, and nascent generic conventions.

Destination Moon was by no means the first trailer to discover the importance of visual effects to lure audiences into theatres, or the first to link effects work and narrative "reality." The 1925 trailer for *The Lost World* centers its stars — stop-motion Brachiosaurs and a Tyrannosaurus Rex — in excerpted scenes that combine animation with live action; while the *King Kong* trailer features its stop motion star from the opening image, as Kong breaks through wooden gates, raises his head and beats his chest. While neither trailer makes any direct reference to the technology that animated these creatures, they both use the technological star to structure their narratives and comment on the ability of those images to interact with reality.[10] Unlike the later technology-centered science fiction trailers, these trailer narratives are about natural wonders, and they make claims of verisimilitude: "we offer you the chance to see it ... this strange and sensational story *lives* before you!"[11] The trailer's call to vision is reflected by shots that place the stop-motion monsters within the normal world of the viewer, with humans shown in the same frame as a Tyrannosaurus Rex, as it roams the London streets. The *King Kong* trailer also showcases its special effects technology by emphasizing Kong's interaction with recognizable New York locations: pulling an elevated train from its tracks, kidnapping Fay Wray from her bed, swatting at bi-planes atop the Empire State Building. Echoing *The Lost World*, these scenes are described as the "stuff for which movies were made ... adventure that will make you wonder if it's true, while your eyes will convince you that it is."[12] Establishing the presentation of a special effects star, both trailers rely on the integration of that monster/image within a realistic milieu, and suggest the importance of audiences viewing, and accepting, this combination of spectacular and mundane. The trailer description of Kong as "the eighth wonder of the world" is also double-edged: Kong is a wonder of stop-motion technology as much as he is a diegetic wonder.[13] The 1950s science fiction trailers would take this notion of a central special effects star, its relation to reality, and the contemporary context of space travel and UFO sightings, to develop a narrative focus on new (and alien) technology.

Destination Moon's trailer suggests the veracity of its opening effects image through the use of newsreel journalism aesthetics and links to contemporary knowledge of rocket science. The bold lettering and graphics recall the first moments of Universal or Movietone newsreels of the 1940s, and the voiceover starts out flat and restrained, not excitable or hyperbolic. This presentation style elaborates on a theme that runs through the film's publicity, an insistence that the film dealt with science fact, not science fiction, citing "years of research, planning and experimentation ... to give the public an accurate and believable account of man's first successful attempt to place a man-carrying interplanetary spaceship upon the surface of the moon."[14] Pal's belief that the visuals could convey a possible reality restricts the fantastic elements of displaying a rocket launch, and its potential as a spectacular star image. By 1950, America and Russia had developed German V2 rocket technology into two-stage vehicles, and were regularly sending these into space. Cinema audiences were familiar with the reality of rocket launches from wartime footage of German V2s even before post-war newsreels showed viewers American V2 rockets taking off from the White Sands research base.[15] The similarity between the *Destination Moon* trailer and the Universal newsreel footage confirms Pal's belief in using special effects to recreate a known reality.

This quest for authenticity reduces any potential the trailer visuals have to display spectacle. The rocket remains the primary generic and effects-based image, but the trailer narrative focuses on the science "fact" of technological preparation as much as the fiction of a journey into space: "It is just one minute before take off in the uninhabited desert of White Sands, New Mexico.... But to reach this dramatic moment takes months of construction, checking every detail a thousand times, and a desperate struggle to convince the skeptical."[16] This opening voiceover (accompanied by images of astronauts, engineers and scientists working on the rocket) has strong ties to the feature's diegetic interest in human science and technology, but the network of influences that surround the trailer reveal that such a quest narrative also reflects on the film's production history. Unified analysis suggests that the

The ***Destination Moon*** trailer (1950) tried to appeal to a wider audience by featuring sales messages and popular periodicals aimed at women.

opening of the *Destination Moon* trailer refers to technological efforts on a diegetic (building a rocket to go to the Moon) and non-diegetic scale (building a model rocket as part of a film production). The trailer can be seen as a commentary on the production: Pal's insistence on realism entailed that each central effect (be it rocket models or stop-motion astronauts walking on the lunar surface) was checked for accuracy "a thousand times" as the special effects team tried to produce more realistic work. The "months of construction" refer to the long preparation involved in testing and experimenting with the film's various visual effects techniques, the "dramatic moment" of presenting those effects to a wider audience, and the "desperate struggle to convince the skeptical," representing Pal's own struggle to finance and make the film, particularly given the recent box office failure of his first feature, *The Great Rupert* (1950).[17]

The heart of the complex layering in the *Destination Moon* trailer is the role of technology: the rocket is a central visual image, an element of the production history, a representation of the known reality of the V2 rockets, and a narrative concern. Yet the narrative is not wholly based around either the rocket, or the technology it represents. In a move that echoes through later genre trailers, and which questions the dominance of visual spectacle, the narrative contains hybrid elements that dilute any narrative based purely around technological display. These additions were presumably intended to broaden the appeal of the film for female and non-genre viewers, particularly given the lack of recent science fiction film successes. Near the end of the trailer, a series of magazine covers are shown: the colorful *Life* and *Parade* publications are particularly prominent, with covers that focus on the film's female cast and costumes—elements that were not dominant in the film's publicity campaign. There are broader narrative strokes within the trailer as well: one scene features an astronaut kissing his wife before boarding the rocket ("Never Before Has Any Woman/Sent Her Man On Such An Exploit!"[18]); while dramatic stakes are heightened post-launch when an excerpted scene reveals the astronauts are trapped on the Moon. Although set within the rocket, the scenes features no display of internal technology, and the astronaut's reference to "going over Niagara Falls in a barrel" is a distinct regression in travel technology from the trailer's opening rocket image.

Similar to the first trailers for CinemaScope (*The Robe*) or 3-D (*Bwana Devil*), *Destination Moon* features an uncertain display of its central technological effects and technology narrative, combining them with hybrid sales messages that lessen the impact of the visual spectacle. As we shall see, later 1950s previews for *Earth vs. the Flying Saucers* and *Forbidden Planet* show that as science fiction films developed, and the genre became more popular, effects-based display began to feature more prominently in trailer sales messages. This development, and the contemporary proliferation of the genre as a whole, is traditionally traced to a confluence of technological factors within social, cultural and historical events: "the bomb, the beginnings of aerospace research, the incipient Cold War, and the perceived presence of extraterrestrial spacecraft."[19] As with our earlier example of the American V2 rocket launches, such a network of influences helps to explain the presence of these narrative and visual elements. What this network fails to consider, however, is why the Hollywood studios moved into the genre so quickly, and efficiently, and what industrial factors contributed to its expansion.

At a time when they were beginning to feel the effects of falling audiences and the growing television market, the place of visual spectacle in both film and trailers was changing. We have already seen the film industry's desire to differentiate television and cinema through the shape and sound of the theatrical screen experience, but the move toward special effects departments shaping this epic, spectacular form of content had been developing over the previous decade.[20] The growing importance (and expansion) of studio effects departments can be largely traced to two elements: the decision by the Academy of Motion Picture Arts and Sciences (AMPAS) to introduce an Academy Award for Special Effects in 1939, and perhaps more crucially, the need to create extensive (and realistic) air, land and sea combat for a cycle of war film productions.[21] As with *Destination Moon*, the role of effects was regarded as the production of realistic visuals, not fantastic ones. Although it rewarded the Technicolor whimsy of *The Thief of Baghdad* (1940), in the 1940s the Academy was more likely to acknowledge the realism of wartime dramas such as *I Wanted Wings* (1941), *Crash Dive* (1943) and *Thirty Seconds Over Tokyo* (1944).[22] Few of these effects sequences were showcased in trailer structures of the time, which favored star and narrative-based hyperbole, but the suggestive influence of realism within these effects departments is important in understanding the initial efforts of producers such as Pal in the late 1940s and early 1950s. With falling revenues and audience levels, studio effects departments were under-utilized and beginning to be downsized: a new direction, and a financially successful genre, offered a reprieve, even if only a temporary one. Unlike the final reel catastrophes of non-genre pictures, visual effects and the technologies they depicted were inherent components of science fiction narratives. The centrality of these effects, the growing need to differentiate the cinema screen, and the established awards-based recognition of the industry fuelled the significant role such effects played in trailer advertising.

The spectacle of Ray Harryhausen's flying saucer effects in the *Earth vs. the Flying Saucers* trailer (1956).

The increase in special effects spectacle—and a newfound interest in extraterrestrial technology—can be seen in the trailer for *Earth vs. the Flying Saucers*. Like *Destination Moon* it opens with a visual effect, but the narrative frames and showcases those effects shots throughout its running time. Three flying saucers glide above the landmarks of Washington DC, the top of each craft revolving as they fly smoothly across the screen: these spacecraft are the central star image, but (unlike the earlier Pal trailer) they represent a fantastic technological sight rather than a realistic human one. The trailer differs from its contemporaries by offering this alien technology as spectacle as well as narrative threat: previous alien invasion trailers for *The Thing from Another World* (1951) or *Invaders from Mars* (1953) had kept the instruments of their global obliteration in reserve, luring audiences in through images of shadowy figures or the strange behavior of brainwashed humans. The *Earth vs. the Flying Saucers* trailer changes that emphasis by immediately centering its stop-motion stars and positioning them as characters at the center of a dramatic narrative: air raid sirens wail, soldiers man artillery guns, and rockets and missiles are fired at the saucers. In the two-minute duration of the trailer, these saucers attack, fire on planes and ships, hover over world capitals, and crash into Washington's most recognizable

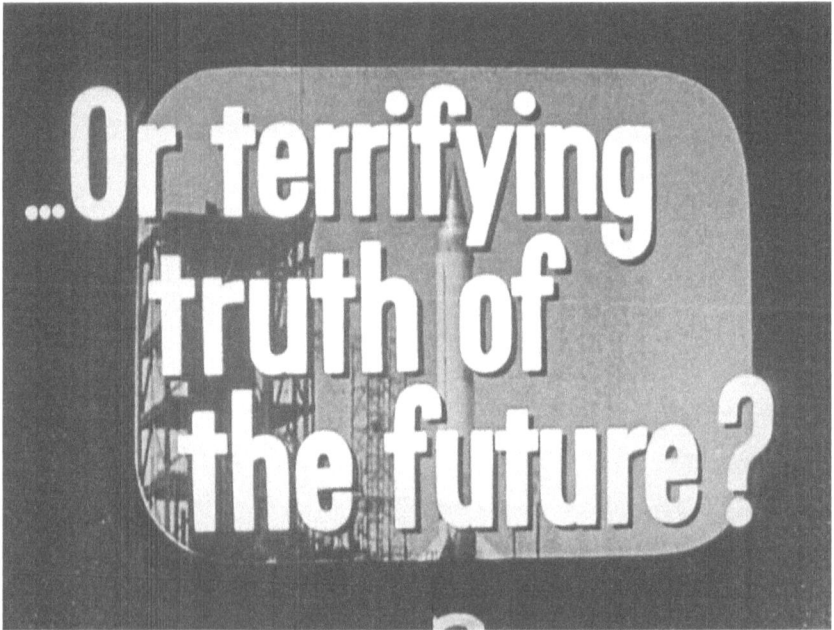

The *Earth vs. the Flying Saucers* trailer centers genre images such as the rocket launch to link back to *Destination Moon*'s earlier success.

monuments and buildings. Unlike the thousands of vague UFO sightings reported in America during the 1950s, these special effects saucers are a spectacular sight and offer a visual synthesis of narrative and effects-based technology.

The centrality of these effects shots may be a reaction to the other cinematic technologies of the era: the spectacle of color film and widescreen. By 1956, wider screen ratios and color film production had begun to dominate Hollywood studio films: unable to compete in terms of screen size, the science fiction film could still fill its screen with fantastic images. The presence of disparate screen technologies becomes a narrative device in the *Earth vs. the Flying Saucer* trailer, which offers what could be seen as a contemporary dismissal of the television screen as a viewing alternative. Like *Destination Moon* before it, the trailer places its opening visual spectacle within a realistic milieu — containing the fantastic within the boundaries of recognizable locations. Many of these first images of saucers hanging over monuments in Washington, Paris and London are seen on a large screen (that remains unidentified, although it is clearly not in a cinema setting). This monitor initially seems to represent a television, showing a news broadcast or newsreel images. This would not be uncommon — effects technology was visually contained by a journalistic aesthetic in *Destination Moon*, and the trailer for *The Day the Earth Stood Still* (1951) opens with a similar device, using a journalistic commentary on the landing of a flying saucer. Unlike these earlier examples, there is no additional title or voiceover work to emphasize the link to journalism, but the newsreel element remains strong — there is a shot of a rocket taking off that recalls both *Destination Moon* and the V2 footage.[23] Each use of these screens within a screen focuses on the special effects shots, particularly the saucers hovering over cities.

The use of this "other" screen to impart newsreel style footage of the invasion takes on a more sinister note as the trailer continues — the monitor showing these images is revealed to be alien, onboard one of the saucers. This knowledge is hidden in the first half of the trailer, which builds up the sense of a fantastic reality, then reveals that the screen is being watched by captive humans on board the saucer (the aliens are, presumably, also watching the success of their invasion). The trailer has put its audience in the position of the invaders, or at the very least, the subjugated humans. The images we have been watching have glorified the destructive power of the alien technology, and been shown on an alien screen technology. The second half of the trailer narrative rejects this alternative screen, displaying its special effects images on the full cinema screen, and presenting a human victory over the alien technology. This also re-centers the special effects spectacle: an animated saucer lands on the White House lawn, a model saucer crashes into the Washington Monument, the Monument topples to the ground, another saucer flies into the Capitol Building. The trailer has changed sides—from the impressive effects shots of the saucers gliding through the sky and effortlessly swatting down planes, the trailer turns to the joy of destroying those same saucers, smashing them into recognizable sites. By rejecting the alternative screen technology, and its suggestion of television, the trailer reasserts the primacy of the cinema screen and its ability to depict such spectacular visuals.

The concern over the alternative screen of television is well established in this time period (there is, unfortunately, no record of any *Earth vs. the Flying Saucers* TV spots), but the trailer also mines contemporary events and fears to add to its claims of veracity. The flying saucer was an established generic image by the mid–1950s, aided by recurring reports about alien abduction and UFO sightings around the world. By placing these familiar images alongside known locations, and presenting them within (what appears to be) television news coverage, the trailer strengthens its claim to verisimilitude, and mirrors Vivian Sobchack's belief that audiences garner satisfaction from "seeing the visual integration of actual and impossible in the same frame."[24] While Sobchack was referring to how effects work in feature films, it seems clear that many trailers attempted to use the same combination of spectacular

Recognizable locations and special effects collide in the *Earth vs. the Flying Saucers* trailer (1956).

special effects and realistic setting to attract audiences. The *Earth vs. the Flying Saucers* trailer offers a journey from the blend of reality/unreality offered by the alien screens to reveling in special effects–inspired destruction. This destructive spectacle is still narrative-based, however, contained within dialogue that explains the alien technology ("They've set up an electronic screen, the artillery doesn't penetrate") and titles that reiterate the importance of viewer participation and acceptance: "See the saucer men's high frequency disintegrator ... see flying saucers travel thousands of miles."[25] The effects sequences do dominate the trailer — soldiers being vaporized, a saucer "buzzing" a car, a glowing energy ball attacking scientists in their lab — but this star attraction does not displace narrative; it remains part of a coherent trailer narrative of invasion and human struggle.

The increasing use of fantastic technological images within realistic settings seen between the trailers for *Destination Moon* and *Earth vs. the Flying Saucers* is absent from the final 1950s trailer in this section, due to its outer space setting. Spectacular visual display remains central to the *Forbidden Planet* trailer, but it is ultimately contained within a more hybrid narrative based around star, story and technology. The *Forbidden Planet* trailer represents a confluence of 1950s cinema technologies: filmed in CinemaScope, Eastman Color and showcasing the work of MGM's special effects department. Unlike the trailer for *Earth vs. the Flying Saucers*, which made no mention of the effects work of Ray Harryhausen, the *Forbidden Planet* preview highlights each of these central technologies: "MGM's great technical staff brings you a magnificent picture of that distant tomorrow.... These magnificent scenes in striking Eastman Color.... Two years in the making in CinemaScope."[26] The combination of these three technologies creates a compelling visual display — never-ending vistas into the futuristic chasms of an abandoned underground city; sparks of green and yellow electricity that leap between pylons on either edge of the frame; the fiery orange and red glow as an invisible monster burns through a door, and screen-spanning images of the planet's red-hued surface. The addition of color and widescreen boost the appearance of the special effects, creating visual spectacle, enhancing narrative information, and displaying generic credentials.

The trailer convention of opening with a strong visual effects image is repeated here, as a flying saucer spins through space, coming toward and passing "over" the camera. After an animated fireball sweeps the title onto screen, the trailer cuts inside the ship, where a model saucer sits in the middle of a complex array of futuristic human technology. This bright red saucer stands out from the utilitarian gray décor, drawing the eye across the image as the CinemaScope camera pulls back to reveal the ship's crew. The voiceover and dialogue impart narrative information, but it has a technological edge that explains these impressive visuals: this is a "faster than light spaceship," it is being "radar scanned," the crew meets a robot, and the planet contains the technological "marvels of a lost, genius race."[27] The visual display underneath this information presents a narrative of special effects: animation, stop motion, matte paintings, set design and optical layering. The trailer narrative even highlights a technologically created character, heralding "The Robot" as a unique star image: not only is it pictured and introduced fourth after Walter Pidgeon, Anne Francis and Leslie Nielson, it shares a credit slide with them at the end. The technological narrative concludes with images of the abandoned Krell civilization: dwarfing characters against immense sets, matte paintings, and miniatures of advanced alien technology. The trailer has established other narrative elements — the story of a father and daughter on this mysterious planet — but the visual spectacle of that planet and the spaceship function as a major audience lure. Indeed, the final images of the trailer, after the voiceover ends, are effects-based: an unseen monster burning through the door, an image of the planet's surface, and the spaceship.

The strong visual effects element present in *Forbidden Planet* seems to confirm the evidence of *Earth vs. the Flying Saucers*, that the use of such technological spectacle was a key structural theme of 1950s science fiction trailers. But there is evidence within the trailer text for *Forbidden Planet*, along with elements of its production history, which complicate that reading. Despite the display of generic visuals — flying saucers, alien planets, robots — the trailer shuns its science fiction roots, describing the film as "the most provocative and unusual ADVENTURE FILM you've ever seen."[28] The opening reference to MGM's great technical staff is not completely supported by the textual evidence: apart from the saucer flying through space, the most impressive effects images use traditional methods (matte paintings, cell animation) rather than stop motion or detailed model work. And despite the star status the trailer gives to "The Robot," its presentation in the trailer confirms that this supposed technological marvel is, like Gort in *The Day the Earth Stood Still* trailer, simply a man in a suit. His status as a piece of futuristic technology is further undercut by the scene he appears in, when Alta demands her new evening dress be "the loveliest, softest thing you've ever made for me — and fit in all the right places, with lots and lots of star sapphires." The Robot whirrs, clicks, then answers that "Star Sapphires take a week to crystallize properly. Would diamonds or emeralds do?"[29] The "man in suit" phenomenon (the most basic special effect given it simply required a costume, of varying degrees of complexity) had given 1950s science fiction audiences a range of destructive capabilities: a shadowy Thing wreaking havoc in an arctic base, silver giant Gort disintegrating rifles with a laser beam, or Robot Monster chasing girls around a desert landscape. Here, despite looking like an amazing technological creation, the trailer presents Robby as nothing more than a glorified sewing machine-cum-butler, the ultimate 1950s labor-saving technology.

The *Forbidden Planet* trailer is best understood as a conflict between nascent science fiction trailer conventions, the display of technological spectacle, and the creation of a broader sales message. The romance sub-plot between Nielson and Francis in the trailer narrative features little or no technological information, or visual spectacle, but it offers a more hybrid appeal to the trailer overall. Released in the same year as *Earth vs. the Flying Saucers*, the big budget grandeur of the *Forbidden Planet* trailer masks a concurrent decline in the science fiction genre's fortunes, with other sales messages moving away from its generic credentials. An earlier trailer for *War of the Worlds* (1953) had featured this more hybrid promotional approach, but its lack of effects spectacle or technological narrative appears to have been a result of special effects production schedules. Trailers could take up to three months to produce, and finished model, stop-motion or optical effects were often not available in time.[30] The decision to reduce some of the science fiction elements within the *Forbidden Planet* trailer also relates to the major studio's uncertainty over the long-term appeal of the genre. In 1955, Paramount (producers of *When Worlds Collide* (1951) and *War of the Worlds*) claimed that "science fiction pictures were a passing fad ... [and didn't] fit with Paramount's economic scheme."[31] The cost of producing the visual effects necessary for larger budget science fiction films was rising at a time when the major studios were facing an uncertain financial future. Like most trailers, *Forbidden Planet* was designed to appeal to as large (and broad) an audience as possible. With the science fiction fad allegedly over, that entailed a hybrid sales message that balanced visual spectacle and a technology-based narrative with human stars and romantic sub-plots.

Although they represent the apex of 1950s science fiction promotion, the trailers for *Destination Moon, Earth vs. the Flying Saucer* and *Forbidden Planet* demonstrate that the central visual effects spectacle was largely contained within strong trailer narratives. Combining reality, fantasy and technology, the special effects star was positioned within a hybrid trailer structure that focused audience attention onto contemporary technological concerns around rockets, exploration and alien invasion. From the positioning of realistic effects as pseudo-newsreel in *Destination Moon* to the more fantastic destruction of *Earth vs. the Flying Saucers* and the outer space exuberance of *Forbidden Planet*, these 1950s trailers represent the growth of visual effects that differentiated the science fiction genre from the concurrent Biblical spectacle of CinemaScope films such as *The Robe* and *Demetius and the Gladiators* (1954). Despite the genre's initial success, the financial situation in Hollywood largely prevented the production of bigger budget science fiction after 1956. Lower budget science fiction continued to depict alien invasion, but through narrative teases rather than visual display: alien mind control and off-screen threats in trailers for *Invaders from Mars* and *Invasion of the Body Snatchers*

(1956), or the man-in-suit phenomenon of *The Giant Gila Monster* (1959) and *Monster from Green Hell* (1957) previews. The corporate downsizing taking place within Hollywood also meant the dismantling of effects departments, with "cameras and optical printers and other finely built instruments ... consigned to scrap heaps, put in storage or sold off cheap."[32] With later trailers (such as George Pal's return to the genre, with *The Time Machine* [1960]) further reducing their visual effects display, and retreating into a hybrid trailer structure, it would be almost twenty years before a new technology promised the return of a visual effects spectacle.

1977–1983: SPACE ODYSSEYS

Star Wars looms large in historical narratives of science fiction and the recent dominance of visual effects in the Hollywood industry. George Lucas' film may divide critics and audiences, but its long-term effect on filmmaking, particularly the blockbuster tendencies of modern film production, has made the film a nexus for discussions of special effects technology and visual spectacle.[33] Yet in 1976, when the film's teaser trailer was released, there was only a muted display of the film's spectacular special effects. Instead of a visual effects star, the teaser offers a layered sales message that harks back to 1950s trailers such as *War of the Worlds* and *Destination Moon*, with their combination of romance, adventure and narrative information. Exploring this paradox, between the accepted image of *Star Wars* and the historical evidence of the trailer, unified analysis challenges our assumptions about *Star Wars* and the use of spectacle in this time period. The emphasis on the moment of production, and the surrounding cultural, social and industrial factors, complicates the view of *Star Wars* as visual spectacle, repositioning it at the center of a complex network of influences. The lack of a special effects star will be traced through unified analysis of trailers for *Star Wars* and its contemporary rival *Star Trek: The Motion Picture* (1979) (as well as their respective sequels, *The Empire Strikes Back* [1980] and *The Wrath of Khan* [1982]). Focusing on the expansion of visual effects houses and the development of new motion control technology, the section will consider whether the 1977–1983 period can truly be regarded as the rebirth of visual spectacle.

The *Star Wars* teaser opens with an image of stars, at the center of which is the film's logo, slowly moving toward camera. From this, the trailer cuts to an escape pod being jettisoned, a gray TIE fighter screams toward camera, closely followed by the white bulk of the Millennium Falcon; a second TIE fighter flies over the Falcon, firing green laser blasts; the camera tracks two TIE fighters as they attack; and a red laser blasts fire out toward a TIE that speeds into the camera. Intercut with two short dialogue excerpts (Leia's

"Here they come" and Luke's "They're coming in too fast"), this short opening sequence relies wholly on the display of spectacular effects technology. The detail and design of the models, and the speed with which they move and spit laser beams, are a forceful demonstration of George Pal's belief in a special effects star.[34] But this display does not last. The remaining ninety seconds of the teaser focuses on character and adventure narrative instead, highlighting gun battles, romance, impressive stunt work, and the villainy of Darth Vader. The emphasis on romantic themes recalls *Destination Moon* and *Forbidden Planet*'s previews, while the imbalance between narrative information and brief special effects shots is more reminiscent of trailers for *War of the Worlds* or *When Worlds Collide*. While the latter section of the teaser does contain brief snatches of laser gunfire and alien creatures, its central effects image — the lightsaber duel — remains incomplete, without the red or blue rotoscoping animation to make the blades shimmer.[35]

The images that stand out in the teaser are the opening shots of the dogfight between the various spacecraft. Even though they flash past too quickly to dominate, this short glimpse of visual spectacle highlights the ability of visual effects houses— in this case, Industrial Light and Magic (ILM) — to create stunning effects work that illustrates the genre's return to fantasy-based narratives. Before *Star Wars*, 1970s science fiction films had featured a dearth of visual effects spectacle: the alien invasion of *The Andromeda Strain* (1971) was at the microbe level, while *The Omega Man* (1971) and *Soylent Green* (1973) set their fictions in realistic near-future Earth environments that resembled contemporary society. In a time period when television regularly broadcast rocket launches and Moon landings, there seemed to be no call for films to depict the realistic space travel seen in the *Destination Moon* trailer. The technological wonder of the 1969 Moon landing and the drama of the 1970 Apollo 13 mission had made American and international audiences familiar with the reality of space travel. Or perhaps over familiar: science fiction writer James Gunn wrote in 1974, only five years after Apollo 11 landed on the Moon, that NASA's popularity was in danger because people saw it as increasingly mundane, lacking adventure or poetry.[36] The *Star Wars* trailer narratives return alien (and human) technology to the stars, the unknown realms of space travel, with no basis in the reality of rockets or Moon exploration.

Nine years before the release of *Star Wars*, another trailer text attempted to revive the science fiction genre, but through an effects spectacle based around a realistic depiction of space travel: closer to *Destination Moon* than the fantasy of *Forbidden Planet*. The trailer produced for the Cinerama launch of *2001: A Space Odyssey* created a unique visual spectacle almost completely composed of effects shots. The trailer is pared down to basic structural elements: there are no graphic wipes, no narrative voiceover, no dialogue, no

Visual spectacle lies at the heart of the *2001: A Space Odyssey* Cinerama trailer (1968).

sound effects, and title work does not appear until the final two images, listing the film title and a quotation from *Time* magazine. What remains is a simple and elegant sales message that places futuristic technology and visual effects at the center of the trailer. Of the 23 images that make up the trailer, 12 are fully effects generated — a combination of model work, motion control technology, and matte paintings — while the others display the technological world of the film's set design and costumes through shots of the interior of immense spaceships, astronauts in spacesuits and the glowing red "eye" of HAL 9000. From the languid rotation of the space wheel and Discovery One's long, thin shape gracefully cutting through space to images of the planets against a vast starfield and the storm of yellow, purple and red stroboscopic light in the Stargate sequence, the trailer centers the visual spectacle of the film with no hyperbole, allowing the stunning imagery to sell itself. Set only to the mounting drama of Strauss' "Also Sprach Zarathustra," the trailer serves two technological masters: the Cinerama process, where such images would overwhelm an audience, and the groundbreaking visual effects that separate the film from its predecessors.

This stark display of effects work creates a strong trailer narrative around technology, literally depicting a futuristic odyssey into space. This simple narrative structure sits between *Forbidden Planet*'s combination of plot, effects and technology, and the *Star Wars* teaser's opening salvo of visual effects. The *2001* trailer emphasizes the verisimilitude of its effects by lingering on the images, while the later *Star Wars* teaser stresses montage, the impact of short bursts of effects-created fantasy. The *2001* Cinerama trailer depicts elegiac effects and spacecraft that travel at a stately pace; the 1970s *Star Wars* and *Star*

Trek trailers replace this with exuberance, speed, and a fantastic view of space travel. As the main trailer for *Star Wars* says, ushering in the preview's main montage of visual effects spectacle, "this is where the fun begins."[37]

The unexpected financial success of *Star Wars* had two immediate results: studios became desperate to greenlight their own science fiction blockbusters, and hundreds of small special effects companies were formed, created in the image of ILM. The popularity of *Destination Moon* in 1950 had been met with a similar production boom: but in the 1950s the major studios already had experienced effects departments able to move into the production of realistic or fantastic images. Economic downturn and the conglomerate takeovers of the 1960s had closed down those same departments, leaving few people (or companies) able to meet this new demand for spectacular visual effects.[38] The production of *Star Wars* had entailed the creation of ILM, and their computerized motion control technology had revolutionized the production of effects. The learning process involved with new companies, new techniques and constant revisions and improvements to technology (including the introduction of computerized systems, a new phenomenon in film production) led to a rash of trailer releases that featured either inferior effects, or none at all. Some of these returned to 1950s concepts such as the "man in a suit" convention: updated with laser blasts and better costumes, these can be seen prominently in trailers for *Battle Beyond the Stars* (1980) and *Battlestar Galactica* (1978). The finished feature may have displayed sophisticated motion control effects, but with such visuals not ready until close to the film's release there was little opportunity for the effects star to shine in advance trailer publicity.

Some film trailers were able to use the lack of effects to their advantage, returning to trailer techniques that teased their central stars rather than displaying them (a concept that can be traced back as far as the *Phantom of the Opera* [1925] trailer, and which was used frequently in 1950s science fiction trailers such as *The Thing from Another World*). Trailers for both *Alien* (1979) and *Close Encounters of the Third Kind* (1977) demonstrate different approaches to this structural conceit. The teaser and main trailer for *Alien* withhold much of the film's effects-based visuals. There is one short motion control image of the *Nostromo* hanging in space, a split-second image of a face-hugger, and a brief shot of the alien landscape and ship. The trailers opt instead to build up suspense and atmosphere through their editing and ominous soundtrack— the effects are a lure, a tease, suggesting the spectacle without displaying it. With *Alien* this structure of concealment rather than visual display may be considered part of its cross-genre appeal, offering horror trailer conventions alongside science fiction ones. The *Close Encounters* trailer also conceals its effects spectacle, showing only a series of colored lights and malfunctioning household objects.[39] Here, this lack is used to promote behind-the-scenes details— a decision that suggests studios were aware of film fans' growing interest in special effects technology. The trailer opens with a sequence that introduces first Steven Spielberg, then Julia and Michael Phillips, before moving on to a fourth "star" image. Pictured on set, giving instructions and peering through a camera, the trailer notes: "Creating special effects is Douglas Trumbull, who in this film goes far beyond his achievements in *2001: A Space Odyssey*."[40] Identifying him through voiceover, pictures and listing a previous genre success—the trailer has marked Trumbull out as a star player. At the same time as Hollywood studios increased their desire for special effects sequences, and visual effects houses expanded, audiences desired to know how effects sequences were produced, and who was responsible. The *Close Encounters* trailer reflects this, and combats the rise of alternative promotional tools—"making of" television specials focusing on special effects, magazines devoted to their production—that were threatening to displace the trailer's status as the main source of film-related information.[41]

Trumbull was also responsible for the most effects-driven trailer of the late 1970s. The *Star Trek: The Motion Picture* teaser makes no mention of his name or achievements, but it showcases his spectacular visual effects.[42] Almost three-quarters of the trailer length is given over to different varieties of visual display, and the overarching narrative is based around the presentation and experience of futuristic outer space technology. Following the lead of *Star Wars*, fantastic images are prominent—motion control, model construction and animated sequences—and there is no suggestion of realism or recognizable Earth locations. Its opening visuals set the technological tone. The Paramount logo, with its arch of stars, is centered in the screen. The mountain logo fades, and another section of stars appears, now forming a complete circle. This begins to stream toward the camera. Concentric circles of white, red and blue stars create a tunnel effect that the camera races down, as a growing whine and rumble grow on the soundtrack. As the screen goes black, Orson Welles' voiceover growls "The human adventure is just beginning."[43] Yet when the next image appears, it reveals that the star of this trailer is not human, but technological: another series of circles, but these are part of a machine or a craft. Like the front of a huge jet engine, this image fills the screen. A soft white glow builds up in the center of this engine, almost as though it were coming to life, and smaller lights spark on around the outer circle. The trailer then cuts to a human star (William Shatner) but the first forty seconds have ensured that technology remains at the heart of this sales message.

After the initial shot of the circular deflector array, the teaser continually returns to this intricately detailed model of the Starship Enterprise, as the camera pans across, around and past it. These images run in parallel with the introduction (or, reintroduction, given their known television status) of the main cast, with their character names, but these short glimpses of the "human adventure" offer nothing to eclipse the technological narrative being developed. The teaser gives viewers no story information, focusing our attention instead onto the ship as the site of effects-based spectacle and narrative interest. Unlike the multiple stars of the *Earth vs. the Flying Saucers* or *Star Wars* trailers, here the special effects star is singular: the teaser builds up glimpses of the Enterprise as various running lights flicker to life. The deflector array, a long white nacelle, the expanse of the white saucer section — and then, as light strikes the ship's registry, another light floods the whole of this intricate and impressive model. Having already displayed two special effects techniques—the innovative computer-animated tunnel of stars and the model of the ship—this stationary tease becomes mobile, with motion control camera shots that track along and around the ship. Cutting back, we see the Enterprise gently pull away from its space dock, sailing gracefully toward, and past, the camera. The teaser lingers on this shot longer than any other, confirming that this image is its audience lure, over and above the nine crewmembers.

This visual spectacle is the heart of the sales message, but it also presents a narrative of technology: a continuation of *Star Wars*' fantasy of outer space travel, but also a development. The ship is both special effect and narrative content: it is visually impressive and is presented as a central character, alongside (perhaps above) the regular cast. Because of the film's nature as a big-screen version of an existing property, the ship is already a known design, but this trailer narrative reintroduces it to the audience. Even when the special effects are not showing the Enterprise, they are emphasizing the narrative purpose of the ship. The two computer-animated sequences that bookend the trailer (the second shows a series of parallel green lines that move up and around the screen, again conveying a sense of forward momentum) visually demonstrate the ship's diegetic technological ability (traveling at warp speed) while displaying the unique trailer spectacle of modern computer graphic techniques (more common in contemporary television advertising than trailers).

The main trailer for *Star Trek: The Motion Picture* also depicts a series of effects images, but it contains them within a strong storyline of exploration and adventure. It is the teaser's depiction of the spaceship, its futuristic design and shape, and its fantastic technological ability that lingers, and that offers perhaps the strongest example of a 1970s effects star. The presence of the different effects techniques in the teaser may well reflect the only production footage that was available at the time, but unlike the *Star Wars* teaser, there was a strong (and existing) technological character and focus to build the trailer narrative around. Spectacle here is intrinsically linked with other concerns, not spectacle for its own sake. As we've seen with the discussion of *Alien* and *Close Encounters*, completed effects footage was often not available.

Delays in producing motion control effects were common, and effects houses were constantly trying to innovate existing technologies to make them more impressive and believable. The reduction in visual spectacle within trailer production that we can see in the late 1970s continues through science fiction trailers of the early 1980s, which feature little or no technological narrative or display. Given the presence of key special effects sequences in *Star Wars* and *Star Trek: The Motion Picture*, analysis of the trailers for their respective sequels (*The Empire Strikes Back* and *Star Trek II: The Wrath of Khan*) will allow us to explore the reduction in visual spectacle as a sales message, and consider how traditional conventions of narrative and generic imagery returned to dominate 1980s trailer structure.

Even when compared to the brief montage of effects spectacle in the *Star Wars* teaser, the *Empire Strikes Back* teaser is a retrograde step. In place of a fast-paced effects montage this teaser offers an array of painted images (by the conceptual artist Ralph McQuarrie) and, toward the end, photographs of the main cast members. The only moving images (in a film series predicated on speed and motion) are the camera flying through a starfield, and moving over the McQuarrie drawings. The lack of visual spectacle in this teaser is a product of two disparate elements of the production process: the effects work being completed by ILM, and 20th Century–Fox's desire to promote the film in theatres as early as possible. Given the feature contained over 400 effects shots (including stop-motion and "go-motion" animation, model work, prosthetics, animatronics, puppetry, and motion control, many of which had to be layered together in the same frame), the teaser trailer was unlikely to have had access to finished production footage for its Christmas 1979 premiere (six months before the film's May 21, 1980, release date).[44] Without access to the known effects star images of the *Star Wars* universe, the teaser trailer relies on two themes: continuing pleasures ("Luke, Han and Princess Leia ... droids and Wookies") and anticipated events ("an awesome confrontation between Luke Skywalker and the master of the Dark Side of the Force, Darth Vader").[45]

The focus on narrative continuation also imbues the main trailer for *The Empire Strikes Back*, which is dominated by a character-based sales message. The bulk of the trailer is structured around medium two-shots, used to emphasize the trailer's romantic theme (Han and Leia on the Falcon) and establish characters in particular locations (Luke being shot at in Cloud City). Effects shots are not as spectacular, or as frequent, as those featured in the *Star Wars* trailers. The sequences that are used — a glimpse of the Hoth Ion Cannon, a tracking shot across the faces of the alien bounty hunters, two quick images from the asteroid field chase — do not offer the unique quality that the motion control images had in the 1977 advertising, or the compelling presentation of the Enterprise in the *Star Trek* teaser. This may again be a result of the limited availability of effects-based images. Trailers are traditionally produced months ahead of films being finished, so for this main trailer to debut in cinemas in April/May 1980 (six weeks to two months before the film was released) it would have been produced in January/February.[46] The effects on display in the trailer suggest this time lag, and lack of finished effects: the base of the cannon appears to be an on-set prop, and the alien bounty hunters are shot live action (wearing masks and prosthetics). The trailer also contains little emphasis on technology as a narrative device, or the fantastic depiction of outer space central to earlier trailers: robots and spaceships continue to function as genre dressing, but they are not central to the trailer narrative. This absence, of a special effects star or a technology-based narrative, made little difference to the film's box-office performance in May 1980, but it is worth noting that both elements are more prevalent in the series of television spots produced and broadcast in May and June 1980, after the film was released. The presence of strong visually arresting effects footage (the AT-AT battle, the Super Star Destroyer, the final lightsaber duel) suggest that the promotional strategy was changed once central effects sequences were complete.

The stronger focus on character or story events over effects-based spectacle is also more noticeable in the trailer for *Star Trek II: The Wrath of Khan*. If we regard the presentation of the Enterprise in the original teaser as the reintroduction of a narrative character, then the difference between trailers may not be quite so distinct. But its emphasis on technology as a diegetic and effects-based display is not repeated here. Instead, the trailer chooses a human character — the villain, Khan — as its central narrative focus. Over the generic image of stars blinking in space, Khan's protagonist role is established: "Khan. A genetically superior tyrant, exiled to a barren planet, banished by a starship commander he is destined to destroy. Left for dead, he has survived."[47] The central sequence of the trailer shows a battle between two starships, but the visual effects are brief and unheralded: the trailer prefers to focus on the dialogue exchanges between the two captains. Rather than functioning as a separate, spectacular image, or within a narrative of technological marvel, the effects repeat a shot-reverse-shot format, showing red laser beams as they rake across the Enterprise. The reactions of the characters are more important to this trailer than lingering on the motion control shots of the starship battle.

There is one moment of unrelated visual spectacle that links the *Star Trek II* trailer back to the original teaser, and its use of computer animation. A line of Khan's dialogue (about marooning Kirk on a planet) runs over the start of a shot of a deserted gray moon — the effects initially appear to be illustrating Khan's words. Yet the positioning of the image immediately before the film's title graphic, along with its use of more advanced technology, highlights this strong final image and suggests something beyond the established trailer narrative. As with the earlier use of computer animation, the sequence suggests movement — the camera tracks a line of fire as it races around the curve of the moon, before swooping down to the surface, panning across the fire, then sweeping back up to show the evolution of green fields and blue rivers. This movement is not motivated — there is no technological source, like the suggestion of the Enterprise going to warp — and it stands as a curious technological and spectacular coda to a trailer narrative otherwise unconcerned with technology or visual spectacle. With no apparent record of its production or why it was placed within the trailer, it must remain a suggestive mystery, possibly a sign of computer-generated images to come.

Unified analysis of these trailers disputes the accepted wisdom that the special effects star was resurgent in the years post–*Star Wars*, offering a more complex reading in its place. The *Star Trek* teaser aside, there are few examples of effects-based spectacle dominating trailer advertising, or functioning as sales messages intended to attract audiences. It may be true that films of the late 1970s were more likely to look to the stars (and *Star Wars*) for inspiration, but the fantastic special effects technologies that fuel the narratives and *mise-en-scène* of *Alien*, *The Black Hole* (1979), *E.T.: The Extra Terrestrial* (1982), *The Thing* (1982), *Flash Gordon* (1980) or the *Star Trek* film series are not reflected or highlighted in trailer production practices. The irony here is that the very technological advances that made those effects possible for feature films restricted their use in trailer advertising. At a time when effects houses and individuals were growing in power and dominance, the texts they used for promotion were not trailers: aside from the features themselves, such companies targeted magazines like *Cinefex*, *Starlog* and *Fangoria*, and television "making of" specials to increase awareness of their work.[48] Douglas Trumbull may have appeared in the *Close Encounters* trailer (and his work may be on display in the *Star Trek: The Motion Picture* teaser) but publicity around him (or ILM) was largely in other media. Without the ability to use central effects sequences, by the early 1980s genre trailer structure had returned to the kind of multiple sales messages familiar from the 1950s: adventure and romance narratives rather than technology or visual spectacle. Some trailers made a boon out of this — previews for *Alien* and *ET* both restrict access to their central effects figure — but most diminish the role of visual spectacle, despite the dominant role it was playing in film production more generally. With visual effects beginning to be central within other genres, particularly popular blockbusters such as *Raiders of the Lost Ark* (1981), *Ghostbusters* (1984) and *Top Gun* (1986), the absence of special effects from advance promotional material was problematic. George Pal's special effects star could not dominate in 1977–1983, but the next iteration of the science fiction genre would ensure that special effects–based spectacle would become more prominent within trailer structure and narrative.

1991–1999: COMPUTER GENERATED

In the early 1990s, computer-generated imagery (CGI) promised to revolutionize film production, particularly the creation of visual effects sequences. The depiction of this technological advance was largely absent from trailer texts—studios were slow to realize the potential of effects technology as a central sales message, despite regular promotion given to special effects houses and practitioners in movie magazines and television specials. Examining 1990s trailers in this final section pulls together three lines of enquiry from the 1950s and 1970s: the possibility of a dominant special effects star, the availability of an effects-based display within the trailer, and the concept of spectacle displacing narrative. Unified analysis of *Terminator 2: Judgment Day, Independence Day* and *Apollo 13* (1995) will consider how changes in special effects technology were reflected in trailer texts, while trailers for *Forrest Gump* (1994) and *The Perfect Storm* (1999) will allow us to reflect on the expansion of CGI into other genres. This analysis reveals that when film production schedules were reworked to create specific effects sequences for trailers, it changed the structural placement of visual spectacle across the whole promotional spectrum. Tracing this development in trailer texts from the 1990s directly tackles the issue of spectacle and narrative, and allows us to see how trailers have positioned these elements for audiences.

The second trailer for *Terminator 2: Judgment Day* begins with a shot of the metal skull of the Terminator T-800 model cyborg, flames raging around it. Fulfilling its status as a sequel trailer by using known imagery from the first film, the placement of the special effects star from *The Terminator* (1984) as its opening image also promotes the continuation of that effects-based lineage. Like many trailers of the late 1980s and early 1990s, the bulk of the *Terminator 2* trailer is devoted to imparting narrative information: Sarah Connor is in a psychiatric institution, her son John is now the target, and the original Terminator is protecting, not hunting, him. By the mid-point of the trailer, the narrative thrust is clear—the T-800 has to battle a second Terminator—and the trailer moves from story beats to a visual depiction of this fight through special effects shots that combine CGI, practical effects and stop motion. Unlike the 1980s sequel trailers for *Star Wars* and *Star Trek*, this trailer uses its visual effects spectacle to tell a narrative about technology. The "liquid metal" T-1000 is described by the trailer voiceover as "the deadliest machine ever built," and the shots support this diegetic claim through a montage of CG images: coalescing into a silvery humanoid shape; its head morphing through a helicopter door; transforming into the human figure of Robert Patrick; Patrick's arms elongating into metal spikes; walking though the bars of a prison door. Each shot offers a believable technological antagonist, interacting with other objects and characters within the narrative. At the same time, the effects work as pure technological spectacle — displaying the ability of the CGI morphing software to create realistic three-dimensional shapes within a live-action environment. This combination of visual spectacle and narrative is summed up by another voiceover comment (that recalls trailers for both *The Lost World* and *King Kong*): "If you thought you had seen it all — think again."[49]

The *Terminator 2: Judgment Day* trailer dramatizes a battle between old and new technology on textual and extra-textual levels: the narrative events of the T-800 and T-1000 fight mirrors the state of the special effects industry in the early 1990s, with practical and computer-generated effects facing off. Not yet up to the dominance of stop/go-motion or motion control technologies, computer-generated images had been present (albeit unheralded) in trailers since the early 1980s. CGI was used to create digital landscapes and vehicles in the trailers for *Tron* (1982), energy shields in the *Dune* (1984) trailer, and the planet creation sequence already discussed from the *Star Trek II: The Wrath of Khan* trailer. The main public exposure to the technology came in James Cameron's *The Abyss* (1989), and its use of a CG "pseudopod," a water tentacle (representing an alien intelligence) that interacts with the crew of a deep-sea drilling platform. In all these examples, the technology behind the computer animation is not heralded, or centered within the sales message, but the introduction of the T-1000 and the revolutionary nature of the effects work heralds a development in 1990s genre trailers. Despite this, the *Terminator 2* trailers still echo the 1980s examples above: the teaser and trailer #1 contain little CGI action, and only trailer #2 (released in the weeks before the film debuted) features a full array of CGI sequences: once again, the availability of state-of-the-art effects technology restricted a full display of the special effects star.

Three years after *Terminator 2: Judgment Day*, a trailer debuted that centered a display of effects-driven visual spectacle as the core reason to see the film. In the process, it rewrote production schedules and transformed the film industry's promotional practices.

> "You want to blow up the White House?" ... We pitched them [20th Century–Fox] the idea of this teaser and at the end of the teaser the White House blows up. "Earth: take a good look — it could be your last."[50]

The teaser trailer for *Independence Day* initially appears to fit into earlier 1990s effects trailer conventions. Like other genre trailers—for example, the *Jurassic Park* (1993) trailer — the opening images convey a narrative thrust rather than a special effects spectacle. Over images of the Iwo Jima statue and a military control room, dialogue establishes that something is approaching Earth. Tension is built by cutting between screen-filling narrative titles and quick shots of the Statue of Liberty, the New York skyline, the White House and the Washington Monument as they are cast into shadow by something passing overhead. Over three-quarters of the way through its running time, the teaser finally reveals its special effects "star"—a shaft of blue-green light descends from a briefly glimpsed shape in the sky, illuminates the White House, which then explodes outward, flames and debris shooting "into" the camera. With no human stars (there is no sign, or mention, of Jeff Goldblum, Will Smith or Bill Pullman) and only the most basic narrative information, the teaser trailer builds to its special effects climax—and its main audience draw. Interviews with the film's producer-director team (Dean Devlin and Roland Emmerich) regularly returned to the White House image. Its reiteration as a central marketing tool always appeared before mention was made of its narrative purpose in the feature. Devlin and Emmerich were so determined to promote this image in the film's advertising campaign that they scheduled the shot early in the visual effects production process.[51] As in the 1950s and *Earth vs. the Flying Saucers*, the desire to combine the real and the unreal, the verisimilitude of Washington locations and the fantasy of alien destruction, repositions the special effects display at the core of the sales message.[52]

This visual effects image—a combination of miniature work, small explosives and CGI — recurs in all *Independence Day* advertising, from posters and "making of" documentaries to the Superbowl TV spots (which Fox paid $1.3 million to air in January 1996).[53] The film's main trailer offers an expansion of the message. From a slow build-up of tension the trailer cuts quickly to its special effects star: a huge flying saucer appears out of billowing clouds over San Francisco, the Empire State Building is destroyed (twice — the trailer replays the explosion from different angles), a wave of CGI fighter planes attack one of the saucers, explosions rip through city streets, alien ships strike an airbase, and Will Smith's fighter plane is pursued by one of the aliens. After its strong narrative opening, the visual effects structure the trailer's spectacle-led sales message. The effects work remains a combination of miniatures and CGI, but the computer-generated elements are more dominant than in any other trailer at this point in the decade. The special effects image, bolstered by the developments in CGI, was now being used as the key element around which publicity narratives were being built: from brief glimpses seen in *Star Wars*, *Alien* or *Jurassic Park*, the special effects spectacle had become the star image George Pal had always insisted it could be. Like a classic star image, the effects shots show key iconic moments— the White House or the Empire State Building exploding — in order to suggest the further pleasures contained within the feature.

Repetition of strong central visuals, so important within *Independence Day*'s teaser and main trailer, would set the tone for many summer blockbuster trailers to follow. With the barometer of Hollywood success now attuned to the first weekend's gross (and the possibility of breaking the $100 million mark), blockbuster trailers needed to create an immediate demand. Following *Independence Day*'s lead, the second half of the decade saw trailers for genre films *Alien: Resurrection* (1997), *Armageddon* (1998), *Men in Black* (1997), *Starship Troopers* (1997) and *Star Wars Episode I: The Phantom Menace* (1999), frontloaded with compelling effects images that echoed throughout their publicity campaigns. The increase in visual spectacle across all forms of promotion — television trailers, posters, "making of" specials, magazines articles, electronic press kits — often reduced the narrative thrust of the image, which was taken out of context and used for display purposes only. This divorcement from a narrative arc (in either trailer or feature) may have fuelled the concept of visual effects sequences as pure spectacle: such images are now designed to be both a narrative event and a promotional entity that can be shown separately to grab viewer attention in other media. The potent television spots for *Independence Day*, designed around a montage of such spectacular scenes, encouraged this practice. Compared to earlier trailers, where trailer narrative contained effects spectacle, the use of high concept imagery such as the White House explosion reduced the importance of trailer narrative. This development can often make watching 1990s trailers an empty experience, with little immediate differentiation between previews. This is particularly clear when compared to the complexity and skill of the 1950s science fiction trailers, or the varied attempts of the 1970s genre trailers to create effects narratives with few effects shots available.

It would be wrong to claim that all genre trailers abandoned compelling narratives. A strong example of balancing effects work with narrative (in this case, based around technology and human endeavor), the *Apollo 13* trailer returns to issues of fantasy versus reality. While both *Terminator 2* and *Independence Day* placed their fantastic images within recognizable settings, the *Apollo 13* trailer uses effects work for purely realistic purposes. Opening with a stunning image of the rocket and gantry silhouetted against a deep orange sunset, the trailer offers a spectacle of real events and a narrative immersed in the technology of space travel. The trailer lingers on 1970s technology: the NASA control room, television broadcasts, computer terminals and, of course, the dials, switches and displays on board the spacecraft itself. Structured around a pre-launch checklist (echoing the opening of the *Destination Moon* trailer) and the introduction of Tom Hanks' character, the trailer's true spectacle begins fifty seconds in, with images of the Apollo 13 rocket launching. Like the Enterprise, the rocket is built up through a montage of separate segments: the slim missile-like body as it rises past camera, the huge boosters as they fire, the gantry falling back, the engines burning, the pointed needle of the cone as it surges into and beyond camera, rising up on a long pillar of fire and smoke. The music, dramatic and low up to this point, reaches a crescendo here, confirming the importance of this effects-heavy display in the trailer narrative.

Effects retain this primacy throughout the trailer: underscored by music and dramatic dialogue, we see shots from outside the spaceship that show it venting oxygen, spiraling through space, or framed against the dark bulk of the Moon and the distant sphere of Earth. Other scenes reiterate the technology-based narrative with talk of malfunctioning instrumentation, trajectory projections and telemetry. However, unlike most genre trailers of the time, this combination of technology narrative and striking visual effects was being used to depict a known event, not the fantasy of alien invasion or *Star Wars*–style space travel. Investigating the network of influences surrounding the production of the effects for *Apollo 13* recalls George Pal's assertion that *Destination Moon* would present science fact, not fiction. *Apollo 13* did not rely on any NASA stock footage for its recreations, but created every special effect through "a combination of live action photography on sets and full-scale mock-ups, practical effects, motion control model work and computer generated artifice."[54] The display of these effects in the film's trailer is impressive: especially considering that Universal shifted the release date forward by four months, moving specific model production and computer work (notably the rocket launch and the animation accompanying the logo) into the first weeks of production.[55] The difference between this trailer and, say, *The Empire Strikes Back* trailer in 1980 or the 1989 preview for *The Abyss* is telling: the completion of particular special effects early in production was a primary issue, not secondary. The effects also had to create realism: rocket and space shuttle launches had been televised for over thirty years, and images of astronauts and ships in orbit were more common.[56] Abandoning the fantastic effects of 1977–1983 and returning to an effects spectacle based around realism initially recalls the structure of 1950s trailers such as *Destination Moon* and *When Worlds Collide*, but the *Apollo 13* trailer represents a larger movement in film production than simple genre reiteration.

Creating realistic locations, events and characters through special effects technology has never been confined purely to the science fiction genre: we discussed earlier the use of such effects in *Noah's Ark* and *Gone with the Wind*, while Biblical epics (*The Ten Commandments* [1956], *Ben Hur* [1959]) and disaster movies (*Earthquake* [1974], *The Towering Inferno* [1974]) have traditionally featured a mix of practical and model effects work. Until the introduction of computer-generated imagery, however, the science fiction genre was the site of most special effects production in Hollywood. As the *Apollo 13* trailer shows, visual effects were increasingly being used to recreate realistic depictions of historical events, and it represents a larger expansion of effects work into other film and television genres. This return to verisimilitude — and the continued success of visual spectacle as a key promotional convention — is reflected in the growth of non-genre trailers that place effects images within their sales messages, creating a heightened reality. While these effects may never reach the level of spectacle seen in *Independence Day*, they reveal the rise of computer-generated effects to situate historic narratives in believable settings.

Many mid- and late-1990s trailers that include CGI effects hide them in plain sight, not offering them as spectacle, but inserting them within trailer narratives. This is the equivalent of the matte paintings of *The Day the Earth Caught Fire* or the rear projection of *How the West Was Won*: the *Forrest Gump* trailer features several images of the anti-war rally at the Washington Monument, where thousands of demonstrators were added in digitally; or the ball that shoots back and forth in the table tennis match of the same trailer, a digital creation that adds narrative detail, not spectacle. In trailers for *Titanic* (1997) and *Gladiator*, location is enhanced and created by computer images of the boat sailing across the Atlantic, or Rome's Coliseum: CGI walls rising majestically in the background of a wide shot of the city, or rows of seats stretching up and around the arena where Russell Crowe and his band of gladiators fight. The trailers are not about these effects, but they are used to situate trailer narratives based around romance, action or nostalgia. Their narrative function may restrict the sense of spectacle they can offer, but contemporary evidence suggests the display of such effects could still be used as an audience lure. Unlike the rear projection and matte painting of earlier trailers, these shots exist in a movie culture that promotes and explains such visual effects through what Barbara Klinger has identified as "self-reflexive ... promotional narratives."[57] While trailers were still in cinemas, magazine articles and television features (as well as a new phenomenon, film websites) were revealing the CGI secrets of visual effects sequences. It is possible that this "hidden" CGI imagery may have featured more prominently for audiences who knew what to look for and were aware of what kind of spectacle computer-generated imagery was capable of.

Trailers outside the science fiction genre often reduced the screen time given over to the display of CGI work, but effects-based images still retained their impact through repetition (the "White House" effect, in posters, television and other media), and placement (with effects images often being the first or last image within a trailer). The teaser for *The Perfect Storm* gradually builds its display of CGI effects, highlighting its recreation of contemporary technology and weather conditions before reaching a crescendo with its promotional "money shot." The teaser opens with images of a weather radar screen, with electronic grid lines tracking storm fronts (suggesting a technology narrative that the trailer does not pursue). The teaser layers further shots of CGI weather, banks of bruised cloud formations, and increasingly unsettled seas, before two effects images illuminate the teaser's sales message—a zoom "down" from a satellite, through the chaos of the storm, to the churning sea below; and the film's "White House" image, of a tiny fishing boat dwarfed by an enormous wave. This computer-generated creation was well promoted via posters and television in advance of the film, and its place at the end of the teaser allows the image to linger in audience's minds. A similar escalation of effects display can also be seen in the *Pleasantville* (1998) trailer. Although it opens with a strong narrative thread (explaining how Tobey Maguire and Reese Witherspoon are projected "into" a black-and-white television program), the trailer gradually replaces this with a montage of colorful images that bloom in the otherwise monochrome world.[58] The escalation of color frames key sequences—a red rose flowering, a glowing housewife confronting her black-and-white husband—that can be found throughout the network of promotional texts that surround the film's release.

By 2000, "virtually every movie—even the most realistic domestic drama or romantic comedy—avails itself of effects technology and the subtle enhancements it can provide."[59] Trailers for films as diverse as *The American President* (1995) and *Godzilla* (1998) featured special effects work that ranged from creating a snowy landscape to placing a rampaging monster in the heart of Manhattan. Unified analysis of science fiction trailers from 1991–1999 has revealed a strong display of CGI visual spectacle in trailers for *Terminator 2: Judgment Day* and *Independence Day*, but contained within a coherent trailer narrative. The major change wrought by trailers in the 1990s was on film production, scheduling the creation of specific effects sequences as early as possible so they could be featured in promotional texts. The White House explosion in *Independence Day*'s teaser, the launch and mishap of *Apollo 13*, the giant wave in *The Perfect Storm* teaser: these powerful effects-driven images can be regarded as spectacle not because of their placement within the trailer texts, but because they existed outside the trailer, in television spots, on posters, in "making of" television specials, and on the Internet. Unlike 1977–1983, when the explosion of effects work was not matched by its availability for promotional purposes, the CGI effects in 1991–1999 were presented as a nascent star image, able to create a strong single image (or sequence) that all trailers, and related materials, could be structured around.

CONCLUSION

It was like selling strawberries. If you want to sell a box of strawberries you make sure the big ones are on the top, the rotten ones are underneath. It was the same when they made a trailer: you pick only the scenes that'll help you sell your picture.[60]

To borrow Paul Lazarus' metaphor, the big strawberries at the top of the box in current trailers are visual effects sequences. Producers talk about "five to ten trailer moments," CGI-based elements that are designed as part of mainstream film projects, finished early in production, then utilized at the heart of the trailer narrative.[61] Film production schedules now revolve around the creation and marketing of these effects-based images for the launch of trailers in cinemas, on television and online (they will also be central components of the film's media marketing and promotional plan). These sequences showcase both fantastic and realistic imagery, placing the unreal within the real, or creating a historical "reality": from the created realism of a moon launch and a historic ship in the *Destination Moon* and *Titanic* trailers, to the fantastic worlds of *Forbidden Planet* and *Star Wars*. Unified analysis of trailer texts from three important moments in the history of the science fiction genre has explored how effects imagery has been positioned through the decades, and challenged the idea that such visual spectacle has replaced narrative as the dominant structural convention. Focusing on these trailers has revealed a complex and shifting interrelation between narrative, character, genre and effects-based elements, with the latter often restricted due to production limitations. Through this analysis, it is clear that visual spectacle, while an important component of the genre trailer, has always functioned within existing conventions rather than displacing them.

The advent of CGI has enabled effects technology to become more widespread in trailer narratives than at any point in film history, but the evidence of trailers from the three decades analyzed here suggest that visual spectacle has never totally dominated. Technological change and the fluctuating availability of an effects-based display has meant that, historically, the heights of visual spectacle seen in the trailers for *Earth vs. the Flying Saucers*, *Star Trek: The Motion Picture* or *Independence Day* were only rarely achieved. Treating those texts as individual sources of information, not simply building blocks in a larger movement, revealed that even the strongest examples of effects-based visual spectacle had a purpose beyond simple display. The *Earth vs. the Flying Saucers* trailer used its effects shots within a narrative of human defeat and then eventual success against the aliens, using the visual spectacle to illustrate a broader narrative arc; *Star Trek: The Motion Picture* lingered on images of the Enterprise to reintroduce both a character and the location of the film's "human" drama; equally, the *Independence Day* trailers relied on blowing up famous landmarks, but (unlike other promotional materials for the film) those images were presented within a narrative progression: the teaser and main trailer built up the tension and suspense using traditional methods, leading the viewer to the point of visual effects display. None of the trailers watched for this survey could be regarded as simply a visual effects spectacle: despite the prevalence of effects-based images in the science fiction trailer, such images are always a part of a larger trailer narrative that includes human stars, romantic sub-plots, generic imagery, and narrative information.

This chapter has argued that analysis of individual trailer texts does not support the belief that spectacle has displaced narrative, but the dominance of these central images within magazine and journalistic coverage may have allowed the spectacular image to overtake the narrative that it originally belonged to. The dominance of theories around the displacement of narrative by spectacle comes from the 1990s, at a time when *Independence Day* revised the production of effects for promotional purposes. These central effects-driven moments (what I have termed "White House" images) can be seen at work in trailers for *Men in Black* (the saucer crashing to Earth), *The Perfect Storm* (the ship and the wave) and *Armageddon* (the shuttle flying toward the asteroid), among others. These moments are the biggest strawberries at the top of the box. The availability and repetition of such imagery underlined its importance, and raised the industrial profile of trailers throughout the 1990s (particularly teaser trailers, which frequently set a film's promotional tone and established key "White House" moments). Appearing on television "making of" specials, entertainment news shows, DVD special features, magazine articles, and, from the late 1990s, on Internet sites, these central special effects images exist independently of the narratives from which they came (either film or trailer).

In 1953, George Pal stated that special effects were the stars of his pictures. Almost fifty years later, at the end of the 1990s, this spectacular star faced an uncertain future. History suggests that effects will remain within a trailer narrative, yet the spread of CGI throughout all genres of filmmaking may yet alter that structure. By the end of the decade, it was clear that an increasing number of different media platforms were interested in film production and forthcoming releases, presenting unique dissemination and aesthetic opportunities for promotional materials such as trailers. The next chapter will continue to explore the importance of visual spectacle in trailer structure, as it examines whether that spectacle is reduced when trailers move from the big screen to the new media screens of video, the Internet, iPods and mobile videophones.

CHAPTER FOUR

The Mobile Trailer

In the 1950s, widescreen trailers promised that "something BIG" was coming. The expansion of the cinema screen became a key sales message, and processes such as Cinerama and CinemaScope became technological stars, enticing audiences with the lure of bigger and better entertainments than they'd seen before (or could see on any other screen). Three decades later, at the start of the 1980s, almost all the big screens were shrinking and the film experience was becoming smaller and more intimate than the colossal theatres of the 1950s. Television had brought films into the living room, but the advent of home video (despite the best efforts of the Hollywood studios to prevent it) made films portable and pliable. For the first time, a feature film could be carried in your hand, taken between houses, rented and returned; paused, rewound, stopped and restarted. Trailers were initially absent from these mainstream video releases—the technology of the video recorder and the notion of the mobile film product appears to have been a strong enough marketing pull in itself—but the exponential growth of the video market necessitated raising awareness of product differentiation and new releases through traditional trailer messages. These video trailers offer more than a simple reiteration of cinema and television trailer conventions: the introduction of home video begins to change conceptions of the trailer, how it interacts with its audience, the temporality of its address, its aesthetic and structural traits, its relation to new media screens and the technology that powers them. The increasing mobility of the trailer from 1980 on intersects with its decreasing visual size: the smaller screens of home video, the Internet and iPods. From the uncertainty over the place of trailers in the home video experience to the revitalization of the trailer in the download generation, the chapter will explore how these smaller, mobile screen technologies have changed the way that modern trailers are displayed, distributed and consumed by audiences.

Given the chronological scope of this chapter, it is important to note that it is not intended as a trailer history of the period 1976–2009. Like the discussion of special effects and visual spectacle in chapter three, the combination of textual and historical analysis in this chapter is used to illuminate key moments and texts that speak to a larger picture based around the increased mobility of the film trailer. The goal of such unified analysis is to consider what this contemporary evidence can reveal about the interaction of trailers and technological change. In place of the assumption that technology easily determines trailer structure and aesthetic change, this chapter investigates how the expansion onto new screens contains a shifting scale of acceptance from the film industry: a reluctance to accept home video; a gradual tolerance of the Internet; and the popular welcome given to iPods and videophones, stressed and promoted as the site of unique trailer content. By expanding the aesthetic debate beyond film onto these new screens, the chapter also offers an alternative view of modern film history, and how these new trailers have been modeled, using these new technologies to appeal to distinct and defined audiences. The different ways in which trailers have navigated across these disparate visual interfaces will allow us to better understand the pliability of audio-visual texts in the world of new media.

The exploration of this thirty-year period therefore focuses on three technological changes: home video (primarily VHS), the Internet, and portable media players (specifically mobile videophones and the video iPod). Each technology raises issues of mobility, screen size and interactivity: key to any discussion around new dissemination avenues, but essential to understanding the changes wrought on trailer structure and aesthetics in this period. Mobility and interactivity combine in the changing role of the trailer audience: from mass spectator to individual participant, video, Internet and iPod create a shifting personal and temporal space within which the trailer message is viewed. These trailers extend the alleged intimacy of the 1950s television trailers by increasing consumer participation: viewers select what trailers to watch (or download) and have control over textual playback. This control is also reflected in the increased ability of trailer viewers to become producers of unique trailer texts, with desktop editing software and multiple websites on which to display their creations. Unified analysis of both varieties of trailer text reveals how this move from the social to the personal has restructured elements of the trailer in order to attract specific fan cultures.

While individual film companies have used new trailer structures to target and attract particular fan cultures, notably those based around established universes such as *Star Wars* and *Lord of the Rings*, those same fans have been empowered to produce and display their own trailer productions. Henry Jenkins' *Textual Poachers* explored the products of fandom, investigating the stories, songs and films that fans have historically produced and circulated amongst their own groups.¹ However, as Jenkins acknowledges in a more recent book, the work of fandom has expanded beyond sharing short stories and poems between a small group of devotees: "the Web has pushed that hidden layer of cultural activity into the foreground."² This chapter will explore Jenkins' concept of a new Internet visibility through the fan-produced trailers for established cultural products such as *Star Wars* and *Back to the Future*, as well as in the efforts of studios and production companies to target and attract that active online fanbase.

This level of interactivity is tied to the technologies that power the smaller individuated screens investigated through the chapter. Video, the Internet and media players emphasize the freedom they offer for trailer viewing, but each format also has a secondary (often opaque) purpose, restricting access to trailer texts by limiting the hardware or software required for playback. Widescreen videos contain a nascent sales message for the new widescreen televisions that can offer the "complete" picture; online trailers can only be viewed if fans download the latest Quicktime player. This synergistic dual role informs the aesthetic component of the trailer text as well as the final viewing opportunity, and awareness of these different levels of sales message will be taken into account when analyzing them.

This duality is best displayed in one of the key examples that the chapter will return to in order to draw out links between formats and historical moments. Given that fan cultures are early adopters of new media technology,³ this investigation focuses on the different trailer options used to promote films with a strong fan-oriented base: primarily, the six *Star Wars* films released since 1977.⁴ Spanning the time periods and technological innovations of this chapter, George Lucas' *Star Wars* films have had a close relationship with technology since the 1976 teaser trailer explored in chapter three. We have already seen that promotional materials for these films often use a display of special effects technology to lure audiences into cinemas. However, trailers for all six of the *Star Wars* films reveal a further layer of technological display: namely, the dissemination technologies deployed to expand this space saga beyond the movie screen. From the advent of home video (for both rental and sale through markets) and the release of widescreen videos, to the use of the Internet and mobile phones as marketing tools, the *Star Wars* trailers have been trailblazers onto these new media screens. They reveal central conventions specific to each technology as well as restrictions and limitations caused by the move onto the diminishing screens. With the launch of the new trilogy in 1998, the trailer text itself becomes a forum for fan interaction and revolution, and allows us to consider the use of trailer aesthetics to empower fan culture. While the chapter will necessarily investigate a wide range of trailers (for pornography, arthouse films and blockbusters), the *Star Wars* saga's use of trailers and technology makes it a crucial textual series in any examination of how visual media have become increasingly mobile and able to colonize the smaller screens offered by new technology.

Video

> *Now The Force can be with you ... on video.*[5]

The first video trailer for *Star Wars* appears on the 1984 video release of *The Empire Strikes Back*. Visually similar to the 1976 cinematic teaser trailer, the video preview differs in its temporal positioning and use of direct address. The trailer addresses its audience in the past tense, assuming prior knowledge of the film, and signifying a sales message rooted in existing appeal not future revelation ("The science fiction blockbuster of the decade ... the film that captured the imagination of millions"). The film is also "now on video," offering a further step away from both "coming soon" (theatrical) and "now showing" (favored by the television trailer), distinguishing the video in its own temporal zone. Meanwhile, the cinema teaser's impersonal tone is replaced in the video version by appeals to individual taste and desire: particularly "The Force can be with you," but also in references to "your favorite renegades" and "exploding onto your screen."[6] The emphasis on personal ownership was unique in its time, three years before sell-through video became a regular feature of video release schedules, but the concept of video as an individual activity rather than a shared experience (i.e., in a cinema auditorium) was common in contemporary video trailers. This section will explore these new developments in trailer production through analysis of three distinct *Star Wars* trailer texts: the 1984 video trailer already mentioned, a 1989 compilation trailer, and a 1991 trailer for the widescreen release of the trilogy. These three video previews allow us to consider why the home video industry attempted to develop an intimacy between videocassette and viewer, and how the smaller screen size becomes a key technological battleground for both film and video industries, from the initial concern over how to utilize the video screen for promotional purposes, to the introduction of widescreen ideology and the rejection of existing video technology.

The growth and success of the home video market in its myriad of technological formats (VHS, Betamax, Video 2000, Videodisc, Laserdisc or DVD) represents a crucial split in the presentation and availability of films (and trailers). For the first time, consumers of film could (legally) own copies of classic and new releases, to be played and replayed at their leisure, and in their own homes. Some scholars have explored the implications of the video revolution of the 1970s and its move from mass entertainment to individualized pleasure. Douglas Gomery claims that "home video is geared to the desires of the individual fan" while Mark Jancovich has explored the social role of the videotapes themselves, "material objects with meanings that exceed those of a mere recording."[7] This focus on exhibition and reception of the home video experience explores an overlooked aspect of film studies, but there is no sense of the content of the videocassette that is central to their work. It may well be impossible to accurately represent the experience of video viewing, given the millions of people and viewpoints that undertaking would involve, but any such attempt also needs to define the unique attributes and qualities of the visual media under discussion. More specifically, what does the video screen look like, what are the differences between that screen and others (the cinema, television), and what restrictions and innovations does it impose on the video aesthetic? This section offers a starting point for such discussions, using the synthesis of historical information and textual analysis to explore key areas that future analysis could expand upon. This initial analysis explores the new mobility video offered, alongside the new opportunities for unique developments in aesthetics (video graphics and fast-paced editing) and structure (compilation trailers).

The 1984 *Star Wars* video trailer remains one of the earliest examples of a specially created video preview (for a mainstream release), but that does not mean there was no market for trailers on video before this. There are examples of cinema trailers being transferred to videocassette — *An Officer and a Gentleman* (1981) on the 1980 video release of *American Gigolo* (1980); *The Empire Strikes Back* on the 1980 release of the documentary *The Making of Star Wars*[8] — while one entrepreneurial UK video company produced and sold *The Incredible World of James Bond (Trailers)*, a collection of cinema previews that were free from copyright restrictions.[9] But in the late 1970s, the main market for video trailers existed outside the mainstream of Hollywood video releases. With the film industry prevaricating over whether to allow their films to be transferred onto home video, pornographic tapes dominated the market in America and Britain: "in 1980 X-rated tapes, by some estimates, accounted for three-quarters of all videotape rentals."[10] Despite the varying quality of the adult films produced and transferred onto tape, they do have one element in common — trailers for forthcoming and currently available video releases. Like the mainstream industry, these pornographic trailers feature visual spectacle and excerpted scenes as a key audience lure, and structure the sales message through a combination of voiceover and excerpted dialogue. Unlike the eventual structure of the Hollywood videos, these adult videotapes feature between five and ten trailers, scattered between short films and features. Even after Hollywood began to dominate the video market, this combination continued: a review of porn release *Electric Blue 004* states that "a large proportion ... is taken up with excerpts in the form of plugs: not only the three previous *Electric Blues* and attendant *Nude Wives*

Special but also for Intervision's *Mustang* (about a legal American whorehouse), VCL's *Amanda Lear* tape and three fairly hardcore looking American films."[11]

The concept of combining trailer conventions within a programming format did not remain unique to the adult industry. After an initial uncertainty over whether to put trailers before or after the feature, by 1983 they were placed at the beginning of mainstream video releases[12] — but in a format that bore a resemblance to existing television programs and the compilation format of adult videos. The 1984 *Star Wars* video-only trailer (on the UK and U.S. video release of *The Empire Strikes Back*) appears as part of a program format called "Time In" used on CBS FOX videos. This distribution company is itself an unlikely combination of media created to exploit the video market: a merger between film (20th Century–Fox Video, formerly Magnetic Video) and television (CBS Video Enterprises) that reflected the contemporary conglomeration of American media industries, with huge libraries of content available for release.[13] It may be that this fusion of different media, and production practices, influenced the programming style of "Time In." The *Star Wars* video preview is one of five trailers in this collection: the trailers are bundled together, linked with the same voiceover, a particular video graphic motif, and similar structural techniques. This unique mix of theatrical trailer structure and video graphic techniques is more familiar to the nascent music video format, but unified analysis of this presentation style allows us to consider how issues of personal address and the aesthetics of the smaller screen are written into this structure.

Opening with a moving wire-frame animation, the company logo appears on screen ("CBS" folds down from the top, "FOX" folds up from the bottom, "VIDEO" is added a letter at a time below) before "Time In" is superimposed on top. The trailer program then begins:

> Hello, and welcome to another great movie from CBS FOX — and to TIME IN where we preview five other great films you won't want to miss! From the special comedy of Mel Brooks ... to the drama of All the Right Moves ...the unforgettable Chariots of Fire ... Star Wars ... and the punchy Cannonball Run — they're all winners.[14]

As each film is named, there is a quick preview of its forthcoming trailer: short images from the film flash up, set in a screen within the larger video screen. The creation of this reduced screen area places the trailers firmly within the aesthetics of the "Time In" program — the images are set within a gray background with bright colored diagonals streaming across it — and reduce their visual impact.[15] A unique development within all branches of trailer advertising, the closest visual antecedent to this presentation appears to be television programs that open with a "coming up" montage of highlights from the show.

After this opening, the individual trailers are introduced. Set in the same gray screen format (the main change is the color of the diagonal stripes), the inset screen now shows a still image from the featured film. The first trailer, for *To Be or Not to Be* (1983), is illustrated with a photograph of Mel Brooks and Anne Bancroft. As the voiceover begins, a bright orange "Z" appears over their image. Followed by a bright red "Z" at a ninety-degree angle. The image is now a multi-colored swastika. Soon, two bright blue boots are added to two of the "legs," as though the symbol is about to march off screen. The trailer imagery, when it begins, emphasizes the setting of the film as a comedy about Nazi Germany, but the video graphics have made that visual point in a simple, yet direct, manner. The layering of simple video graphics on top of photographs continues: three blue lines are superimposed over an image of Tom Cruise from *All the Right Moves* (1983), then disappear one by one (an excerpted scene shows the American football players with similar lines painted on their faces); the *Chariots of Fire* (1981) image of two runners adds blue, red and yellow circles over their faces that join up to form part of the Olympic logo. In the case of *Star Wars*, the still image of Obi-Wan Kenobi facing off against Darth Vader is augmented by first Kenobi's, then Vader's, lightsabers being painted bright blue, before the Death Star background flashes a violent cerise pink (perhaps suggesting an explosion or laser blast). Unlike the earlier examples, the addition of video graphics to this *Star Wars* image does not stress narrative or thematic tropes, but a focus on special effects and action.

Analysis of the actual trailer footage reveals that these video previews are heavily edited versions of longer trailers, no doubt theatrical ones: the *Star Wars* video preview excises four sequences and pre-existing title work from the film's 1976 teaser, then reduces the remaining dialogue by fading it down under the voiceover (only four lines remain intact). Having made these deletions, the trailer then creates its own video-specific sales message through the voiceover's direct address to the audience. The tone of the voiceover remains constant throughout all five trailers, with no attempt to vary it for the film or genre being advertised — this more casual attitude (in keeping with the television adverts of the 1950s) creates an intimacy that binds the disparate film clips together. In the case of *Star Wars*, by adding video graphics onto the lightsaber image, and excising dialogue scenes from the excerpted footage, the video trailer is even more dominated by special effects: but the use of the brightly colored graphics may have been intended to add visual interest given that some of the spectacle is reduced by panning and scanning the trailer footage to fit it within the smaller video screen. The addition of the personal layer — the calls for video ownership and the notion of "your screen" — reiterates the journey the film has made from large-screen spectacle to small-screen individual enjoyment.

By the mid–1980s, the creation of a trailer gallery at the start of each videocassette was an established convention. Structurally similar programs to "Time In" can be found on Warner Home Video releases. The 1984 video release of *The Right Stuff* (1983) features a series of linked — and shortened — trailers under the heading "for your next night in"; while 1987's *Heartbreak Ridge* (1986) video begins with a "Coming Soon" feature.[16] Even once the video format reverts to stand-alone trailers (more akin to the "trailer park" collection of trailers in cinema exhibition), the introduction of the video sell-through market continues the theme of compilation trailers, often based around individual stars or movie genres: The Video Collection used a compilation montage to sell a series of films starring John Wayne and Cary Grant, as well as 1950s science fiction films; while early Disney home videos stressed the range of Disney classics through a montage of clips from films such as *Robin Hood* (1973) and *Sleeping Beauty* (1959).[17] Despite the success in placing trailers at the beginning of the video exhibition format, there was still some uncertainty over their effectiveness: the individual control offered to viewers by the video recorder also contained the possibility of skipping trailer messages entirely, fast-forwarding to the beginning of the movie. Viewer dissatisfaction with this pre-film section was only increased with the addition of non-film commercials: a trend begun with the 1987 sell-through release of *Top Gun* that featured a Diet Pepsi commercial "tied to the theme and images of the feature that followed."[18] Although many trailers were now specially commissioned for video releases (either for films released "straight-to-video," or films whose sales message was tweaked for a video audience), film companies were unsure about the potency of trailers on videocassettes.

A desire to attract viewer attention within trailers, to stop them fast-forwarding to the film, returns us to issues of visual spectacle. Video trailers for known products, films that already exist in the public consciousness, could play on that knowledge, using established visual spectacle to hold viewer's attention. The Video Collection and Disney video trailers discussed above suggest the potential of this approach, but they are too quick to move onto the next product; there is little chance for individual film spectacle to impress. A compilation trailer from the 1989 *Return of the Jedi* (1983) video release presents a development of this, structuring a sales message purely around visually striking imagery from *Star Wars*, *The Sound of Music* (1965), *My Fair Lady* (1964), *The Longest Day* (1962), *The Cannonball Run* (1980), *Butch Cassidy and the Sundance Kid* (1969), *M*A*S*H* (1969) and others from the CBS FOX "All Star Classics" range. An abrupt opening explodes with images of the Star Destroyer and Death Star from *Star Wars*, cuts to wartime explosions, car chases, dance numbers, aerial battles (both above the Earth and in space), helicopters, and surfing. The whole trailer is edited to John Williams' *Star Wars* score, and the clips reflect it: the dramatic opening is about war and fighting, the quieter moments feature singing and dancing, a romantic refrain accompanies famous screen kisses, and the crescendo returns to drama and farewells. The only direct sales message comes at the end, with the film titles scrolling up a blue screen while the voiceover notes they are "yours for all time."[19] In this video trailer, the sales message relies purely on known visual spectacle, the recognizable imagery of existing products.

The reliance on sound and images to structure this video trailer may reflect a different expansion of trailer aesthetics and structure from the 1980s: the music video channel, MTV, and the opportunities it offered for film promotion and exploitation. Although too extensive a topic to cover here, it is worth noting the similarities between the two branches of video production, and the potential for overlap between the industries. Andy Kuehn, head of U.S. trailer company Kaleidoscope, believed trailers and music videos shared stylistic traits: "The only other thing I can think of that has a two-and-a-half to three-minute format is a song ... MTV ... just contributed to the speeding up of the cutting style that we had already started with trailers."[20] The trailer tradition was most strongly evident in one particular genre of music video: the movie theme song. During the 1980s popular music began to become more dominant in feature film production. On aesthetic and financial levels, music powered montage sequences and introduced a new breed of soundtrack albums for film fans to purchase.[21] The combination of music and film led to music videos that merged film footage and band performances using editing techniques familiar from trailer structure: see, for example, the music videos for Berlin's "Take My Breath Away" and Kenny Loggins' "Danger Zone" from *Top Gun*; "Footloose" from *Footloose* (1984); or Ray Parker Jr.'s "Ghostbusters" from *Ghostbusters*. Each video features excerpted film images edited into the kind of visual spectacle we would expect from a movie trailer (and which can be seen in the CBS FOX "All Time Greats" video trailer). The music video offered a new avenue for film promotion, targeting an audience that video trailers might not be providing. Although the music video also had an impact on theatrical trailer production in the late 1980s, its main influence would come in another iteration of the mobile trailer, and the introduction of trailers for mobile videophones and the video iPod.

By 1991, the early video trailer conventions had faded — there was little sign of unique video graphics or the "program" format. Video trailers had reverted to the stand-alone status accorded the cinema trailer. However, the success of the sell-through market and the introduction of new television technology led to the return of a cinema-specific ideology: widescreen aesthetics and their impact on the video screen. At the forefront of this new revolution: a compilation trailer for the widescreen release of the *Star Wars* trilogy. This trailer (and a structurally similar preview advertising the widescreen video releases of *Alien* and *Die Hard*) raises both video- and cinema-specific issues: the size of the smaller television screen, pan-and-scan techniques, and the suitability of video technology to transfer the spectacle of cinema imagery into an individuated experience. Widescreen video also raises an issue over industrial context that lies outside the scope of this book, but remains tangentially useful. The *Star Wars* video trailers discussed above were used on both British and American releases, but there is no conclusive proof that the widescreen trailers were used in the UK and the U.S. Both countries introduced widescreen videos in the late 1980s, but the UK embraced widescreen releases more quickly than the U.S. (where full-screen DVD releases remain a common sight in video stores). The 1991 *Star Wars* widescreen trailer, with its compelling argument against pan and scan (in the service of commercial success), is such a strong piece of advertising that its duplication on all widescreen releases would seem likely. For the purposes of this section, however, it is worth remembering that this analysis may only relate to early British widescreen trailers.

The "*Star Wars* Trilogy Widescreen Collection" trailer opens with a standard rectangular 1.33:1 shot of the underside of a huge star destroyer passing over camera.[22] Its triangular gray bulk fills well over half of the screen, the rest filled with a starfield and a thin curve of blue planet at the bottom of the image. John Williams' "Imperial March" theme accompanies the image as the voiceover asks, "So, you think you've seen the whole of the *Star Wars* legend on video?" As we watch, the full-screen image shrinks into the center of the screen, a black frame all the way around it. Simultaneously, the music and voiceover lose some of their luster, becoming more tinny and thin. With a grinding, wrenching noise, the left and right edges of the image expand to the horizontal edges of the screen (with black stripes above and below), revealing

The curving Widescreen video logo (1991) recalls the famous CinemaScope logo from the 1950s.

the heretofore hidden image of a half-completed Death Star hanging in the extreme left of the frame. The music surges back into stereo as the voiceover adds: "Well, think again."[23]

Dating from 1991, this trailer recalls the issues and conventions of the 1950s Cinerama and CinemaScope trailers, while building on the unique nature of home video trailers. By opening with such a dramatic presentation of the difference between the standard and wider screen sizes, the trailer prompts memories of Cinerama's expansion from one screen size into three; or the trailer for *Knights of the Round Table*, where superimposed banners were lifted up, turning the 1.33:1 image into the wider 2.55:1 ratio of CinemaScope. Like all CinemaScope trailers, this Trilogy trailer selects the most compelling horizontally composed images to stress the wider screen ideology: a desert skiff that flies right to left across the image, while explosions rock the huge barge behind it (the flames also move right to left, following the skiff, and leading the eye); an Ewok is pulled across the width of the screen by the acceleration of the speeder bike it is riding; and when Luke and Leia swing across a chasm aboard the Death Star, they also travel the width of the letterboxed frame.[24] Even the font and typeface for the "widescreen" logo recalls the curving letters of the CinemaScope trademark. Returning to these 1950s widescreen trailer conventions is not simply a nostalgic echo, but the ability for television and video screens to reference the technological revolution they were about to enter into themselves, and impose the belief that widescreen is the correct viewing format.

A Fox Video booklet included with the *Alien* "Widescreen Collection" video demonstrates this more conclusively, and suggests the problem facing the developed video market as it attempts to expand its offering. On the second-to-last page, the booklet notes that you can "experience the Wonders of Cinema at home.... Wide Screen is the future of the viewing experience ... televisions which for the first time imitate the wide screen that can only presently be seen in the cinema."[25] There are further iterations of the widescreen principle: claims that these widescreen videos imitate the natural field of vision, give greater involvement, and are closer to the director's original intention. The addition of an auteurist sales message aside, the language is a direct echo of CinemaScope's trailer advertising of the 1950s: emphasis on enhancements, realism, panoramic views, dazzling landscapes and "greater involvement" (known as envelopment in the days of 3-D and CinemaScope). But there is a crucial difference: these improvements are being offered to an individual home viewer, not to attract a mass audience back to cinemas. There is an emphasis on home viewing, having "cinema in your own home" and "your viewing enjoyment."[26] The trailer is being used to advertise a new technology — but it is not cinema or video-specific. The trailer is designed to sell the widescreen televisions that will properly display this new generation of video releases, including the Phillips television pictured in the Fox Video booklet that came with each widescreen videocassette.

These widescreen trailers may promote widescreen television technology, but they also problematize the place of video trailers and home video in general, because they present established video technology as inferior to cinema. The trailers of the early 1980s use video graphics and video-specific sales devices to combine the unique conventions of video and cinema trailers, and they stress the innovation that home video offers. By 1991, and the *Star Wars* widescreen Trilogy trailer, the emphasis on the wider screen size and scale is offered as a solution to the problem of the standard screen. The booklet describes panning and scanning — the central device in the transfer of modern widescreen film production onto videocassettes— as "a loss of up to ⅓ of the picture information" and that only widescreen keeps "all the enjoyment."[27] The *Star Wars* and *Alien/Die Hard* trailers visualize that argument in simpler terms—the expansion of the smaller, tinny screen into the superior, widescreen stereo experience is compelling evidence — then reiterate it by referring to the *Star Wars* videos as "the complete saga in the complete format."[28] The suggestion that the previous releases—and home video itself— were incomplete and unworthy may undermine the existing video market, but the trailers are more likely aimed at the collector's market. The promotion of special widescreen editions encourages fans to buy multiple copies of sell-through videos: an initial full-screen release before the eventual widescreen (and superior) release a few years later. The financial success of trailers such as these, despite their reduction of the video experience, can perhaps best be seen in its modern mirror with multiple DVD releases of the same film, repackaged with better transfers and unique special features.

The history of video trailers from the early 1980s to the 1990s is more complex than this section can completely cover, but analysis of the three *Star Wars* video trailers reveals key areas and conventions that suggest the ways in which the technology interacted with the trailer text. The move from a "trailer program" (or compilation) to stand-alone trailers is a reassertion of the cinema trailer aesthetic, but there are still elements of the early experiments in video trailer production: the appeal to an individual experience, the use of unique graphic techniques, direct audience address and a distinct temporal mode. The mobility that the home video format brought to film viewing may not ultimately have helped the growth of video trailers, now that viewers were in control of the exhibition experience and could fast-forward to the beginning of the film. To combat this, many video stores played looped tapes of trailers in the store, in order to retain some element of the "trailer park" feature from theatres. The growth of Laserdisc — and eventually DVD — brought new technological options for the placement and display of trailers, with some discs programmed to automatically load trailers before the film could be accessed. In each case there was an assumption that video had to follow the lead of cinema or television, with distribution establishing a set time and place for trailers to appear in, suggesting audience consumption of trailers should resemble the cinema experience. Removing trailers from this concept of a linear programming structure and allowing audiences to have access to trailers whenever (and wherever) they wanted them would lead to a revitalization of interest in the trailer text.

Online Trailers: "The Most Anticipated Two Minutes of Film Ever"

> *[Because of the Internet], we're really able to talk one-to-one with a potential customer ... there's an opportunity to create trailers for the Internet that would be completely different from the trailer you would create for a theatrical experience.... To just run the same trailer on the Internet, even though it gets four gazillion hits, may not be the best use of the footage that was selected for a theatrical experience.*[29]

The first teaser trailer released for *Star Wars Episode I: The Phantom Menace* (1999) in November 1998 is a representative example of trailer production of the late 1990s. There is no structuring trailer voiceover, no screen-filling titles, and no hyperbole of star names. Instead, the trailer focuses almost purely on narrative revelation and the visual spectacle afforded by state-of-the-art digital special effects. Fuelled by simple inter-titles and dialogue excerpts, the narrative comes alive through a succession of fantastic scenes and glimpses of widescreen action — space battles, alien landscapes, lightsaber duels — with CGI offering a special effects star on par with the original film's special effects focus. A strong example of the teaser structure, it reveals central concepts (the first meeting between Anakin Skywalker and Obi-Wan Kenobi) while teasing audiences with new, unknown elements (a red-and-black-faced villain, different locations and creatures). Unlike many of the trailers analyzed in the preceding chapters, the notoriety and impact of this teaser trailer is not derived from its aesthetic or structural conventions, but from the prominence it gave to a new form of trailer distribution and exhibition: the Internet.

On November 17, 1998, the teaser debuted in selected cinemas across the U.S. As the first new footage from George Lucas' *Star Wars* universe since *Return of the Jedi* in 1983, the trailer was heralded as the "most anticipated two minutes of film ever."[30] But with no apparent media plan to disseminate the trailer beyond the cinema screen, it was only available theatrically, playing with other trailers before *The Siege* (1998) and *Meet Joe Black* (1998).[31] Tens of thousands of fans flocked to these screenings — but by the evening of the November 17, there was a non-theatrical venue for the trailer. Seven years before the advent of video-sharing sites such as YouTube and MySpace, several *Star Wars* fans recorded, digitized, uploaded and shared the teaser to an exponentially increasing number of websites. Lucasfilm, in an attempt to curtail these low-quality bootlegs, eventually posted the trailer online at www.starwars.com: 450 *Star Wars* fans a second attempted to download the trailer from the official site, over 200,000 in forty-eight hours, rising to an estimated 3.5 million in total: shattering all previous Internet download records.[32] Offering a potent combination of fan power, new distribution technology and Hollywood promotional techniques, the dissemination of the *Star Wars Episode I: The Phantom Menace* teaser signals the beginning of a new period of trailer dominance in Hollywood. While video trailers ultimately made only minor adjustments to established trailer conventions, this section will explore the changes wrought by the new media screen of the Internet. Three specific areas will be examined: the aesthetic content of the trailer, the interaction with fan culture, and the synergy that has been created between downloading trailers and selling new software. The ability to download, display and save complex visual information via the computer screen has altered trailer dissemination and structure, possibly forever.

The *Star Wars Episode I: The Phantom Menace* trailer was not specially designed for the Internet, but its appearance online firmly established two key features that originated with the video preview: the trailer was now mobile (with the potential to save it to disc or hard drive, accessible by any computer with the right software) and the viewer was in control of trailer exhibition (able to pause, stop and re-watch the footage whenever they desired). These features promoted the trailer to a high position within fan culture, which could now scrutinize the montage of imagery laid out for them, and share their findings. Within days of the trailer appearing online, websites such as www.theforce.net had a detailed breakdown of trailer scenes, while web forums were full of other fans desperate to debate the footage and what the disparate images might refer to in the feature. Unlike any other time in trailer history, content analysis was now something that could be done by the most casual fan with access to a computer. This desire to excavate and interact with a cultural text has been described as a key element of fandom, "a model of interactivity as well as a mode of consumption ... the fictions it dedicates itself to are modeled accordingly."[33] The idea of "modeling" texts for the fan/cult audience can be seen by the rise of more intricate, complex and layered montage sequences within trailer structure. As trailers were debated and pieced apart online to reveal potential "spoiler" information,[34] trailer production complicated the process, adding in more images and increasing the pitch of editing to a point where the casual viewer might miss a piece of information. The dedicated fan would, however, be able to discover it through downloading, pausing and re-watching the trailer text.

This idea of specially designing trailers to appeal to the Internet audience was seized upon by studios and filmmakers. Less than a year after the appearance of *The Phantom Menace*, five Internet trailers for *Fight Club* (1999) were made available through the Fox website, appearing in small pop-up windows above the main page. Processed to look like old, scratched and badly projected film stock, these Internet spots are more thematically reminiscent of the feature than the cinema trailers. The theatrical teaser and main trailer position the film as an offbeat action thriller, built around the "rules" of Fight Club, with excerpted scenes dominated by a montage of explosions, men fighting, and interaction between Brad Pitt and Edward Norton. The five online trailers, by contrast, feature a simple set-up: Norton's character speaking directly into the camera. But this description belies the complexity of the editing and the innovative sound mixing in these spots, overlaying and complicating the levels of information they contain.[35] The use of direct address suggests a link between these *Fight Club* trailers and early television advertising, but the function of that address is thematically and structurally unique. In early TV spots, the presenter was inclusive and personal, but the trailer narrative was always sales-based: when *Bedtime for Bonzo*'s Percy Kilbride told viewers how good the film was, or columnist Erskine Johnston promoted Rock Hudson in *Captain Lightfoot*, the address was inclusive, but their words were direct sales messages about an aspect of the film. The *Fight Club* online spots differ by being narratively inclusive, where the character addresses the viewer, talks to them about everyday issues. There is no hyping of the film, because these trailers exist within the diegesis. They build up a friendly, one-on-one relationship between trailer and audience. Rather than a mass of people, these spots are designed to work on one person at a time — like the insidious nature of the diegetic Fight Club, the intimacy of these trailers suggest a word-of-mouth campaign, spread person to person.[36]

This convention may have been thought necessary because of the technological restrictions of the computer monitor: the average screen size was fifteen inches (diagonal). The pop-up window for each trailer took up less than a quarter of that space: it may be that intimate close-ups and voiceover were considered more suitable for the small screen than the visual spectacle of explosions and street fighting seen in the theatrical trailers. The use of personal address does not detract from the (often frenetic) montage that structures these trailers and encourages repeat viewings. In keeping with many trailers of the time period, the editing structure has a playful relationship between soundtrack and image, sometimes to create humor or to suggest deeper narrative concerns. In the online trailer "Change Your Life," the structure and editing offer clues (and potential "spoilers") to the schizophrenic nature of the Pitt/Norton relationship. During Norton's comment that "All the ways you wish you could be ... that's me" there is a brief cut to an image of Pitt on "me," then back to Norton, suggesting an uncertainty over the identity of "me"; in the "I Know You" trailer, Norton's direct address is momentarily interrupted when the film stock jumps to Pitt, also staring at camera; we see Norton's point-of-view of his dull office, where a ghostly image of Pitt flickers in and out of existence; and over the lines "deliver me from clean skin and perfect teeth" the trailer offers images of Norton, Pitt then back to Norton — the dialogue once again suggests one person, while the figure of Pitt is literally spliced into Norton's life. Many of these instances rely on the trailer's use of specific cinematic imagery — the processing of the images to look battered and worn, the suggestion that this old and tattered film is coming loose in a projector — alongside advanced modern editing techniques and frame-by-frame manipulation (made possible through non-linear editing technology such as Avid or Apple Final Cut). The trailers seem to relish this dichotomy: designed for downloading/viewing through the technology of the Internet and created by advanced editing technology, their aesthetics foreground a false depiction of decrepit cinema projection.

The *Fight Club* Internet spots demonstrate the ability of modern editing software to produce compelling and intricate layered texts that can target a distinct group of fans. Another online trailer, for *Star Wars Episode 2: Attack of the Clones* (2002), demonstrates the interaction between fan culture and a cultural text, while also solidifying the place of the George Lucas universe as a nexus for fandom. Debuting at www.theforce.net in October 2000, the trailer eschews the close imagery and direct address of the *Fight Club* online adverts and returns to epic widescreen spectacle (the downloadable trailer was only made available in the letterbox format). The trailer features sweeping helicopter shots over locations that appear familiar from the previous films (the desert of Tatooine, the mountains of Naboo, the city-planet of Coruscant), quickly edited images of the cast, and several special effects shots, including a horde of lightsaber-wielding Jedi attacking an unseen enemy. A more detailed examination of the trailer — an activity that online previews were now arguably designed for — revealed more questions than answers. Many of the space battles were from earlier films, some of the actors did not appear to be in known *Star Wars* locations, and elements of the footage were taken from other feature films (most notably, the Jedi attack was actually a scene from *Braveheart* (1995) with lightsabers added digitally). The trailer was quickly revealed to be an unofficial preview cut and created by a single fan. It highlighted the fact that fandom had evolved "beyond zines and collectible figurines" and was now "a new breed ... empowered by desktop technology to create participatory works."[37] Within eighteen months, Internet fandom had expanded from sharing the *Star Wars Episode I: The Phantom Menace* trailer to producing its own unique trailer creations. The trailer, already a major online promotional tool for the Hollywood studios, was now being used to promote fan interactivity with cult texts.

In November 2001, when the official marketing campaign for *Star Wars Episode II: Attack of the Clones* began, an online teaser trailer titled "Mystery" expanded on the notion of modeling trailer texts for multiple viewings. Yoda's line "Dangerous and disturbing this puzzle is" foregrounds (along with the teaser title) the structural tease offered by the preview footage.[38] Online fans watching (or downloading) the trailer were given a narrative puzzle rather than the linear narrative that much contemporary trailer advertising relied upon. The earlier cinematic teaser "Forbidden Love" had built a trailer narrative around the romantic pairing of Anakin and Padme: in contrast, "Mystery" presents an enigmatic montage of footage and dialogue excerpts, a fragmented narrative that encourages detailed examination rather than cursory viewing. The trailer is not completely opaque: broad clues—an attack on Padme, a return to Tatooine, a chase through the skies of Coruscant— are littered throughout, and key characters are pictured to suggest the traditional sequel trailer reliance on known pleasures. There are two levels of mystery here: a diegetic one based around the identity of Padme's attempted assassin (established by dialogue excerpts), and a non-diegetic one, constructed through the montage of new and strategically familiar images. These latter shots, like in the *Fight Club* online trailers, are barely on screen long enough to register, and require (and reward) a frame-by-frame analysis: a space battle reveals a spaceship not seen since *The Empire Strikes Back*; a one-second sequence shows a bar fight similar to the original "cantina" scene in *Star Wars*; there is a lightsaber battle between Anakin and an unseen opponent; an oceanic world with flying sea creatures; Christopher Lee (as new villain Count Dooku) lurking on the far edge of one frame; and a half-second image of Anakin wreathed in Force electricity (not seen since *Return of the Jedi*). This online trailer develops the notion of what the Internet preview can do: offer the audience more questions than answers with an exciting (if vague) collection of narrative events, and beyond that, a layered text (based around montage editing) that can be excavated for further detail.

This expansion of online trailer content can be linked to how the *Attack of the Clones* teaser was made available on the Internet. As the online marketing environment grew, a synergy began to develop between studio franchise properties such as *Star Wars* and technological developments in online video software (similar to the widescreen *Star Wars* Trilogy trailer and its— unspoken—promotion of the new visual platform of widescreen television). "Mystery" debuted online in November 2001, but its appearance was directly attributable to two other technologies: DVD and Apple's Quicktime playback software. The trailer was (initially) only accessible through a weblink built into *The Phantom Menace* DVD release: fans had to buy the DVD, and then play it through their computer in order to unlock the trailer via the *Star Wars* website. In order to view the trailer once they reached the website, fans then had to download Apple's latest version (5.02) of Quicktime. Available in three sizes, "Mystery" was heralded as being free to view: however, only the small and medium "screens" were actually free. Following the Internet interest in *The Phantom Menace*'s teaser, fans had to pay for the third trailer option. The website referred to it as a "large and clear version ... for maximum quality and careful inspection,"[39] official confirmation that the producers expected this new level of fan interaction with the text, and that trailers were being modeled accordingly. Payment gave fans access to Quicktime Pro 5, a more advanced playback system that also allowed them to download and save the trailer to watch as often as they desired. By combining their technological resources, Lucasfilm and Apple were able to nurture the growing online demand for *Star Wars* content and expand the dominance of Quicktime software.

New Line Cinema used a similar synergy when launching the first online trailer for the *Lord of the Rings* trilogy, offering it only to people who downloaded Real Player 8, a competing online video player to Quicktime. The trailer they offered through this new software was a different approach to online trailer structure and content, although one that proved equally adept at "modeling" trailer content for fan culture. The preview available in April 2000 was not an early teaser for the first film in the series, *The Fellowship of the Ring* (2001), but a broader look at director Peter Jackson's vision for the whole trilogy. The trailer replaces the fast-paced montage of *Fight Club* or *Star Wars* with a collection of interview footage of Jackson, production clips that show actors on set, performers in half-assembled creature costumes, early pre-visualization computer images of huge armies pouring across landscapes, and some short clips of finished footage (notably the Fellowship themselves, and the One Ring). These short segments are intercut with a blood-red graphic of the Ring, and a voiceover reciting the "one ring to rule them all" poem from the novels. Referring to the trilogy as "J. R. R. Tolkein's Lord of the Rings," with release dates for all three films, and concluding with the title, "Now in Production," the trailer demonstrates another option in targeting online fandom: the montage of completed imagery is replaced here by a slower selection of behind-the-scenes shots and suggestive comments. The trailer offered the same sense of reward as the *Star Wars* teaser, with fans re-watching it, trying to place the images, imagine what the complete monster might be, and discussing what battle the pre-visualization footage might show.

The effect of this early preview on online trailer structure is difficult to ascertain, mainly because it appears to have had more influence on the growth of behind-the-scenes features on movie websites. The structure of the *Lord of the Rings* preview was influenced by the original purpose of some of the footage: the interviews and early computer animation came from Jackson's original pitch for the trilogy, while the production shots were shown to fans at the San Diego Comic Con (a comic convention that has become a major venue for launching new film titles—and trailers—with a link to cult fandom). The success of the trailer—1.7 million people downloaded the trailer in the first 24 hours, in comparison to 1 million for *The Phantom Menace* over the same timeframe in 1998[40]—did not lead to a flurry of "behind-the-scenes" online trailers. Instead, the aesthetic offered by the *Lord of the Rings* preview was taken up by Internet production diaries: normally three to seven minutes of footage shot on set, interviews with cast and crew, or glimpses of completed scenes, these diaries were first made popular by www.starwars.com on all three of the most recent *Star Wars* films, then taken up by similar effects blockbusters *King Kong* (2005) and *Superman Returns* (2006). Available as downloads from official websites, and then transferred onto the DVD release, they have extended this early online trailer concept into weekly installments designed (and modeled) to target the same fan community who eagerly consume Internet trailer texts.

These online trailers demonstrate a new complexity in trailer editing and structural techniques, but they also show the rising interest of trailer texts within movie and fan culture. In chapter three, we discussed the possibility of demographic targeting, with reference to *Spartacus* and *The Day the Earth Caught Fire*: in a similar way, many of these unique Internet trailer texts target specific elements of fan culture. This is not restricted to the dominant online fan cultures—the science fiction/fantasy genres of *Star Wars* and *Lord of the Rings*, for example—but can also be used to target fans of particular directors. The *Elizabethtown* (2005) website offers three online trailers that combine interview footage (mainly director Cameron Crowe, or stars Orlando Bloom and Kirsten Dunst talking about Crowe), behind-the-scenes production footage, and a montage of excerpted scenes.[41] All three trailers are distinct from the cinematic teaser and trailer, and set up the film as "a Cameron Crowe film," targeting the romantic comedy aspects and the director's particular use of soundtrack to set tone and emotion: demonstrated most clearly in one seven-minute trailer, "First Look," whose montage of images set to Elton John's "My Father's Gun" mixes online trailer with music video aesthetics. This internet targeting can also model trailers to appeal to sub-groups of fan culture: the *Hitchhiker's Guide to the Galaxy* (2005) online trailer is designed to appeal to fans of the original radio, television and novel versions of the story through its mocking of blockbuster trailer aesthetics and structure—"The goal [of a movie trailer] is to create a piece of advertising that is original and exciting, yet intelligent and provocative ... in other words, lots of things blowing up."[42] This self-aware trailer structure combines this (reflective) content with more traditional online aesthetics—a series of fast-paced montage sequences lead up to an even more frenetic final montage ("designed to blow away whatever synapses you have left in your brain"[43]) in which over thirty separate images explode onto the screen in under five seconds. The trailer attracts the fan culture audience through its reference to the humor of the books, but also retains its online audience through the creation of a sequence so quickly edited that multiple viewings are required, increasing fan activity with the text.

The ability of online trailers to target and retain such a fan audience — as well as a more casual audience who may only watch the trailer once, rather than excavating it — has been a factor in the resurgence of interest in trailer releases. Although many of the trailers that appear on the Internet are simply advance previews of a cinema trailer about to debut, their appearance is chronicled daily on film websites such as www.aintitcoolnews.com, www.empireonline.com and www.ign.com. Generally targeting the more rabid end of the fan spectrum, the trailers regularly dominate message boards, fan forums and blogs with speculation over film's plots, character arcs and the chance to discover "spoilers" in new trailers. Aside from this strand of online promotion, the Internet-only trailers have developed unique aesthetic options that have impacted back on the cinema previews that spawned them: the fast-paced montage that encourages (often requires) multiple viewings, the importance of the soundtrack to structure modern trailer messages, and the use of behind-the-scenes sequences. Perhaps most importantly, the online trailer has given control over trailer viewing into the hands of the audience, the individual who can choose which trailers to download, when to watch them, and whether to archive them in a personal library. While films have been collectable since the advent of video (and before, if you take into account 16mm collections), the availability of trailers online has increased their profile in marketing departments and in film culture generally, freeing them from their pre-film position in theatres and confirming their existence as unique short films in their own right.

THE MOBILE TRAILER: FROM VIDEOPHONES TO THE VIDEO IPOD

> *Being able to carry the Star Wars universe around with you wherever you go is pretty compelling.*[44]

From video through DVD and on to the Internet, trailers have become increasingly mobile, freed from the confines of the cinema program or the set schedule of television broadcasts. Yet this mobility was finite — the physical DVD with its trailer gallery, or the downloaded trailer saved onto a CD or memory stick — and was further constricted by the need for a larger visual interface: a television, DVD player or computer system was required to actually play back the trailer. The next extension of the online trailer, explored through this last section, is the recent developments in portable media that have made the trailer text truly mobile. The advent of mobile videophones, and the growth of portable media players such as Apple's iPod, has once again altered our ability to interact with trailer texts. Because the effects of these new technological developments are still largely unknown, and aesthetic and structural conventions are more fluid, this section will explore a selection of trailer texts that have debuted on these new media screens: the *Star Wars Episode III: Revenge of the Sith* (2005) trailer viewable via the Orange mobile phone network in 2005, and *King Kong*, *The Chronicles of Narnia: The Lion, the Witch and the Wardrobe* (2005) and *Marie Antoinette* (2006) which were released via Apple's iTunes trailer site in 2005 and 2006. With no established equilibrium or historical perspective on these events, unified analysis remains well placed to examine how these texts were produced and displayed, interrogating the discursive network that surrounds their dissemination and the ways in which audiences have responded to them. This analysis will consider the possibilities and restrictions of these mobile screens, and suggest what aesthetic and structural opportunities they may offer to future trailer structure.

The teaser trailer for *Revenge of the Sith* that was made available for download to Orange mobile videophones in November 2004 was not a unique phone-only trailer. Echoing earlier transitions between cinema and new media screens (the re-editing of the *Star Wars* teaser trailer for its video release; the digitization of *The Phantom Menace* teaser for its Internet appearance) the *Revenge of the Sith* teaser was a reformatted version of the cinematic text. Available "free" for Orange customers with compatible videophones, it demonstrates some of the limitations of the phone screen.[45] The visual restrictions of the videophone screen are striking: the images are often blurred, with digital artifacts producing an image made up of block-like segments rather than fluid motion. The quick style of editing developed for the cinema and computer screen does not seem suited for this smaller screen — complicated shots are reduced to simple concepts (an explosion, a space battle), reducing the clarity and impact of the digital cinematography. As with early television spots, or the online *Fight Club* trailers, the strongest images are close-ups, particularly in dialogue exchanges where the camera does not pan or cut quickly, but allows the eye to linger on the image. Unlike almost all previous *Star Wars* trailers, the special effects star does not dominate — the videophone image affords no spectacle of spaceship dogfights, fantastic landscapes and digitally created panoramas. The strongest structural element of the videophone trailer is the soundtrack. With the lack of clear visuals, the music, sound effects and dialogue sell the developing narrative, clarify some of the onscreen action and suggest (if only partially) the excitement the visual montage is attempting to create.

The appearance of the trailer on this small screen may offer the chance to carry a unique piece of the *Star Wars* universe around in your pocket, but it does not correspond with the 1991 *Star Wars* widescreen Trilogy trailer, and its dogmatic insistence on cinematic scope and seeing the "complete" film. Released to cinemas, the Internet and Orange mobile phones on the same day, the videophone trailer is a reduction of the theatrical or online experience in more ways than one: a smaller image area and a trailer reformatted by Lucasfilm in order to fill the 1.33:1 screen. Given that the other trailers available on Orange phones were letterboxed, further analysis of the differences between the full-screen phone trailer and the widescreen cinema and online trailer may illuminate Lucasfilm's decision to experiment with this format. Watching the videophone version is almost a reversal of the 1991 widescreen trailer: aside from the blurred imagery and artifacts, it is clear that the framing has been recomposed. Two-shots of Anakin/Palpatine and Yoda/Obi-Wan can only contain one full figure, with the other head cut in half by the edge of the frame. It makes it more difficult to identify the figures until they speak, or we are shown the reverse shot. Images that utilize widescreen composition are missing elements, reducing planets in scale, cutting off large portions of buildings and excising figures completely: a shot of a group of Jedi confronting the Chancellor features three (possibly four) indistinct figures, and a green lightsaber blade that appears to be hanging in mid-air on the far left of the 1.33:1 screen. Comparison with the Internet version of the trailer reveals that the lightsaber-wielding Jedi on the left of frame has disappeared in the full-screen version (leaving only his blade on screen), while the vague fourth image is actually a tall ornament between two other Jedi. The scene is still intelligible with these omissions, but it relies on dialogue, sound effects and the appearance of three bright lightsaber blades to distinguish the onscreen action. Some of the changes wrought by the full screen reformatting offer more positive developments: cutting extraneous detail adds emphasis to close-ups of Palpatine, Anakin and Obi-Wan Kenobi. In the online trailer the characters are more distant, but in the videophone version, the faces fill the small screen, underlining the narrative intent of their excerpted dialogue. Centering these closer images pushes them forward in the midst of the unclear and fast-moving imagery.

This aesthetic boon is undermined by the very nature of the *Star Wars* trailer, unable to balance the severe diminishment of the sweeping visual spectacle the preview relies on to construct its message (and which is effectively conveyed on other screens). The focus of the trailer is panoramic adventure and screen-filling wonder. The close-ups are effective, but because the trailer was not designed for the restrictive videophone screen, they are few and far between. The Quicktime screen available through the Internet may be only two or three times the size of the Nokia 6630 screen, but the increase in size and the sharp clarity of the image make it appear bigger again. The difference in quality resides in the technological basis of these playback options: most phone memory currently restricts the size of video files that can be stored and played back. The size of file in the current comparison is telling — Orange's *Revenge of the Sith* trailer is 580KB, the online version is 31.9MB (or 31,949KB), over fifty-five times larger (the advent of higher Broadband connections and speeds also means that the download rate is similar in both cases, despite the size of file). In order to keep data transfer fees as low as possible, videophone files are also encoded at a far smaller rate — approximately 100kbps rather than the Internet, which goes up to 1500kbps.

The introduction of new technologies on 3G videophones and the Apple iPhone has revised some of these data storage and transfer issues, but the *Star Wars* teaser release in 2004 demonstrates the standing of both technological options at that time. Trailers may remain an important tool in demonstrating the desirability of the mobile videophone screen: Orange has been targeting trailers on videophones since 2004 as part of their continuing association with the film industry.[46] The company sees trailers as "free, promotional content ... a short video format that customers were already familiar with" in order to encourage customers to pay for the other exclusive video footage that was becoming available (including Premier League goals and news bulletins).[47] Once again, trailers were a lure for forthcoming cinema releases and a new form of technological display. Since 2004, when Orange first made trailers available for download (the first ten were the nominated films for the 2004 Orange Film of the Year award[48]), trailers have consistently been among the most popular downloads via Orange World, with the *Episode III: Revenge of the Sith* teaser rated "[the] most popular video clip of the year" for Orange in 2005.[49] With no other trailers attempting to create a videophone aesthetic, the *Episode III* videophone trailer remains a unique attempt to create a different trailer experience for phone consumption — even if that experience was simply the reformatting of a trailer from another medium. With phone users already successfully downloading letterboxed trailers, Orange believes that most film companies regard mobile phones as being "on the periphery" of promotional sites, with the future lying not in videophone-specific trailers, but in "user-generated content ... like YouTube."[50] With 3G phones offering a better video experience — streaming video rather than downloading increases the size of media file that can be accessed — the quality of trailer viewing may increase on videophone screens, but their availability will likely remain cinema or online trailers transferred to the smaller screen.

> This is going to be the coolest way to watch movie trailers in the world.[51]

Steve Jobs singled out trailers as a unique content option for the Video iPod when it was released in October 2005.[52] Within two months, twenty trailers were available to download (via the Apple website and iTunes) including the blockbusters *King Kong* and *The Chronicles of Narnia: The Lion, the Witch and the Wardrobe*.[53] Alongside music videos, podcasts, short animated films, and television shows (all largely fee-driven), trailers have remained a popular download option — partly because they are seen as free content, they offer a good display of the player's attributes, and their short length suits the iPod experience (traditionally based around the short form of music tracks and/or videos). Like the Nokia 6630 videophone, the iPod has a small screen size — marginally larger than the average mobile phone at 5cm by 3.8cm (320 by 240 pixels) — but unlike the phone, the quality of the image is much higher, partly due to the processing power, screen resolution and playback software contained within the iPod.[54] Within a year of its release, the iPod had grown in dominance as a vehicle for trailer dissemination: online marketing campaigns for major releases regularly included a downloadable iPod version of all available trailers. The 2006 London International Film Festival also underlined the importance of the iPod screen as a promotional interface when it made 62 trailers available for video iPod download via its website.[55] The "coolest" way to watch movie trailers was now on the move, in crisp digital quality and presented in widescreen: the mobile trailer was now a reality.

The prevalence of trailers for video iPods does avoid one key question: what should an iPod trailer look like? In the time since its release, there have been no iPod-only trailers produced that deliberately target the smaller screen size, personal interaction, or aurally dominant technology. Unlike the videophone, there have been no experiments in re-framing or creating new content specifically for the iPod screen: Walt Disney's "full screen" release of *The Lion, The Witch and the Wardrobe* promotional material from 2005 offers a suggestive step in this direction, but the selection of clips and behind-the-scenes features that were made available were no different to the online production diaries for *Lord of the Rings* or *Star Wars* — and the film's iPod trailer remained in its widescreen format. With no trailer text yet created specifically for the iPod, the section will conclude with a selection of potential routes the iPod-only trailer could take in the coming months and years, based on the restrictions and capabilities suggested in the iPod trailers for *King Kong, The Lion, the Witch and the Wardrobe,* and *Marie Antoinette.*

All three trailers are identical to their cinematic and online versions: audio and visual information is the same, all use widescreen formatting (although this is most obvious on the iPod screen, which retains the black bars above and below the image), and the basic difference remains the available screen size. The use of the letterbox reduces the iPod screen from 5 × 3.8cm to 5 × 2.7cm (approx.), but none of the trailers attempt to address this lack of visual area. The trailers for *The Lion, the Witch and the Wardrobe* and *King Kong* represent the basic structural devices of modern blockbuster previews: a series of establishing images that set up a narrative device (shots of Jack Black, Naomi Watts, a map, and the ship setting sail; the four children exploring the magical wardrobe that draws them into Narnia); dialogue excerpts that explain those images (Jack Black's voiceover; the Beaver's excerpted lines about the children's destiny); a suggestion of narrative complication (Kong's roar interrupts filming; the White Witch appears); before the trailer moves into a montage of CGI-created visual spectacle (Kong, dinosaurs, the native people, giant insects, Kong fighting a T-rex; Aslan, centaurs, sweeping images of a huge battle). The intent of this simplistic formalist schema is not to reduce these trailers, but to demonstrate that the cinematic and online trailer conventions remain strong structural devices. Most of the images are medium, long or establishing shots—particularly in landscape-building films such as *The Lion, the Witch and the Wardrobe* and *King Kong* that want to make their fantastic landscapes believable (including the effects-created 1930s New York of *King Kong*). Close-ups are used throughout, but unlike the dialogue sequences in the videophone version of *Revenge of the Sith*, they do not dominate the screen: the widescreen aesthetic reduces the close-up to one area of the screen, alongside background detail. The only exceptions to this rule are two incredibly close images of Kong's face, particularly focused on his eyes: filling whatever screen the trailer was played on, they demonstrate the ability of the CGI technology to create enhanced realism. On the iPod they are particularly effective because they are one of very few images that speak to the alleged intimacy the more mobile screen can create between screen and individual viewer.

Both *The Lion, the Witch and the Wardrobe* and *King Kong* rely on their soundtracks to create scale and excitement, most notably in the montage sequences that build to the conclusion of the trailer narrative. The third iPod trailer, a teaser for *Marie Antoinette*, uses music for a deeper purpose, thematically linking music and image to create mood and association as much as scale or visual grandeur. Again, the content of the trailer matches online and theatrical versions: mostly medium and long shots that display the excess of the French court, a focus on Kirsten Dunst as the title character, and the suggestion of a romantic triangle between Marie, the king and another nobleman. With no reliance on close-ups or dialogue exchanges, it is the soundtrack that ties it to a potential iPod aesthetic convention, and an existing strength of the iPod: the music video. Under two minutes in length, the *Marie Antoinette* teaser is cut to the New Order track "Age of Consent." This link between trailer and music video aesthetics has already been raised in relation to video trailers in the 1980s, but it may suggest a stylistic convention that future iPod trailers could follow, given the popularity of both forms on current video iPods. In the *Marie Antoinette* teaser, the juxtaposition of the 18th-century clothes and locations with the 1980s music promotes the eclectic nature of the feature, but also raises thematic parallels between those periods in history. The iPod screen may reduce some of the visuals—the palace of Versailles, the party scenes—but the music remains dominant, propelling the images, and giving the teaser a coherent structure.

The creation of a unique iPod trailer may occur at some point in the future, but like a videophone-specific trailer, such a preview would need to consider the use of widescreen imagery, whether a full-screen image allows more opportunities for direct address, and the exploitation of the intimate nature of the small screen/viewer experience. Although the iPod offers clearer and better quality than the videophone screen, the smaller frame is not best designed for the speed of montage seen in the online spots for *Attack of the Clones* or *Hitchhiker's Guide to the Galaxy*. In contrast to the current modeling of online trailers for playback and multiple viewings, perhaps iPod or videophone trailers should linger on images rather than rush from one to the other—as the close-ups in the videophone preview of *Revenge of the Sith* demonstrate. In addition, the use of the soundtrack becomes central: not simply the current mix of excerpted dialogue and (occasional) voiceover with music, but the interplay of music and imagery that lies at the core of the iPod's current appeal, and of which *Marie Antoinette*'s teaser offers a suggestive example. Whether these aesthetic elements come into play or not, the growth of mobile media in both videophones and portable music players suggests that the introduction of a specific trailer that targets the smaller screens of these dissemination technologies will happen, and that trailer production techniques may be altered once again.

Conclusion

The technological advances that have expanded the range and number of media screens on which filmed images can be played (and replayed) have decreased the size of those visual interfaces, but increased the mobility that they offer to audiences. The size of the potential audience has shrunk from hundreds to one, while the level of interactivity and control offered to that audience has increased exponentially. The technologies that have made trailers mobile have removed them from the traditional programmed place within a film or television schedule: videocassettes offered an early degree of control, where viewers could choose to watch or fast-forward trailers (or re-watch them later), while the Internet and portable media players actively encouraged fans to download a library of current and classic trailers, to be played whenever the viewer wanted, rather than at a pre-set time and place.

These issues of trailer dissemination and fan interactivity are crucial to the unified analysis of the selected video, Internet, phone and iPod previews that illuminate recent changes in the aesthetic and structural qualities of the trailer text.

Ironically, although offering the opposite of CinemaScope's promise of "something BIG," these smaller screen trailers have re-emphasized the ideological issue of the wider screen image: what the *Star Wars* widescreen trilogy trailer describes as "the complete experience." From the appearance of widescreen video trailers in 1991, the letterbox image has been elevated above the full-screen pan-and-scan that had been dominant since the 1960s due to television screenings and the first decade of video releases. From those *Star Wars* video trailers, through the Internet and onto the iPod, widescreen has been the *de rigueur* trailer format: only the *Revenge of the Sith* videophone trailer offers an experiment in full-screen visuals and because of file and format issues, it is not entirely successful. So, the expansion onto new media screens has been undertaken in terms that reinforce the theatrical trailer aesthetic and presentation. With the introduction of the touch-screen iPhone and its more letterboxed screen size, it appears that widescreen imagery will remain dominant on these small, mobile screens. These new screens have not overhauled trailer aesthetics — but they have developed the existing conventions and taken them into new directions.

Perhaps the most compelling development offered by these new trailers is the online concept of modeling trailers to attract particular elements of Internet fan culture. The creation of fast-edited sequences that contain a flurry of images that can only be properly appreciated (and understood) through multiple viewings is an extension of the contemporary theatrical trailer aesthetic, but only the advent of trailer texts that can be paused, rewound and advanced frame-by-frame allowed these montage grids to increase the rapidity of the editing. This awareness of fan interaction has led online trailers to experiment with jump cuts and less structured trailer narratives (based around the collision of images rather than a cohesive collection of story-related scenes). Alongside this level of textual interaction, consumers are more involved than ever before, downloading trailers, building up personal archives, controlling the texts, analyzing them and sharing this knowledge with other fans. The advent of MySpace and YouTube means more fans are making more trailers available to download and watch (for classic films as much as new releases). With the availability of digital editing tools, new trailer texts have also entered the online world: taking a leaf from the "fake" *Star Wars Episode II* trailer, these unique texts offer parodies of classic film trailers. From "George Lucas presents *Singin' in the Rain*" (complete with laser blasts and TIE-fighters) to the recent run of *Brokeback Mountain* trailer parodies (starting with *Brokeback to the Future*), these demonstrate that online fan interaction with trailer texts remains strong. The production of short trailers also allows fans that are amateur filmmakers to disseminate their work, expand their reputation within the fan community. Henry Jenkins suggests that in order to retain their audiences, studios need to give fans a "stake in the survival of the franchise ... creating a space where they can make their own creative contributions": but the evidence of the trailers analyzed here suggests that the studios are more content to encourage trailer producers to model trailer texts that encourage audience interaction with licensed product, creating online excitement through official montage sequences and imagery than fan-produced works.[56] The degree of interactivity these texts allow — pausing and sifting through the trailer — may also be complicated by the growth of videophone and iPod trailers, where the control offered by these portable screens is not currently as tactile or accurate as a computer interface. However, with technology constantly developing, it is likely that fan-created trailers and trailer modeling will both continue for some time to come.

The other aesthetic strands of these trailer texts also draw on existing trailer conventions, but develop them in unique ways. The use of behind-the-scenes images can be traced back to trailer texts as early as *Citizen Kane* (1941), and formed a major part of television coverage of movie production in "Making of" specials from the 1960s on. In the modern era, such footage goes beyond the awareness-raising promotional role of previous decades: the intent is still to increase knowledge of a forthcoming film, but now it is modeled and presented to actively encourage debate and controversy in online forums and blogs. The *Lord of the Rings* online trailer may never have created as strong a convention as the montage editing, but the influence on Internet production diaries and the recurrence of such imagery in the *Elizabethtown* trailers suggest that it remains central to modern marketing techniques. The third stylistic trait, a reliance on soundtrack elements (particularly music and dialogue) to structure its sales message, also has earlier antecedents. Music was being used to structure trailers as early as the teaser for *The Public Enemy* (1931), where "I'm Forever Blowing Bubbles" punctuated the gangster imagery, but the introduction of the music video in the 1980s increased the potency and possibilities of music in trailer texts. While music videos borrowed trailer aesthetics, modern trailers often position music within their narratives to suggest genre, mood or emotion. Dialogue meanwhile has replaced both the narrative voiceover and inter-titles as the dominant storytelling device within trailer narratives. Not a development that has its ties in technological changes, the use of dialogue nonetheless will remain a crucial tool, particularly if the smaller screens of iPods and videophones continue to dominate trailer dissemination.

In the thirty years since the introduction of home video, the trailer has successfully moved from one media screen to the next, revising and changing its basic structural and aesthetic conventions to fit within that new technologically created frame. Theatrical trailer tenets remain strong — the basic construction of many trailers relies on elements found in silent trailers of the 1920s — but the new media have allowed trailers to expand and develop from this base level. Trailers are no longer cinema or television specific, their release from the set patterns and schedules of theatrical exhibition or commercial breaks has revealed them to be unique layered texts in their own right. The modeling of online trailers (and the iPod technology that allows them to be truly mobile) may have targeted specific fans, but it also raised trailers above the level of being "simply" commercial, just an advertisement. Viewing any trailer from throughout their long history shows that this has always been the case, but the increased mobility offered by these new screens has increased awareness of this aspect of the trailer text, and made it into a text that can be archived, discussed, interacted with, and re-positioned. In becoming more mobile, trailers have been able to assert a unique identity, apart from the cinema screen that created them.

Conclusion

> *The production of a film, then, includes the making of its "consumable" identity. Promotion acts on this aspect of a film's design by providing designated elements with an inter-textual destiny: certain filmic elements are developed into a premeditated network of advertising and promotion that will enter the social sphere of reception. Such an intricate relation between film and promotion has been intensified historically: every new invention in the media, from radio to TV, to cable TV and videocassettes, has provided new forums for advertising. (Barbara Klinger)*[1]
>
> *We cannot standardize our pictures as a soap manufacturer standardizes his soap. They must all be different. So must all our advertisements. Each picture requires a new advertising treatment, a new approach. (Robert Cochrane)*[2]

Trailers are everywhere. Confirming Barbara Klinger's notion of historical "intensification," trailers have expanded from the cinema screen onto television, radio, the Internet, mobile phones, iPods, videogame consoles, DVDs, and, most recently, in London Underground tube stations and on public transport. Despite claims that they have become too predictable and formulaic (a timeless charge that recurs throughout the decades, from the 1930s on), trailers remain Hollywood's foremost promotional text, helping delineate and define each new release. But although trailers are more visible, mobile and omnipresent than at any point in their history, they have fallen through the cracks of film and media studies. The purpose of this project has been to revitalize interest in the film trailer, and to show how essential this text is to any full understanding of film history. *Coming Soon: Film Trailers and the Selling of Hollywood Technology* has demonstrated the important, often dominant, role the trailer has played within film promotion: helping to create a feature film's "consumable" identity, and defining historically distinct changes in marketing, narrative and technology. Often created well in advance of other promotional materials, the trailer establishes a visual and generic identity echoed in later posters, TV spots, and lobby cards. As Klinger identifies above, and in her work on Douglas Sirk, the trailer (as part of the network of advance advertising and promotion) shapes particular ideas about the forthcoming film in audiences' minds, foregrounds particular themes, stars and images.[3] Designed to be the first entry point viewers have into the world of the feature film, the trailer is a crucial textual bridge between film studio and audience.

The preceding chapters have revealed the trailer to be an intricately layered text, a complex fusion of sales messages and meaning that belies an apparent simplicity based around structural elements of excerpted scenes, graphic title work, music and voiceover. Throughout, my analysis has been predicated on the basis that these trailers are a unique source of historical and textual information, adding new layers to our understanding of the film industry, its promotional strategies, and the larger relationships between media. Detailed examination of trailer texts has cast fresh light on key topics within film studies. While technology has been the main focus, the book has shown how trailers helped maintain the star system, with distinct structural approaches displaying the appeal of Gene Kelly, Marilyn Monroe or Robby the Robot. Images of rocket launches and alien worlds (*Apollo 13, Star Wars Episode III: Revenge of the Sith*), gunfights and Indian attacks (*How the West Was Won*), vampire bats and haunted castles (*The Maze*) have depicted and delineated generic tropes for trailer viewers. Television spots teased out notions of both technological and national differences, with uniquely British and American approaches to aesthetic content in *Smiley* and *Born Yesterday*. The use of the female form in trailers as disparate as *Sangaree*, *Singin' in the Rain* and *Marie Antoinette* tells a story of shifting modes of representation and power (although perhaps not as progressive as might be hoped over the course of fifty years). Trailer analysis reveals how individual texts present and structure these elements, but the trailers are also historical markers of the moment of their production, containing specific social, cultural, and industrial information and attitudes.

Dealing with the complex layers of this textual resource required a theoretical approach that could tease apart and comprehend the strata of visual and aural information contained in each trailer. My belief in treating trailers as highly structured texts in their own right, rather than precursors or lesser adjuncts to the feature, led to the concept of "unified" analysis, and the synthesis of close textual and historical analysis. In the 1980s, Thomas Elsaesser said that film history had moved away from interpretation toward analysis of alternative archival sources, and that "the films themselves ... [were] not the object of study"[4]; more recently, B. F. Taylor called for each film to be treated "as an individual object of critical scrutiny"[5]: film history without consideration of the film text itself, or film analysis without a sense of the historical moment, the specific circumstances of production. I hope this book has proven that it is possible to fuse these different approaches; to root interpretation, or close readings of film sequences, within meticulous historical research, to underpin strong *mise-en-scène* analysis with equally strong analysis of archival information. Similar aims were expressed in *The New Film History*, where essays by Jonathan Munby and Sarah Street merged aesthetic and historical work around cinematography, editing and color, but the overall focus of the edited collection fell mainly on contextual work, not film analysis.[6] This book has concentrated on the possibilities of unified analysis, and what a combination of close analysis and historical context can reveal.

The emphasis that unified analysis places on scrutinizing the individual trailer text, and building a network of the unique historical influences that surrounded its production, does not preclude the use of larger themes within trailer production. Similar to Richard Maltby's work on 3½ seconds of *Casablanca* and the influence of the Production Code Administration, this project has seen the wider historical context as a potent source of information that constantly underpins close analysis.[7] This move from larger industrial and historical context down to individual trailer text also works in reverse, allowing trailer analysis across a historical period to reveal similarities in depicting stars, defining genre imagery, or investigating the place of visual spectacle in trailer structure throughout the years. Unified analysis begins with the unique and complex trailer text but can expand out to consider the impact of other elements: this movement from historical framework to historically informed analysis allows unified analysis to sift the trailer for possible meaning.

Applying the theory of unified analysis to the initial sample of trailers identified the technological underpinnings of the trailer text, and revealed the pivotal role that new technology has played throughout trailer history. Important though stardom, genre, national identity and representation are, each of these areas relies on the technologies that underpin trailer production, distribution and exhibition. The 1927 trailer for *The Jazz Singer* offered an early demonstration of how new technology introduced innovative creative and stylistic options for trailer production. The direct audience address from John Miljan could be seen as a backwards aesthetic step from the flamboyant editing patterns, graphic wipes and animation of the mid-1920s trailer, but the display of synchronized sound actually introduced new layers to the trailer text: musical punctuation, dialogue excerpts, and a narrative voiceover that could sit alongside the existing tools of the trailer business. From synchronized sound to CinemaScope, from television to special effects and from videocassettes to mobile videophones, screen technology has continually altered where trailers have been seen, what trailer narratives are about, and how trailers can look. The trailers analyzed through the previous chapters have revealed the importance of technology within trailer structure. This focus allowed unified analysis to expand and challenge existing notions within film and media studies, particularly the interaction between disparate media screens. Unified analysis of the first years of television trailer production reassembled unique evidence that broadened the academic view of the relationship between the film and television industries of the 1950s. The investigation of textual detail and contextual background confirmed that there existed a productive cross-fertilization of style, structure and content between the rival screens. Without the dual approach intrinsic to unified analysis, and the central role played by technology, reassessing this moment in cross-media history would not have been possible.

Technological change has been the one constant throughout much of trailer history, with new screen processes and technical platforms that have complicated the production, distribution and exhibition of these texts. Because of its combination of text and context, unified analysis provides a way of dealing with these technological changes, exploring the range of future aesthetic and structural possibilities suggested by the recent development of popular media screens such as the iPod and videophone technology. Given the rapid expansion of technology beyond the limits of chapter four, this conclusion will consider some of the relevant advances that have taken place, and how they reflect on the larger remit of this book.

The advent of video billboard technology in the past months now allows trailers to appear on the high street and on public transport: trailer advertising for *Ocean's 13* (2007) in summer 2007 made use of the array of video posters at selected London Underground stations. As passengers traveled down the escalators at these stations, video screens on their right and left showed advertisements. As with television and video, this new adaptation of dissemination technology offers new possibilities for trailer aesthetics. With sixty-six screens in total (thirty-three each next to the "up" and "down" escalators respectively), the viewing experience is distinct from any other form of screen covered in previous chapters. Passengers are continually moving past each individual screen, but the trailer has been designed to combat this movement and use it to structure the trailer visuals. As the short *Ocean's 13* trailer begins, we see images of Las Vegas, casinos and gambling across thirteen distinct screens. There is music, and inter-titles: "When you cross one Ocean, you cross them all." At this point in the cinema and online trailers, there is a long series of star images, from George Clooney through Al Pacino. On the video posters, the cast list is split between the thirteen screens, each depicting a close-up and identifying title for one actor. As the escalator descends, passengers would see all thirteen star names and images displayed across the multiple screens. An earlier trailer on this system, for the release of *Rocky Balboa* (2007), featured eleven separate images on the "up" escalator that showed the famous sequence of Rocky running up the steps of the Philadelphia Museum of Art. In the Underground version, the images of Rocky kept pace with the passengers, as the theme tune played, and the release date was displayed.[8] Rather than the singular screens of cinema and television, these billboards allow for titles, images and animation to extend across multiple screens at one time. As such screens become more common (they are already popular in Europe and Japan, but only now becoming available in Britain and the U.S.) they open up new areas for trailer production and dissemination.

As each chapter has shown, talking about how trailers utilize new technological possibilities is not restricted to the new display opportunities of the television or mobile phone. Changes in screen technology necessarily affect aesthetic and structural parameters: how existing trailer conventions are used, and what new stylistic avenues are opened up. In the case of the London Underground video posters, images are no longer restricted to one screen; they can move with the viewer, literally jumping between screens to keep pace: the dissemination and display technology has again influenced how trailers are produced. From *The Jazz Singer*'s 1927 trailer to these *Ocean's 13* video posters in 2007, such examples have fuelled the book's central belief that technology has played a central role within trailer history: often a star figure within sales messages, as seen in Cinerama, 3-D, CinemaScope and many science fiction trailers; occasionally the force that defines trailer aesthetics, such as early television spots, Internet and mobile phone trailers; always opening up the tools that trailer production could play with, and use.

Alongside new screen opportunities, old technologies have recently reappeared in cinemas. The growth of IMAX 3-D has popularized 3-D filmmaking, with specific sequences of blockbusters *Superman Returns* (2006) and *Harry Potter and the Order of the Phoenix* (2007) produced for 3-D screenings. This renaissance has been promoted through a new generation of 3-D trailers, with previews for *Happy Feet* (2007), *Meet the Robinsons* (2007) and *Beowulf* (2007) demonstrating that sales messages based around a free sample of 3-D photography have not dramatically changed since 1954. Dancing penguins, spaceships and monsters lunging out of the screen; arctic, futuristic and fantastic landscapes containing different layers of activity; these mirror the trailer conventions that unified analysis reconstructed and identified in chapter one. Future 3-D filmmaking and distribution may also affect the temporal address of trailers, again through the lens of new technology. The Introduction discussed how technology had changed the temporal address of a trailer, from "Coming Soon" to "Now Showing" or "Now Available." In the 1950s, widescreen re-releases of classic films were promoted as new, or better, because of the application of new technology: the 1950s trailer for *Gone with the Wind* (1939) was "more spectacular, more stirring" in widescreen, while the *Fantasia* (1940) trailer claimed the 1950s SuperScope version reflected how the film "was originally conceived."[9] The return of 3-D production and theatrical projection may contain an echo of this temporal repositioning. In 2005, Lucasfilm announced that they plan to release 3-D versions of all six *Star Wars* films, applying a new digital process to the existing footage.[10] Over a decade after the 1997 release of the CGI-enhanced *Star Wars* trilogy "Special Editions" (whose preview offered the temporally opaque instruction "see it again, for the first time") it seems clear that trailers for these 3-D releases will follow Lucasfilm's policy of re-presenting something old as something new, through the lens of new technology.[11] The 1977 and 1997 texts will be temporally repositioned again, this time in a 3-D format.

Throughout, this project has been cautiously optimistic about the role of technology in opening up new frontiers for trailers. Perhaps this is because trailers are always early adopters of technology, invariably among the first texts used by film studios to test the technological waters, continually trying out new styles, structures and screens. Technology has also allowed fan cultures to re-imagine the trailer format as a site of empowerment, creating participatory works that still reflect dominant trailer conventions, while gently mocking the format. YouTube has revolutionized how fans access a variety of trailer texts, while sites such as www.trailermash.com display fan creations that "mash" (or combine) different genres and films to create new trailer texts. One of the most potent examples, *Brokeback to the Future*, takes the storyline and music from *Brokeback Mountain* (2005) and grafts it onto a montage of scenes lifted from the *Back to the Future* trilogy, creating a trailer that is structurally indistinguishable from a mainstream ("real") preview. Other fan-produced texts include *The Shining* (1980) as a romantic comedy, and *Scary Mary* (*Mary Poppins* [1964] as an *Exorcist*-style horror trailer).[12] Created (or recreated) by fans purely to share with the online community (and, in some cases, to demonstrate particular editing skills), these trailers exist because of the changing technological opportunities open to trailer producers, both amateur and professional, and the development of new dissemination avenues.

The combination of technology and trailer production demonstrated in fan cultures has also expanded out into other arenas, offering a possible future for technology in trailer production. A team from the University of Bremen developed a piece of production software designed to automatically generate a trailer from any action movie inputted into their computer system. With little or no human involvement — beyond instructing the computer what star images to look for, or giving it narrative information — the Semantic Video Pattern (SVP) software was programmed to select appropriate action and dialogue sequences, and edit them together into a coherent whole. Having created an online database of trailers, existing trailer patterns were identified and used as the basis for the computer models. The project is illuminating in terms of what elements the team identified as necessary for their action movie trailers—faces, image motion, soundtrack elements, quotations (selected through interaction with a quotation database at www.imdb.com), and explosions, gunshots, and screams. The use of generic (active movement, violent actions) and star images (the selection of particular faces) compares with mainstream trailer production, but the finished product lacks the complexity and narrative development that marks out the contemporary trailer text.

The project's central "generated" trailer was for *Transporter 2* (2006) a modern action sequel. With only two short dialogue excerpts and one title card, the SVP trailer is almost wholly structured around a frenetic montage of explosions and gunplay. Unlike the display of science fiction spectacle seen in chapter three, these action-packed elements have no narrative purpose, and are used purely as an action spectacle. The sequences conform to genre expectations, but the trailer construction is limited to this concept, offering none of the layers that "real" trailers display. Comparison with the "real" trailer for *Transporter 2* is telling: while it also features action tropes, and many of the same spectacular stunts and fighting, the authentic trailer contains its spectacle within a trailer narrative. Alongside the stunts, the trailer sets up its star (Jason Statham), status as a sequel ("I'm looking for a Transporter," "The best in the business is back in the game"), and basic narrative events—Statham as a special kind of driver, the kidnapping of a young boy under his protection, his promise to rescue him. The "real" trailer also adds a sexual element to the action conventions, suggesting a relationship between Statham and the boy's mother, and by focusing viewer attention onto a seemingly ordinary nurse, who (in slow motion) shrugs off her uniform to become a half-naked femme fatale, complete with stockings, tattoos and semi-automatic machine pistols (a visual change summed up by the trailer narrative as: "In his line of work ... nothing is ever what it seems").[13] The trailer includes several montage sequences of spectacular stunts, but the set-up of the trailer has justified their inclusion, and given them a purpose that the SVP trailer montage lacked.

The difference in style and content between the two different trailers appears to be rooted in two concepts: removing the human element from the production, and the possibility of reducing the trailer text to a list of structural elements. In the supporting materials on their website, the Bremen SVP project states that a trailer is "a piece of art produced by creative humans" but that the team were "curious to see how close algorithms could get to this goal."[14] On the evidence of the trailers they generated, what the software currently lacks is a comprehension of narrative events and how they relate to the presentation of visual spectacle. The creative, or "human," element added in the "real" *Transporter 2* trailer is not easily defined, but there is a playful and humorous relationship established between titles, voiceover and imagery, particularly when breaking up destructive action with comic interludes. Not part of its programming, the computer ignores such moments in favor of more destruction and mayhem.

The Bremen experiment proves that reducing trailer structure to three or four conventions ignores the range of external aesthetic, structural and contextual elements that this project has explored, and which feed into the network of influences surrounding the trailer. Generating a trailer by computer highlights the importance of the network of influences central to unified analysis, because it removes many of the shifting factors that shape and guide trailer production, be they cultural, social, industrial or historical. In their place is a strict and unchanging list of conventions of what (in the case of SVP) an action trailer should contain. Modern critics have often complained that trailers have become too simplistic, reliant on a repetitive format of explosions, dialogue cues and loud music (the elements mocked so effectively in the *Hitchhiker's Guide to the Galaxy* trailer discussed in chapter four): the SVP project reduces all trailers to one formula. This is not to state, as the Bremen project does, that all trailers should be considered works of art, but this book has argued throughout that they should be recognized as unique products of a particular time, place, and industry. Chapter three noted the lack of originality in many late–1990s science fiction trailers, but that period of relative stagnation was challenged by the appearance of trailers for *The Matrix* and George Lucas' attempt to create "tone poems" with the advertising for the *Star Wars* prequels.[15] Attempting to pin down a master structure for trailers over the last century, or for any period within those hundred years, is a thankless and ultimately empty task. The Bremen experiment proves that each trailer is unique and needs to be watched, analyzed, and debated as a unique text, not simply as a cog in some larger trailer machine. Given the SVP project is no longer active, it remains a unique experiment and, potentially, a compelling future technological development within trailer production.

A further contemporary development — perhaps the most useful one to occur during the writing of this book — has been the resurgence of trailers within popular culture. While there is a financial and legal element to this— many trailers remain outside of copyright law, making them perfect material for televised biographies, documentaries and entertainment news channels— the advent of DVD and the Internet has helped promote awareness of the trailer. Most DVD releases include at least the film's trailer, and many have Trailer Galleries of previews related by genre, star, or studio. Warner Bros. has even begun including historically accurate trailers, cartoons and short material on their archive DVDs, intended to recreate what a "night at the movies" would have been like in the year the film was released to cinemas—a partial suggestion of the historical moment of production and release. Outside of this, there are now trailer compilations on DVD, focusing on film studios (Hammer Horror), genre (film noir, science fiction), technology (3-D and CinemaScope) or larger film cultural movement (exploitation or "grindhouse" movies). Meanwhile, the Internet has become an unofficial trailer archive, with fans and studios uploading new and classic previews to a variety of sites, from the Internet Movie Database to YouTube. Creating a personal trailer archive, either online or on DVD, is now a genuine possibility, and will hopefully drive more writers to consider the historical importance of these unique texts to film and media studies.

Culturally and industrially, the potency of the trailer text is also on the increase. During the writing of this book, the BBC was criticized over a trailer for a television documentary about the Queen that misrepresented the temporal order of events surrounding a photo shoot; a new viral marketing campaign for *The Dark Knight* (2008) (featuring the first teaser trailer for the film) was the talk of Internet forums and chatrooms; and the MPAA (Motion Picture Association of America) and the ESRC (Entertainment Software Ratings Board) sparked a debate about access to Internet downloads of violent film and video game trailers (the video game industry represents a vast new area of trailer production and dissemination that warrants its own study), and whether underage viewers could be restricted through technological "age gates."[16] Cinemas, television, DVD, the Internet, videophones, public transport, iPods, videogame consoles: trailers are, indeed, everywhere.

Almost twenty years ago, Janet Staiger called for a history of film advertising that considered its social, cultural and historical situation.[17] Her concern was motivated mainly around reception studies, but this book echoes her call for academics to scrutinize the practices of film advertising, and to situate that scrutiny within aesthetic, historical, social, cultural and industrial terms. This current study has attempted to advance that debate, demonstrating how important trailer analysis can be for all areas of film and media studies. As this work has proven, trailer analysis has only begun to scratch the surface of what these texts can reveal around issues of access, censorship, fan participation, and the past and future of film promotion. Focusing on trailers has also demonstrated the desirability of unified analysis, that fusion of close analysis with historical and contextual approaches, synthesizing and using the best elements of each to inform the other. This exploration of the coming attraction trailer offers this unique text as a revelatory journey into both new and familiar areas of film and media studies.

Appendix I
Interview with Bill Seymour
January 24, 1995, at
Screen Opticals, Perivale, London

Bill Seymour worked at British trailer company National Screen Services until the late 1980s, then their successor, Screen Opticals, in the 1990s.

Q: Can you tell me something about the history of National Screen here in London, how they went about the process of making a trailer?
A: When the war started they came down here [Perivale] in 1942 and of course those were the days of black and white so the trailers that were made in those days were for no charge — National Screen didn't charge for the actual producing of the trailers 'cause they had their own laboratory out the back. They had an agreement that they made all the prints that were required for going round the circuit so they made their money that way.

They would make money if they had a hundred prints to make and then they'd also make money on the distribution ... they had all the contacts tied up so that they could produce the trailers, make the trailers and distribute them. But then as times got on they [inc. Esther Harris] found that ... they were virtually telling the producers ... how best to sell it, coming up with the ideas but then gradually they wanted two-penneth ... they were sticking in, getting more sophisticated, finally costing more money. Then they started introducing small charges — I think the first one was about £200.... It was peanuts when you consider what had to go into it.

They never have worked from a print. What happens, even today, the negative — when they get a finished feature they screen that and decide how they're going to make the trailer and then whoever is producing the trailer then logs where all those scenes that they require are in the feature and then that list of material goes to the laboratory which is holding the negatives and they make inter-positives of those sections. They then come to a place like this to assemble them and cut them down the finished length that they've got and do any opticals or titles ... whatever goes into it. And while they're doing that the other arm of the production — the editing side — they pull the same sort of things out of the track side: they get magnetic tracks and go through a similar procedure, laying the tracks and getting any commentary they want done and any effects, and the editor lays these to the cutting copy he has made and then they go to a dubbing session. Simultaneously, the negative is being made from the master. When that negative is finished it goes off to the laboratory to be married up with the track neg. and they can churn off as many copies as they like.

In the early days they used to work it that if they had sixty features of the film going round the circuits one week that feature would play North London, South the next week — the same right through the country so that they had these features going round the cinemas week after week after week. The same sort of thing happened with the trailers — if they were working on fifty features they'd need eighty trailers — every week they'd go out to the cinemas a week or two before the feature was due they'd show them. When that week was finished the trailers came back to National Screen on a Thursday night — all those trailers went back out again on Friday morning to the different areas.

They only made a small number of prints, whereas today, over the last six years, with these multiplexes and things like that they flood the market — a film comes out and its all over the country; there's none of this crossover now; it's a terrible waste but it averages out. I mean, for a big film you're talking about 750–1000 trailers. They go out in blanket distribution from National Screen. They're going out two months in advance — trailers are going out now for the summer. What's happening is that these trailers are shown at one cinema, one multiplex, then they're sent back here and thrown away. They do keep a few of each because sometimes they're called for abroad. We still get calls — two or three a year — from people who want trailers back to 1931, 32...

The video companies have got people who ring up National Screen and say, "Can we have a trailer for this, that and the next thing" and they just put them on tape. They go to a video edit — they can cut out whatever they like. There's some cinemas in town have got a big screen in the foyer where the company borrows the trailer and makes tapes.

What happened here — when color started coming in, National Screen found that they didn't have the facilities to start making the color negatives so they were having to go out to places like Technicolor, who had an optical department. The producers want the maximum advertising they can — National Screen were getting a lot of stick from producers and distributors saying "we want it on the screen now," so NS in 1952 decided that they would buy a color printer and started making [printing] their own trailers. They kept buying printer after printer — and cameras — because there was no one making opticals in those days. In the end they were making all the feature titles for every film that was made in this country. They got very big indeed — we had seven printers and three cameras. Until the crash came in 1986, of course. When color came in, the costs started rising and rising — in the end National Screen didn't have anything to fall back on.

You're talking about £25 – 30,000 to produce a trailer negative. National Screen didn't have any competition in the early days but in 1962 a couple of the editors who used to do all the Rank trailers—like all the Carry On's, things like that—they, with backing from Peter Rogers and Jeremy Thomas, went out and set up a company called General Screen Enterprises and they started making all Rank's trailers. Another company called Creative Partnerships set up in the late 70s—they were in town and had a place in Hollywood. About the same time a company called Picture Productions also started making trailers. So National Screen's monopoly was gradually eaten away. [Picture Production Company] now creates the trailers and we [Screen Opticals] put them all together and produce a negative at the end of the day, just like National Screen did.

Q: How many trailers are adapted from the American versions? Are there often changes made for the different audiences?

A: In total, we're only talking probably ten a year—which isn't a lot when you consider the number of trailers—ones that are drastically overhauled that is. The Americans still like to keep a finger in the pie. They always have to okay it, to ensure that the publicists here are going along the right lines.

Q: Has the influence of the trailer maker on the finished product been eroded over the years as marketing and publicity practices have evolved?

A: Esther Harris and people like that decided what they wanted to do but nowadays before they start creating the trailer the publicist of the studio would go down and view the feature and they would give them a rough idea of what they think. Now, the creative people might say "well, we disagree"—they'd have a discussion to set out what they think, how it should be done. This is submitted to Fox, say, who will make a few suggestions; then it comes back and is made to that script.

Q: What about approval from the BBFC?

A: Nowadays, every trailer has to go to the BBFC to be classified. It's always been like that. Sometimes you get the ridiculous thing: the feature will get a "PG," you'd make a trailer, submit it to the board and they would give the trailer a "15" because they'd say you condensed all the violence or whatever that was strung out through the feature. You'd have to go back and start all over again.

But nowadays ... they started having complaints because although all the trailers have certificate bands on the front when they go out from National Screen these trailers would get to the cinemas and these bands would be thrown away, discarded—they were running into complaints that when they were making their cake stand the certificates were getting cut off and showing "15" trailers when the feature showing was a "PG." Three or four years ago they introduced a system where you actually color code the side of the trailer with the same brand as the certificate.

[On Screen Opticals work for BBFC] These days the BBFC recommend us to shoot the certificates ... we get about 95 percent of them.... There's a lot of people chasing after the prestige main titles ... well, it's my 42nd year in the film industry, if they want to come to us, they will. We don't go out chasing them.

Q: What was National Screen responsible for in terms of exhibition materials?

A: Well, National Screen, apart from the trailers, would send out the posters, all the front-of-house materials, lobby stands ... these days they send out the *Flicks* magazine.

Q: **How did the introduction of different technology affect the trailer makers? Things like television, video, widescreen?**

A: If the feature is shot in widescreen or 'Scope ... well, these days there are no 'Scope trailers, only in specialized circumstances will cinemas show 'Scope trailers.... What happens now is if they shoot a feature in 'Scope the same thing happens—we get the inter-positive and we have to unsqueeze it and pan-and-scan whatever we have to ... [in terms of TV trailers] twenty-second spots, we'd do them all the time. For each trailer you'd produce a TV spot [in NSS days]. The thing is the cost of transmitting them has gone out the window—you'd talking a prime time spot of £10,000 every time it's shown. [London area rate?]

Q: **What are the different costs involved in trailer production?**

A: I would estimate that ... well, what normally happens is when the creative people order the sections of the picture and the track, that tab is picked up by the production company anyway so that is an "add on" cost. A trailer might average 250 feet—when they order the sections in the first instance and the labs overprint ... we get in excess of 1,200 feet—you're talking 1,200 feet of inter-positive at £1.30 a foot. Off of that they take a black-and-white reversal to give them a cutting copy (black-and-white reversal is thirty pence a foot) so say 2,500 grand extra.

For putting the whole trailer together—the creative side, our side, all depends on the amount of opticals (dissolves, fades, titles) that are added on. You're talking between £1,000 to £2,000. But with all the editing—in the National Screen days, which is going back nine years, it was working out for the whole thing about £15,000. So up that to at least £25,000. It's cheap publicity when you consider you've got 700 trailers going out—250 feet, the printing cost is nearly £17,000—each trailer costs you £22. They've got to add that on to their bill for publicity—it's not a lot when you think of how much a film costs, and the revenue they hope to make.

Q: **What trailers did you work on over the years at NSS? What trailers did you particularly admire?**

A: There are two or three... The Bond trailers ... they cost a little bit more because of all the stuff Maurice Binder put into them. They weren't National Screen trailers as such, but Maurice Binder created the main titles, the teaser trailers and the main trailers, all at National Screen. He used to create them, National Screen put them together for him.... Stanley Kubrick did it on *Clockwork Orange* as well ... he got Pablo Ferro from the States, he came here—created something completely out of the ordinary. Two or three frame cuts ... eyes and whatever, colors all flashing ... a one-off, when the studio get their own man in.

In terms of my own work ... well, up to 20, 25 years ago, almost any film you can think of was probably a National Screen trailer. That would include films like *Zulu* (1963), *Fall of the Roman Empire* (1964), *Help* (1965), *Guns of Navarone*

(1961), *Force 10 from Navarone* (1978), *Anthony & Cleopatra* (1972), *Day of the Jackal* (1973), *Four Musketeers* (1974), *At the Earth's Core* (1976), *Are You Being Served?* (1977), *Death on the Nile* (1978), *Flash Gordon* (1980), *Ghandi* (1982) and *Greystoke* (1984).

Q: What about directors? How closely were they involved?

A: Apart from Kubrick ... Hitchcock and Kubrick ... they were big enough to do what they wanted.

Q: Over the years what have been the biggest changes in trailer style?

A: You never have all these big titles saying "Exciting," "Big Romance" and all that anymore, all the gregarious kind of effects and wipes — question marks zooming in and out. Trailers tend to follow a trend — we've found recently we have to put a lot of "slow mos" in a lot of them.

Q: How did the British NSS differ from the American one?

A: National Screen in the States wasn't producing the trailers in the end, not like we were over here ... they had the similar set-up but they packed that up a long time ago — the trailers were just coming to them for distribution.

APPENDIX II

Interview with John Sittig
May 31, 2005, at Pacific Winnetka
21 Theatre, Los Angeles

John Sittig, as part of his responsibilities with Pacific Theatre, is closely involved with Pacific's Cinerama Dome as well as the Cinerama Archive. During the interview he was also able to show me two original trailers, for the 35mm release of *Seven Wonders of the World* and the 1962 release of *How the West Was Won*.

Q: How did trailer advertising work for the initial Cinerama films?
A: For the first five Cinerama releases—the narrative travelogues—there was no trailer advertising at all. This was partly because the process launched with such good publicity, but mainly because of the structure of the company. In the mid–50s there were only 24 Cinerama theatres in the U.S., maybe 50 around the world, and many of these were either run by independent exhibitors, or were four-walled theatres that Cinerama owned, and not part of a circuit. This set-up meant there wasn't much room for synergy; you couldn't cross-promote your product across theatre chains. There was also a problem with the system itself—it was so cumbersome to run the three-projector system without trying to insert something like a trailer into the program.

Q: When did this set-up change to include trailers? What caused the change?
A: The main difference came when we partnered with MGM. The original contract between Cinerama and MGM was for four films to be produced in the three-strip process. By this point there were 260, maybe 280 Cinerama screens worldwide and it was decided to launch the first two films, *The Wonderful World of the Brothers Grimm* and *How the West Was Won* at the same time, *Brothers Grimm* debuting in the U.S. and *How the West Was Won* launching in Europe. The MGM films changed the Cinerama process as well, moving from 26 frames per second to 24, allowing the films to become longer. Cinerama had always had 26 f.p.s. to try and

cut down on shutter flicker at the edges of your peripheral vision. To avoid this, the Cinerama screen had a 146 degree curve to it. When we cut it down to 24 f.p.s. the screen curvature had to be reduced to 120 degrees to avoid the shutter flicker.

Q: How were these trailers inserted into a standard Cinerama program?

A: If we take the example of *Brothers Grimm*, you would walk into the theatre. The Overture for the *Brothers Grimm* would be playing, then the curtains would open and the film would begin. The Cinerama films always opened with a big bang, like the rollercoaster at the start of *This is Cinerama*, so they didn't want to take away from that impact by showing a trailer ahead of the film. The first half would play — about 45 to 60 minutes — then the screen would say "Intermission," the curtains would close and there would be a 15-minute break for people to go back to the snack bar, have a cigarette, whatever. Every film had a built-in intermission so the projectionists could rethread the four machines. After ten minutes or so, an usher would walk to the front of the theatre, they would announce that the next film they were going to be playing was *How the West Was Won*, and here's a trailer for it.

The curtains would open, the five-minute trailer would play, the curtains would close again, the lights would come up, there'd be silence in the theatre for about two minutes then the callback music would start playing, people would be back in their seats, and the second half would begin. It was easier to put the trailers here, because the three-projector technology was cumbersome, and no theatre could afford to have six projectors for seamless changeover.

Q: Given that none of the original five Cinerama productions had trailers, why does one exist for 1956's *Seven Wonders of the World*?

A: *Seven Wonders* played in conventional cinemas in the early 60s, combining the three-strip process into a 35mm anamorphic print. Because there were still large groups of people who didn't live near a Cinerama theatre but were interested in the films, the film was released this way. The trailer, also showing the three-strip process, was produced for this release, not the original Cinerama-only release.

A similar thing happened with *This is Cinerama* in 1972, when a 70mm print of the film was exhibited in normal theatres. A one-minute trailer was made for this release, not using any footage but instead featuring a painting of the famous rollercoaster sequence, printed titles and a voiceover saying "for the first time you can see *This is Cinerama* in 70mm." The Cinerama footage didn't transfer well to regular theatrical or television — they were trying to sell the name without showing anything different to what people were used to looking at.

Q: How did the Cinerama release pattern work?

A: Generally, a film would open at one theatre a week — open in New York at the Warner Theatre or Warner Cinerama in Hollywood. Open in New York, then one week or ten days later, open in Hollywood, then week/ten days later, somewhere else — the roll out over three or four months. The field guys for the Cinerama theatres did great work; they made it an event; they would arrive in town with stars;

they would turn up in schools, would do tie-ins with libraries, women's clubs, just to launch the new film.

Q: Did the competing technology of CinemaScope affect the fortunes of Cinerama?

A: Not so much CinemaScope — it was Cinerama for the masses. While Cinerama took the camera on location to Rome, or flew over Niagara, or went down to South America, most 'Scope films were filmed in Hollywood, Culver City, with maybe some second unit location work for backgrounds.

CinemaScope and Cinerama were providing different things — Cinerama was the thrill ride, what you didn't see every day. Cinerama had 260 screens worldwide, but CinemaScope films had 230 prints in circulation at once, going round the circuit, getting out to the regions ... the film would launch on the coasts, and maybe not getting to Ohio for six months.

What hurt Cinerama was Todd-AO, Panavision, Technirama — they took the camera out onto location, to the actual places, and they were showing on "roadshow" presentations, using a single print, no joining lines, just one piece of film. Much easier. Because Cinerama was so expensive to produce and exhibit — you needed five projectionists just to show the film — and you could see the lines in Cinerama, people realized they could see *Ben Hur* or *South Pacific*, in 70mm with stereophonic seven-track sound. Hollywood saw the difference, realized there was money to be made, even with an expensive movie like *Lawrence of Arabia*. Cinerama just became too technologically cumbersome.

Q: Can you see the influence of Cinerama on the CinemaScope films and trailers?

A: Well, yes, the opening of *Three Coins in a Fountain* with its five-minute travel round Rome, while Sinatra sings ... that's a tie to Cinerama. *Boy on a Dolphin* (1957) had a travelogue prologue, tying it back to Cinerama.... Cinerama had a significant impact on Hollywood; you look at the composition in *Beneath the 12-Mile Reef*, if Terry Moore is on the bow of the boat, Robert Wagner had to be on the stern, so you'd think "that's really wide."

Q: What happened to Cinerama after *How the West Was Won*?

A: Although the deal with MGM for was four three-strip films, *Brothers Grimm* did not do well at the box office. *How the West Was Won* did well, but it was extremely over-budget — $15 million, well over. It was decided that the next two MGM Cinerama films — *Grand Prix* and *2001* — weren't going to be three-strip, but filmed in conventional 70mm. They were released to Cinerama theatres first with the Cinerama title on the front, then they went to non–Cinerama theatres as 70mm prints, then 35mm prints for smaller theatres. *Battle of the Bulge* (1965), *Mad World* [*It's a Mad Mad Mad Mad World* (1963)] and *Hallelujah Trail* (1965) were all 70mm releases, then 35mm. The advertising material would often change between the Cinerama, 70mm and 35mm releases; I mean they would drop the Cinerama name but they would also make other changes to the footage.

APPENDIX III

Interview with Paul N. Lazarus

February 5, 1994, at the University
of California, Santa Barbara

Paul N. Lazarus, a former movie advertising and promotions executive, started his career in 1933. Having worked at Warner Bros., United Artists, and Columbia, he became executive Vice-President of National Screen Services Corporation from 1965 until he moved into teaching at UCSB.

Q: Can you tell me about the formation of National Screen Service?
A: Well, National Screen Service [N.S.S.] was set up as a way of getting the eight major companies out of the nickel-and-dime business of selling trailers and posters and stills to individual theatres. This was back in 1918 when these companies had to do it all themselves—Herman Robbins, he was the guy who came up with the idea. He was working in the sales department at 20th Century, and he put it all together, around about 1919, 1920. At that time all the companies had their own trailer departments which created and produced trailers—which weren't all that established, these were the real early days of advertising. Now, as the years went on and as N.S.S. grew to a sizeable company representing all the industry the companies began to phase out their own trailer departments and asked N.S.S. to provide a talent base in each studio which would create and produce the trailers. This man was on National Screen's payroll but he was exiled to the respective studios—these were National Screen employees, paid very well because there were not that many of them about. These were specialists; these were men who could work on a picture from the time it got started, picking out key scenes, work with the director and producer and sales department and come up with a format which was acceptable to the company. Once that had been approved by the company the negative was turned over to N.S.S., who then made prints and supplied them to their own exchanges around the country.

Q: How did National Screen make money? Did they charge the studios?

A: No, no—National Screen set up their own distribution contracts, renting the trailers to the theatres and arranging for delivery. During that period every theatre played about four pictures a week, a double feature on Monday, Tuesday and Wednesday and then it changed to another double feature on Thursday to Sunday. So, these theatres needed four trailers for the next week's program. N.S.S. set up what we called a T-deal. These theatres made an overall contractual commitment to National Screen, and they paid per week as a regular fee. In return, National Screen agreed to fulfill all of their trailer requirements, which if they were playing four pictures a week could be 208 trailers a year. These days N.S.S. is just a distribution service, the creative work has gone to new companies set up just for that purpose, not like the early days.'

Q: So how did National Screen work with the studios?

A: N.S.S. was created to get the major companies back into their primary business of making movies and not selling trailers or posters or anything else. But none of the companies had a contractual relationship with National Screen—this was set up originally as a loose confederation—any company could pull out whenever it liked. And periodically one of the companies in the N.S.S. spectrum would decide that N.S.S. was screwing them and would pull back—they'd suddenly discover they wanted N.S.S. to handle posters but didn't want them to handle trailers—which became difficult. Warner's was always a problem—they eventually set up their own trailer department in the mid–30s. Ed Selzer was head of their press book department and he was moved up to be head of the trailer department. Columbia was another one, though Arthur Houseman did most of their trailers, whether through N.S.S. or not.

Q: What was the financial advantage of the studios using National Screen?

A: National Screen paid a royalty to the companies based on the amount of business done on trailers and posters—the percentage was established early on. The more theatres wanted to run the trailer the more money the studios would get.

Q: Where did trailers come in a theatre's program?

A: Between the films. Between double features, and normally after the better picture, the one people came to see. They would run the trailers after the good picture was over, and before the second.

Q: How were trailers regarded in terms of other advertising materials?

A: There was a general consensus that the trailer was the most important: there was no waste; you had a captive audience in a movie theatre; every one of them was a potential customer. If you could intrigue them with what you showed on the screen, they'd come back the next week. The only 100 percent motion picture coverage was the trailer. It was like selling strawberries. If you want to sell a box of strawberries you make sure the big ones are on the top, the rotten ones are underneath. It was the same when they made a trailer: you pick only the scenes that'll help you sell your picture.

Q: How much scope did trailer makers have to be individual or unique?

A: The studios retained control, from the very start of N.S.S. Every trailer had to be approved. Not just by the studios; there was the AAC as well, the Advertising Board. If you put in something that was questioned you'd have to take it out, get it re-edited. You had to get approval on every piece of advertising, every poster.

APPENDIX IV

Interview with Simon Ashberry
December 21, 2006

Simon Ashberry is Orange Film Channel Manager, and was responsible for overseeing the unique videophone campaign for *Star Wars Episode III: Revenge of the Sith*.

Q: Can you give me some background as to why Orange decided to make trailers available for download onto phones? Was there a reason why trailers were considered suitable — consumer demand, a convenient file size for the technology?

A: When videophones first came onto the market, few commercial deals were in place for premium mobile video content so trailers—which are viewed as free, promotional content by the film industry—were an ideal place to start. It is a short video format that consumers were already familiar with and most trailers are around two minutes or less, which is ideal for phones.

Q: What were the first trailers to be downloadable on Orange phones?

A: The very first were for the ten films nominated for the Orange Film of the Year at the Baftas in February 2004. These were provided as part of our sponsorship of the awards.

Q: In 2004, Orange made trailers and movie clips from *The Incredibles* (2004) and *Shrek* (2004) available for download. Why were these films chosen? Were they successful with consumers?

A: By the end of 2004 Orange had a deal in place with MyMovies.Net to supply us with trailers for all films which made the UK box office top ten. *The Incredibles* and *Shrek 2* were supplied as part of that agreement and both proved among our most popular trailers of the year. Animation has always worked well on mobile.

Q: How successful are trailer downloads? Are there figures available for amount of downloads for each trailer, or in comparison with other phone content?

A: Downloads of trailers are generally higher than those for content such as Java games, True Tones, etc., simply because they have no premium charge attached to them — though there is in fact a cost incurred because of the data transfer.

Star Wars

Q: What content was included in the initial phase of the *Star Wars* campaign (i.e., video clips, ringtones, imagery)? Why were these chosen?
A: From the very start, the campaign included all available content types — video clips, ringtones in all formats including sound effects and voicetones and wallpapers. The aim was to offer different content types to ensure there was something for everyone regardless of what type of phone they had.

Q: What was added to the *Star Wars* package over time? Were these items chosen by Orange/selected by Lucasfilm?
A: We later added to the suite of content several Java games once they were developed and also an avatar messaging product. These ideas were developed by Orange in conjunction with Lucasfilm.

Q: For what length of time were these elements downloadable? Are they still available through Orange World?
A: All *Star Wars* content is still available and still sells really well! We had another surge of interest when the original films were released on DVD on September 11, 2006.

Q: How is the success of this kind of project rated? Is it number of downloads, new phones sold, awareness of new packages?
A: My team were judged on the amount of revenue generated; however, other parts of Orange were more keen on brand awareness, the positive effect of being associated with *Star Wars* and we did also sell specific handsets packaged as *Star Wars* phones.

Q: When did the *Episode III: Revenge of the Sith* trailer debut for videophones?
A: It was first available on all phones including 3G in November 2004.

Q: Was the content the same as the cinema trailer?
A: No, it was a simultaneous release of the same trailer in cinemas and on phones.

Q: Were any changes made to the content for its 3G screening? How was it formatted — widescreen/full screen? Was the formatting done at Orange, or by Lucasfilm?
A: It was made available in full-screen format by Lucasfilm.

Q: Were other trailers added at any point?
A: Further trailers were added and the same [format issues] applied to these as above.

Q: What was the goal of adding/promoting the *Episode III* trailer?

A: Orange aims to make its film channel the most compelling in the mobile marketplace and having the best trailers is part of that. Also, trailers may not carry a premium charge but there are data costs incurred.

Q: How successful was it? Are there download figures available?

A: Unfortunately this is commercially sensitive but I can say that the *Episode III* trailer was by far our most popular video clip of the year.

Q: What other features/downloads were added with the promotion of *Episode III*?

A: There were other video clips, both from *Episode III* and the earlier Star Wars films, plus behind-the-scenes clips of the making of *Episode III*. Again, these were generally available to video-enabled customers but the experience for 3G phones was undoubtedly superior.

Q: A similar campaign was launched to promote *Superman Returns*— was this film chosen to fulfill a particular marketing strategy?

A: I wasn't personally involved in the early part of this deal but essentially we hoped to repeat the success of *Star Wars* by offering content for a new, much-anticipated cinema release together with a package exploiting the franchise's back catalogue.

Q: Was the choice of film fuelled by Orange, or Warner Bros.' willingness to move into the 3G market?

A: 3G was only a contributing factor in this decision as Orange's aim was to provide compelling *Superman Returns* content to all customers whatever phone they had.

Q: When did the trailer go live, and which version was used? Again, were there format issues, and was the formatting done at WB or Orange?

A: The trailer went live in the autumn of 2005. WB supplied the trailer in a master format which was transcoded by Orange's systems into versions which could be supported by our range of handsets.

Q: What other features were available for *Superman Returns*?

A: It was a similar package to that for *Star Wars*: wallpapers, video clips, ringtones, voice tones and a Java game plus some new content types that have come on stream more recently such as screensavers, videotones and calling tunes.

Q: What do you see as the next step in terms of trailers on 3G videophones?

A: 3G opens up many more possibilities because of the option of streaming rather than download which limits the size of video clips according to the memory capacity on each phone. Orange TV, which streams video content in different channels, is already beginning to show the potential for having trailers shown in that format.

Q: Presuming trailers are still part of the 3G experience, do you think companies will ever produce 3G-specific trailers to fit with the smaller screen? Would this be something Orange would actively pursue, or would it be left to the film companies who supply you with content?

A: It's possible, although mobile generally is very much on the periphery for most film companies at the moment. What is more likely is that Orange will actively pursue user-generated content in the same way that websites like YouTube have made a success of.

Q: What attributes does Orange look for in order to publicize a film through its 3G offerings? Is it brand led?

A: To a certain extent, although we are also likely to go for content we think is a good match for our user profile. In recent months we have found funny and/or edgy films such as *Borat* to have particularly captured our users' imagination as much as big brands such as James Bond.

Q: How can people get hold of any of this material? Is the content only accessible through Orange videophones, or is it available elsewhere?

A: Many of the trailers we carry on Orange World are also available in a similar format on *www.orange.co.uk* but obviously the customer experience is very different. To see 3G in action for yourself it really is best to try to get an Orange 3G phone!

Chapter Notes

Introduction

1. Only two books, and a handful of academic articles, have considered the trailer as anything other than a loud, over-revelatory nuisance. See, for example, Lisa Kernan, *Coming Attractions: Reading American Movie Trailers* (Austin: University of Texas Press, 2004); Mary Beth Haralovich and Cathy Root Klaprat, "*Marked Woman* and *Jezebel*: The Spectator in the Trailer," *Enclitic* (Fall 1981/Spring 1982): 66–74; Michael Goodwin, "The Lost Films of Alfred Hitchcock," *New West* (April 1981): 84–87, 142; Paolo Lughi, "When Saying Is Getting Somebody to Do Something: Manipulations and Speech Acts in Verbal Language of the Trailer," *Semiotic Enquiry/Recherches Semiotiques* 4, 3–4: 356–371; James P. McElwee, "The Trailer," *Films in Review* 39, 10 (October 1988): 472–479; Alain Kerzoncuf and Nándor Bokor, "Alfred Hitchcock's Trailers," *Senses of Cinema* 35 (April–June 2005).

2. Howard T. Lewis, *The Motion Picture Industry* (New York: D. Van Nostrand Company, 1933), p. 248.

3. Andy Medhurst, "The Big Tease," *Sight & Sound* 8, 7 (July 1998): 24–26.

4. Although his book on film trailers has been available in German for several years, Vinzenz Hediger's work on trailers has, at the time of this writing, been unavailable in translation. His forthcoming *Nostalgia for the Coming Attraction: American Movie Trailers and the Culture of Film Consumption* will reveal his approach to trailer study in more depth, but it was not available at the time of this writing.

5. Janet Staiger, "Announcing Wares, Winning Patrons, Voicing Ideals: Thinking about the History and Theory of Film Advertising," *Cinema Journal* 29, 3 (Spring 1990): 3–31.

6. Barbara Klinger, "Digressions at the Cinema: Reception and Mass Culture," *Cinema Journal* 28, 4 (Summer 1989): 3–19.

7. Haralovich and Klaprat, "*Marked Woman* and *Jezebel*: The Spectator in the Trailer."

8. Lisa Kernan, *Coming Attractions: Reading American Movie Trailers* (Austin: University of Texas Press, 2004), p. 3.

9. Robert C. Allen, "From Exhibition to Reception: Reflections on the Audience in Film History," in *Screen Histories: A Screen Reader*, ed. Annette Kuhn and Jackie Stacey (Oxford: Oxford University Press, 1998), p. 13.

10. Thomas Elsaesser, "The New Film History," *Sight & Sound* 55, 4 (Autumn 1985): 247.

11. Elsaesser, "The New Film History," 247.

12. David Bordwell and Noel Carroll, "History and Analysis," in *Post-Theory: Reconstructing Film Studies* (Madison: University of Wisconsin Press, 1996), p. 405.

13. Richard Maltby, "'A Brief Romantic Interlude': Dick and Jane Go to 3 ? Seconds of the Classical Hollywood Cinema," in *Post-Theory: Reconstructing Film Studies*, ed. Bordwell and Carroll, pp. 434–459; Donald Crafton, "*The Jazz Singer*'s Reception in the Media and at the Box Office," in *Post-Theory: Reconstructing Film Studies*, ed. Bordwell and Carroll, pp. 460–480.

14. Bordwell and Carroll, "Introduction," in *Post-Theory: Reconstructing Film Studies*, pp. xvi–xvii.

15. Jeffrey Richards, "Rethinking British Cinema," in *British Cinema: Past and Present*, ed. Justine Ashby and Andrew Higson, pp. 21–34 (London: Routledge, 2000), p. 21.
16. B. F. Taylor, *The British New Wave: A Certain Tendency?* (Manchester: Manchester University Press, 2006), p. 129.
17. John Gibbs, *Mise-en-scène: Film Style and Interpretation* (London, New York: Wallflower Press, 2002), p. 5.
18. Susan Hayward and Ginette Vincendeau's collection, *French Film: Text and Context*, also stresses the desirability of combining these approaches, describing "Film *texts* emerge from a complex network of *contexts*, or determinants, which include the aesthetic project of their author(s): industrial and financial constraints, historical circumstances and discourses about history, the presence (or absence) of stars, generic patterns and critical discourses." The essays in their book focus on individual film analysis, and consider the ways in which these films "textually inscribe and rework these contexts." The focus on textual analysis here is strong, but the range of work within the actual essays reveals a lack of a central methodological approach to how this combination of text and context can actually work. It is this attempt to theorize the process that *The New Film History* develops.
19. James Chapman, Mark Glancy and Sue Harper, "Introduction," in *The New Film History* (Basingstoke: Palgrave Macmillan, 2007), p. 1.
20. Chapman, Glancy and Harper, "Introduction," p. 7.
21. Chapman, Glancy and Harper, "Introduction," p. 7.
22. Chapman, Glancy and Harper, "Introduction," p. 7.
23. Chapman, Glancy and Harper, "Introduction," p. 8.
24. Mervyn Stokes, "*Gone with the Wind* (1939) and the Lost Cause: A Critical View," in *The New Film History*, ed. Chapman, Glancy and Harper, pp. 13–26; James Chapman, "'This Ship Is England': History, Politics and National Identity in *Master and Commander: The Far Side of the World* (2003)," in *The New Film History*, ed. Chapman, Glancy and Harper, pp. 55–68; Laurie Ede, "Art in Context: British Film Design of the 1940s," in *The New Film History*, ed. Chapman, Glancy and Harper, pp. 73–88; Mark Glancy, "*Blackmail* (1929): Hitchcock and Film Nationalism," in *The New Film History*, ed. Chapman, Glancy and Harper, pp. 185–200.
25. Sue Harper, "History and Representation: The Case of 1970s British Cinema," in *The New Film History*, ed. Chapman, Glancy and Harper, pp. 27–40; Jeffrey Richards, "The Politics of the Swashbuckler," in *The New Film History*, ed. Chapman, Glancy and Harper, pp. 119–136; Jonathan Munby, "From Gangsta to Gangster: The Hood Film's Criminal Allegiance with Hollywood," in *The New Film History*, ed. Chapman, Glancy and Harper, pp. 166–179; Sarah Street, "British Cinema, American Reception: *Black Narcissus* (1947) and the Legion of Decency," in *The New Film History*, ed. Chapman, Glancy and Harper, pp. 201–214.
26. Chapman, Glancy and Harper, "Introduction," p. 7.
27. Chapman, Glancy and Harper, "Introduction," p. 8.
28. Thomas Elsaesser, "The New Film History," 247.
29. Richards, "Rethinking British Cinema," p. 22.
30. Barbara Klinger, "Film History Terminable and Interminable: Recovering the Past in Reception Studies," *Screen* 38, 2 (Summer 1997): 127–128.
31. David A. Cook, *A History of Narrative Film*, 2d edition (New York: Norton, 1981), pp. 480–481.
32. Title cards, *Singin' in the Rain* trailer.
33. Title cards, *Singin' in the Rain* trailer.
34. Title cards, *Singin' in the Rain* trailer.
35. In a filmed interview, trailer academic Vinzenz Hediger commented that the introduction of innovations such as CinemaScope and color "did not significantly change either the structure, or the look, of trailers—you would still get, for example, wipes, roll-on titles, and narration." Although he has never expanded on this (unlikely) opinion, this book will demonstrate that the reverse of this is, in fact, more accurate. *Coming Attractions: The History of the Movie Trailer* (DVD, Kaleidoscope Creative Group, 2005).
36. *Coming Attractions: The History of the Movie Trailer* was financed and produced by the Andrew J. Kuehn Foundation. Kuehn, and his company, Kaleidoscope, become the focus of this individuated narrative when it covers the 1960s.
37. John Belton, *Widescreen Cinema* (Cambridge, Mass.: Harvard University Press, 1992), p. 6.
38. John Miljan narration, *The Jazz Singer* trailer, 1927.

39. John Miljan narration, *The Jazz Singer* trailer, 1927.
40. Scott Eyman, *The Speed of Sound: Hollywood and the Talkie Revolution, 1926–1930* (New York: Simon & Schuster, 1997), p. 14.
41. Trailers for *Lion and the Mouse* and *Tenderloin*, quoted in Donald Crafton, "Enticing the Audience: Warner Bros. and Vitaphone," in *History of the American Cinema: 4: The Talkies — American Cinema's Transition to Sound, 1926–1931*, ed. Tino Balio, pp. 120–126 (New York: Charles Scribner's Sons Macmillan Library Reference USA, Simon & Schuster Macmillan, 1987), p. 122–123.
42. Crafton, "Enticing the Audience: Warner Bros. and Vitaphone," p. 120.
43. Steve Neale, *Cinema and Technology: Image, Sound, Colour* (London: MacMillan Education/BFI, 1985), p. 1.
44. Kernan, *Coming Attractions: Reading American Movie Trailers*, p. 1.
45. The growth of the multiplex, which helped establish the cinema program into its current "advertising/trailers/feature" format, effectively ended the double feature and with it, any sense of these short films "trailing" after the A film in a cinema program.

Chapter One

1. Title card, *The Swan* trailer (1956).
2. Voiceover, *Beneath the 12 Mile Reef* trailer.
3. Voiceover, *Night After Night* trailer (1932); Title cards, *Jezebel* trailer (1938); Voiceover, *Casablanca* trailer (1942).
4. Widescreen formats such as Fox's Grandeur and Paramount's Magnafilm had attempted to increase screen and image width in the late 1920s and early 1930s. No trailers from this early "wide film" period exist for the purposes of comparison.
5. Many 1950s technological advances were either publicity gimmicks designed for a particular film, terms for specific special effects techniques, or cheaper versions of the main studio processes. A full list would include (in alphabetical order): Amazoscope, Aromarama, Cinema-Scope, CinemaScope-55, Cinerama, Dynamation, DuoVision, Emergo, Horrorscope, Hypno-Magic, Illusion-O, Mattascope, Mystimation, Naturama, Panavision, Percepto, Regalscope, Regiscope, Smell-O-Vision, Spectarama, SuperScope, Technirama, Terrorscope, VistaVision, and Wide Vision.
6. See, for example, articles by John Belton, J. Spellerberg and R. Hincha in the special CinemaScope issue of *Velvet Light Trap* 21 (Summer 1985); H. E. Bragg, "The Development of CinemaScope," *Film History* 2, 4 (1988): 359–371; S. Huntley, "Sponable's CinemaScope," *Film History* 5, 3 (September 1993): 298–320.
7. Charles Barr, "CinemaScope: Before and After," in *Film Theory and Criticism*, 4th ed., ed. Gerald Mast and Marshall Cohen, pp. 139–163 (Oxford: Oxford University Press, 1992); André Bazin, "Will CinemaScope Save the Film Industry?" in *Bazin at Work*, ed. Bert Cardullo, pp. 77–92 (London: Routledge, 1997).
8. Barr, "CinemaScope: Before and After," p. 155.
9. Bazin, "Will CinemaScope Save the Film Industry?," p. 90.
10. John Belton, *Widescreen Cinema* (Cambridge: Harvard University Press, 1992), p. 2.
11. Belton, *Widescreen Cinema*, p. 10.
12. Title cards and voiceover, *Beneath the 12 Mile Reef* trailer.
13. www.redballoon.net/~snorwood/book/index.html, accessed August 11, 2006.
14. John Miljan dialogue, *The Jazz Singer* trailer.
15. Voiceover, *Becky Sharp* trailer.
16. *The Search for Paradise* (1957) publicity material, quoted in Belton, *Widescreen Cinema*, p. 95.
17. Voiceover, *How the West Was Won* trailer.
18. Voiceover, *How the West Was Won* trailer.
19. Author interview with John Sittig, May 31, 2005. See Appendix 2.
20. *How the West Was Won* press book, p. 5.
21. Voiceover, *How the West Was Won* trailer.
22. The active sequences feature heavily in the film's promotional material. The press book relies on images of the buffalo stampede to "explain" the Cinerama process, and the buffalo,

Indian attack, train and river rapids are all featured in images that illustrate screen elements jumping out of the widescreen ratio—a further emphasis on the importance given to the audience envelopment aspect of Cinerama.

23. Voiceover, *How the West Was Won* trailer.
24. Author interview with John Sittig, May 31, 2005.
25. Voiceover, *Grand Prix* trailer; title cards, *2001: A Space Odyssey* Cinerama trailer.
26. Richard Carlson, *It Came from Outer Space* "flat" trailer.
27. Richard Carlson, *It Came from Outer Space* 3-D trailer.
28. Richard Carlson, *The Maze* 3-D trailer.
29. When titles are used in the *It Came from Outer Space* trailer, they tend to sell narrative events over technology: "Sights human eyes have never seen ... one of the most suspenseful stories ever filmed."
30. William R. Weaver, "Arch Oboler Will Make 3-Dimension Picture," *Motion Picture Herald* 186, 6 (February 9, 1952): 35.
31. Title cards, *House of Wax* "flat" trailers.
32. Belton, *Widescreen Cinema*, p. 98.
33. "Theatre Publicity using 3-D," *Today's Cinema*, 80, 6704 (February 25, 1953): 15.
34. www.rollanet.org/~vbeydler/van/vmcolect.htm, accessed July 4, 2006.
35. The third, the use of graphic title design, was impossible to judge based on the flat trailers that have survived. Unlike the use of depth photography or items thrusting at the screen, the titles in a 3-D trailer look exactly the same as in a flat one.
36. Quotations taken from written description on scripts for the *Creature from the Black Lagoon* "flat trailer" and "TV trailer #1 (60 seconds)"; *Revenge of the Creature* "script #1 (flat selling 3-D)," "teaser trailer" and "60-sec TV #1." Universal Script Archive, Margaret Herrick library.
37. Voiceover, Arlene Dahl and Fernando Lamas dialogue, *Sangaree* trailer.
38. Randolph Scott, *The Stranger with a Gun* "flat" trailer; title cards, *Those Redheads from Seattle* trailer (possible 3-D trailer).
39. "CinemaScope, *Robe* Triumph," *Hollywood Reporter* 126, 9 (September 17, 1953): 1.
40. Title card, *How to Marry a Millionaire* trailer.
41. Letter from Zanuck to Jerome Edwards, July 26, 1965. Fox Legal Files Box 1353, File 8087, "CinemaScope Short Subjects."
42. Title card, *How to Marry a Millionaire* trailer.
43. Author interview with John Sittig, May 31, 2005.
44. Daryl F. Zanuck, *The CinemaScope Parade* script, 20th Century–Fox Archive, UCLA Arts Special Collections.
45. Belton, *Widescreen Cinema*, p. 117.
46. "American Commentary," *Today's Cinema* 80, 6694 (February 11, 1954): 8.
47. Voiceover and title cards, *The Robe* trailer.
48. Tom Milne, ed., *Time Out Film Guide*, 3d ed. (London: Penguin, 1993), p. 599.
49. Memo from Darryl F. Zanuck to Spyros Skouras, July 3, 1953. Fox Legal Files, UCLA Arts Special Collections, File 8087 "CinemaScope."
50. Title cards, *How to Marry a Millionaire* trailer.
51. Title card, *The Great American Past-time* trailer.
52. Memo from Donald A. Henderson on "The Todd-AO Matter," September 16, 1963. Quoted in John Belton, *Widescreen Cinema*, p. 178.
53. Title card, *It Started with a Kiss* trailer.
54. Letter from Daryl F. Zanuck to Jerome Edwards, July 26, 1965. Fox Legal Files, UCLA Arts Special Collections.
55. This policy was discovered in original trailer scripts in the MGM, Universal and Paramount script archives at the Margaret Herrick library. Trailer scripts for *Bad Day at Black Rock* (1954), *The Cobweb* (1955), *Captain Lightfoot* (1955), *Rose Marie* (1954), *Seven Brides for Seven Brothers* (1954), *The Student Prince* (1954) and *Wings of the Hawk* (1953) all demonstrate this policy regarding widescreen, 3-D, and stereophonic sound.

Chapter Two

1. "Wide Vision and Stereophonic Sound" 1953 TV trailer, Universal Pictures Trailer Script Collection, Margaret Herrick Library, Los Angeles.

2. Lisa Kernan, *Coming Attractions: Reading American Movie Trailers*, p. 1.
3. Ed Buscombe, "All Bark and No Bite: The Film Industry's Response to Television," in *Popular Television in Britain: Studies in Cultural History*, ed. John Corner (London: BFI, 1991), p. 206.
4. Su Holmes, *British TV and Film Culture in the 1950s: Coming to a TV Near You* (Bristol: Intellect, 2005), p. 14. Other books that have deepened understanding of the Hollywood/television relationship include Tino Balio, ed., *Hollywood in the Age of Television* (Boston: Unwin Hyman, 1990), and William Boddy, *Fifties Television: The Industry and Its Critics* (Chicago: University of Illinois Press, 1993).
5. Christopher Anderson, *Hollywood TV: The Studio System in the Fifties* (Austin: University of Texas Press, 1994).
6. Anderson, *Hollywood TV: The Studio System in the Fifties*; Karel Ann Marling, *As Seen on TV: The Visual Culture of Everyday Life in the 1950s* (Cambridge, Mass.: Harvard University Press, 1994).
7. Holmes, *British TV and Film Culture in the 1950s*.
8. Holmes, "Looking At the Wider Picture on the Small Screen," *British TV and Film Culture in the 1950s*, pp. 219–250.
9. Jason Jacobs, *The Intimate Screen* (Oxford: Oxford University Press, 2000), p. 14.
10. Jacobs, *The Intimate Screen*, p. 10.
11. Jerry Wald, quoted in Alan Ames, "Utilizing Video," *New York Times* (September 16, 1951), 6X.
12. Nigel Kneale, "Not Quite So Intimate," *Sight & Sound* 28, 2 (Spring 1959): 86.
13. This was common practice in Hollywood trailer-making from 1912 through the 1960s.
14. *Born Yesterday* press book, p. 9.
15. Ames, "Utilizing Video," p. 6X.
16. *Born Yesterday* press book, p. 9.
17. Fred J. MacDonald, *One Nation Under Television: The Rise and Decline of Network TV* (Chicago: Nelson-Hall, 1990), p. 19.
18. Brad Chisholm, "Red, Blue, and Lots of Green: The Impact of Color Television on Feature Film Production," in *Hollywood in the Age of Television*, ed. Tino Balio, pp. 213–234, Boston: Unwin Hyam, 1990, p. 228.
19. Orrin E. Dunlap Jr., "Television Show Reveals Current Stage of the Art," *New York Times*, February 21, 1937.
20. www.tvhistory.tv/FergusonAd2UK.JPG, accessed November 7, 2006.
21. Anderson, *Hollywood TV: The Studio System in the Fifties*, p. 62.
22. Maurice Gorham, quoted in Buscombe, "All Bark and No Bite," p. 201.
23. Percy Kilbride became famous in 1947 as the character Pa Kettle, who then featured in a successful series of seven films between 1947 and 1955. *Bedtime for Bonzo* TV trailer script, Universal Pictures Trailer Script Collection.
24. Ames, "Utilizing Video," p. 6X.
25. en.wikipedia.org/wiki/Film_tinting, accessed November 9, 2006.
26. Ames, "Utilizing Video," p. 6X.
27. Ames, "Utilizing Video," p. 6X.
28. Tim Bell, "The Agency Viewpoint 3," in *British Television Advertising: The First Thirty Years*, ed. Brian Henry, pp. 437–453 (London: Century Benham, 1986), p. 438; David Bernstein, "The Television Commercial: An Essay," in *British Television Advertising: The First Thirty Years*, p. 254.
29. Bernard Charman, "Commentary," *Daily Film Renter* 7175 (July 24, 1956): 2.
30. Simon Brook, "The New Medium: Television Survey," *Daily Film Renter* (March 1, 1957): 8.
31. Bernard Charman, "Commentary," *Daily Film Renter* 7166 (July 11, 1956): 2.
32. Anon, *Kinematograph Weekly*, August 2, 1956, p. 5.
33. Bernard Charman, "Commentary," *Daily Film Renter* 7193 (August 20, 1956): 2.
34. *Jeopardy* 60-second TV script #1, Universal Pictures Trailer Script Collection.
35. Ames, "Utilizing Video," p. 6X.
36. Anderson, *Hollywood TV: The Studio System in the Fifties*, p. 134.
37. Chisholm, "Red, Blue, and Lots of Green: The Impact of Color Television on Feature Film Production," p. 224.

38. *Wings of the Hawk* 20-second trailer script "TV#3 (3-D Adventure)," Universal Pictures Trailer Script Collection.
39. *Wings of the Hawk* 20-second trailer scripts "TV#3 (3-D Adventure)" and "TV#2 (Sex)," Universal Pictures Trailer Script Collection.
40. *Abbot and Costello Go to Mars* trailer script "60 second TV#1," Universal Pictures Trailer Script Collection.
41. *Wings of the Hawk* 20-second trailer script "TV#2 (Sex)," Universal Pictures Trailer Script Collection.
42. *The Creature from the Black Lagoon* trailer script "60 sec TV#3," Universal Pictures Trailer Script Collection.
43. *The Black Shield of Falworth* trailer script "TV spot #1 (60 sec)," Universal Pictures Trailer Script Collection.
44. *Black Widow* press book, p. 8.
45. *Black Widow* press book, p. 8.
46. Observer, "Up and Down the Street," *Today's Cinema* (January 30, 1956): 4.
47. Belton, *Widescreen Cinema*, p. 218.
48. *The Black Shield of Falworth* trailer script "TV Spot #1 (60 sec)"; *Captain Lightfoot* trailer script "Trailer #1-A"; *Sign of the Pagan* trailer script "TV Trailer #1 (60 seconds)," Universal Pictures Trailer Script Collection.
49. Voiceover, *The Day the Earth Caught Fire*, "U.S. TV spot 1."
50. "Third Renter Uses Plug TV For Film," *Today's Cinema* 87, 7577 (August 1, 1956): 3
51. *Away All Boats* trailer scripts "TV #1 (60 seconds)," "TV#3 (20 seconds)" and "TV#8 (20 seconds)," Universal Pictures Trailer Script Collection.
52. For more on the introduction of feature excerpts into television program structures, see Holmes, *British TV and Film Culture in the 1950s*.
53. "Return to basic showmanship is needed—Al Duff," *Today's Cinema* 87, 7611 (September 19, 1956): 8.
54. Leo McKern dialogue, *The Day the Earth Caught Fire* "U.S. TV spot 1."
55. Voiceover, *The Day the Earth Caught Fire* "U.S. TV spot 1."
56. "The fate of the world was decided that day ... The Day the Earth Caught Fire. Provocative. Superb." Voiceover, *The Day the Earth Caught Fire* "U.S. TV spot 3."
57. Title cards and voiceover, *The Day the Earth Caught Fire* "U.S. TV spot 4."
58. Voiceover, *The Day the Earth Caught Fire* "U.S. TV spot 1."
59. Title cards and voiceover, *Wings of the Hawk* "TV#2 (Sex)," Universal Pictures Trailer Script Collection.
60. *Spartacus* trailer scripts, "TV Spot #1 60 second Woman Appeal Spot For Daytime Use," "TV Spot #2, 60 second Action," "TV Spot #3 60 seconds, Teenage Appeal," Universal Pictures Trailer Script Collection.
61. Voiceover, *Spartacus* trailer scripts, "TV Spot #1, 20 second (cast and action)," "TV Spot #2, 20 second (action)," "TV Spot #1 60 second Woman Appeal Spot For Daytime Use," "TV Spot #2, 60 second Action," "TV Spot #3 60 seconds, Teenage Appeal," "TV Spot #5, 20 second Action Appeal," "TV Spot #6, 20 second Teenage Appeal," Universal Pictures Trailer Script Collection.
62. Voiceover, *Spartacus* trailer script, "TV Spot #1 60 second Woman Appeal Spot For Daytime Use," Universal Pictures Trailer Script Collection.
63. Title cards, dialogue and voiceover, *Dr. Strangelove* trailer.
64. Steven Heller, "Mr. Roughcut," *Eye* 32 (Summer 1999): 1.
65. Voiceovers, *Dr. Strangelove* trailer.
66. Title cards, *Dr. Strangelove* trailer.
67. Philip H. Dougherty, "First Bang of a Big Bang Bang," *New York Times* (April 30, 1968), p. 75.
68. *Wings of the Hawk* trailer script "TV#2 (Sex)," Universal Pictures Trailer Script Collection.

Chapter Three

1. Neale, *Cinema and Technology: Image, Sound, Colour*, p. 2.
2. Kristin Thompson and David Bordwell, *Film History: An Introduction* (New York: McGraw-Hill, 1994), p. 715.

3. Vivian Sobchack, *Screening Space: The American Science Fiction Film* (New York: Ungar, 1988), p. 282.
4. Miranda J Banks, "Monumental Fictions: National Monument as a Science Fiction Space," *Journal of Popular Film and Television* 30, 3 (Fall 2002): 141.
5. Geoff King, *Spectacular Narratives: Hollywood in the Age of the Blockbuster* (London, IB Tauris, 2000), p. 2.
6. King, *Spectacular Narratives: Hollywood in the Age of the Blockbuster*, p. 42.
7. Although science fiction was a well-known literary genre through the popular success of writers H. G. Wells and Jules Verne, filmed science fiction remained scarce. Despite films such as *A Trip to the Moon* in 1902, *Metropolis* in 1927, and an adaptation of Wells's *Things to Come* in 1936, the genre's strongest motion picture tradition in the years before 1950 was the serialized screen adventures of pulp characters Buck Rogers and Flash Gordon.
8. *War of the Worlds* press book, p. 6.
9. Title card, *Destination Moon* trailer.
10. *The Lost World* trailer does refer to the length of its production ("Seven years to bring it to you — seven years of hard work") but does not link that to the creation or animation of its central technological star.
11. Title card, *The Lost World* trailer (original emphasis).
12. Voiceover, *King Kong* trailer.
13. The "eighth wonder of the world" line is also central to the trailer's balance between Kong as a larger-than-life figure (the extravagant spectacle rampaging through the city) and part of life (the wonder of the Kong "effect" as it interacts with New York scenes and locations).
14. George Pal, quoted in the *Destination Moon* press book, p. 3.
15. "First Pictures Nazi Rocket Bomb in U.S.," Universal Newsreel, available online at www.archive.org/details/1946-05-13_1st_Pictures_Nazi_Rocket_Bomb_in_US, accessed May 21, 2007.
16. Voiceover, *Destination Moon* trailer.
17. *The Great Rupert* was Pal's first attempt to combine live action and animation techniques, although *Rupert*'s animated squirrel was a fantasy creation, a cartoon, rather than the detailed "realism" of *Destination Moon*'s rockets, take-off gantries, and lunar landscapes. Pal's standing at Paramount was shaken by the failure of *The Great Rupert*, making *Destination Moon* that much more of a gamble against the "skeptics" at the studio. Jan Alan Henderson, "Lunar Ambition," *American Cinematographer* 81, 3 (March 2000): 111.
18. Title card, *Destination Moon* trailer.
19. James Wierzbicki, "Weird Vibrations: How the Theremin Gave Musical Voice to Hollywood's Extraterrestrial 'Others,'" *Journal of Popular Film and Television*, 30, 3 (Fall 2002): 127.
20. Effects departments were largely a creation of the 1930s, building on techniques (trick photography, miniatures and optical work) that can be seen as early as *A Trip to the Moon* in 1902. While visual effects work is most obvious in genre films such as *Metropolis* and *Things to Come*, it also added scale to Biblical epics (the flood in *Noah's Ark*) and historical melodrama (the burning of Atlanta in *Gone with the Wind*, the earthquake in *San Francisco*). Few of the non-genre films placed their special effects technologies in their trailer sales messages: despite their central disaster sequences, *Gone with the Wind*'s trailer focuses on Vivien Leigh, Clark Gable and David O. Selznick; and the trailer for *San Francisco* chooses Gable and a singing Jeanette MacDonald as its audience lures in place of its earthquake effects work.
21. 1950s science fiction films, with their visual spectacle, were popular with the Academy. Winners include: 1950: *Destination Moon*; 1951: *When Worlds Collide*; 1953: *War of the Worlds*; 1954: *20,000 Leagues Under the Sea*. As the popularity of science fiction faded, more "traditional" effects films got the Academy Award: 1956: *The Ten Commandments* beats *Forbidden Planet*; 1958: *Ben Hur* beats *Journey to the Center of the Earth*.
22. That is not to say that fantasy films did not remain popular — *Jungle Book* was nominated for the Academy Award in 1942 — but that the verisimilitude of recreated wartime battles dominated effects work for several years, resulting in nominations for *Foreign Correspondent* (1940); *Flight Command, Sea Wolf* and *A Yank in the RAF* (1941); *Flying Tigers, Mrs. Miniver, One of Our Aircraft Is Missing* (1942); *Air Force, Bombardier, So Proudly We Hail, Stand by for Action* (1943); *Days of Glory, Secret Command* (1944); *They Were Expendable* (1945). A post-war return to fantasy is arguably reflected by the award-winning success of the ghostly *Wonder Man* (1945) and *Blithe Spirit* (1946).

23. Not all of the rocket images are special effects; some were stock footage of American Viking missile tests, as well as V2 launches.
24. Vivian Sobchack, *Screening Space*, p. 141.
25. Dialogue and voiceover, *Earth vs. the Flying Saucers* trailer.
26. Voiceover and title cards, *Forbidden Planet* trailer.
27. Voiceover, *Forbidden Planet* trailer.
28. Title card, *Forbidden Planet* trailer — original emphasis.
29. *Forbidden Planet* trailer.
30. Gail Morgan Hickman. *The Films of George Pal* (London: Thomas Yoseloff Ltd., 1977), p. 69.
31. Hickman. *The Films of George Pal*, p. 99.
32. Patricia D. Netzley, *Encyclopedia of Movie Special Effects* (Phoenix: Oryx Press, 2000), p. 5.
33. References to the importance of *Star Wars* and special effects in the Hollywood industry can be found in Neale, *Cinema and Technology*, p. 2; Thompson and Bordwell, *Film History*, p. 715; Gregg Rickman, "Introduction," p. xiv; Thomas Schatz, "The New Hollywood," in *Film Theory Goes to the Movies*, ed. Jim Collins, Hilary Radner and Ava Preacher Collins, pp. 8–36 (New York: Routledge, 1993).
34. Mark Hamill and Carrie Fisher dialogue, *Star Wars* teaser. The special effects images are created by motion control, a technique that refers to the layering of effects shots (e.g., model spaceships, star backgrounds, matte images) through the repetition of camera movements, in order to create the illusion of a spaceship passing by the camera. Mechanical motion control was used on *2001: A Space Odyssey*, plotting each movement frame-by-frame then manually moving the camera on each "pass." For *Star Wars*, a computerized motion control system was created — it stored and exactly duplicated the camera movement in order to produce the fast-moving space dogfights required for the film.
35. The trailer features no John Williams score, and many of the effects shots are unfinished, but the trailer does link each image with its unique sound effect: the hum of the lightsaber, the sizzling whine of a laser bolt, the low throb of the Falcon's engines, and the thin whine of a TIE fighter. These help highlight the effects and were also used as the basis of the 1977 *Star Wars* radio trailers.
36. James Gunn, "A Short History of the Space Program; or, A Funny Thing Happened on the Way to the Moon," *Vertrex* 2, 1 (April 1974).
37. Voiceover, *Star Wars* main trailer.
38. Mark Cotta Vaz and Patricia Rose Duignan, *Industrial Light and Magic: Into the Digital Realm* (London: Virgin Publishing, 1996), p. 4.
39. Later trailers for "Special Editions" of both *Alien* and *Close Encounters* abandon this approach, assuming prior knowledge of the main visual effects work. The *Close Encounters Special Edition* (1980) trailer displays small alien figures, and a long shot of the model mothership as it rises into frame. A similar concept can also be seen in *ET* and *Star Wars* special edition trailers, where the re-mastered effects become the main, sometimes only, reason to re-watch the film in a cinema.
40. Voiceover, *Close Encounters of the Third Kind* trailer.
41. *Starlog* and *Cinefex* magazines, with their focus on the genre and the production of special effects, launched in 1976 and 1980, respectively.
42. The film credits him as "special photographic effects director" and "2nd unit director."
43. Voiceover, *Star Trek: The Motion Picture* teaser trailer.
44. Howard Maxford, *The George Lucas Companion* (London: B. T. Batsford, 1999), p. 87.
45. Voiceover, *The Empire Strikes Back* teaser trailer.
46. Iain Blair, "Film Trailers: Attracting Audiences With Style," *On Location* (January 1983): 46.
47. Voiceover, *Star Trek II: The Wrath of Khan* trailer.
48. The late 1970s also saw the introduction of "Making Of" videos, behind-the-scenes production documentaries that were released concurrently with the film's theatrical debut. As with many things in this period, this move was spurred by *The Making of Star Wars* video, released in 1979. www.davisdvd.com/misc/starwars/ep_misc.htm, accessed January 10, 2007.
49. Voiceover, *Terminator 2: Judgment Day* trailer #2: "Same Make, New Mission."
50. Dean Devlin, quoted in Tom Shone, *Blockbuster: How Hollywood Learned to Stop Worrying and Love the Summer* (London: Simon & Schuster, pp. 233–234).

51. Tom Shone, *Blockbuster*, p. 237
52. The lack of agency responsible for the destruction of the White House adds a curious layer to the trailer. Appearing before the title "The Day We Fight Back," the meaning of the image is obtuse: was the White House blown up because "we fight back" or do "we fight back" because it was blown up?
53. Tom Shone, *Blockbuster*, p. 239.
54. Tim Prokop, "Launching *Apollo 13*," *Cinefex* 63 (September 1995): 60.
55. Prokop, "Launching *Apollo 13*," p. 62.
56. Comparison with the 1983 trailer for *The Right Stuff* is also telling: the earlier trailer focuses on patriotism and character, with only brief glimpses of its rocket launch special effects, and little mention of the technological narrative underpinning the story.
57. Barbara Klinger, "Digressions at the Cinema: Reception and Mass Culture," *Cinema Journal* 28, 4 (Summer 1989): 15–16.
58. Despite being the trailer that features the most visual effects shots—almost every image was digitally manipulated by correction-correction technology—the *Pleasantville* trailer makes no reference to the behind-the-scenes process. Netzley, *Encyclopedia of Movie Special Effects*, p. 169.
59. Jody Duncan, "A Look Back," *Cinefex* 80 (January 2000): 161.
60. Author interview with Paul N. Lazarus, February 5, 1994. See Appendix 3.
61. Jason Silverman, "Meet Avi Arad, the Man Who Launched the Superhero Craze," *Wired*, www.wired.com/entertainment/hollywood/news/2007/05/spider_aviard?currentPage=2, accessed May 7, 2007.

Chapter Four

1. Henry Jenkins, *Textual Poachers: Television Fans and Participatory Culture* (New York: Routledge, 1992).
2. Henry Jenkins, *Convergence Culture: Where Old and New Media Collide* (New York: New York University Press, 2006), p. 133.
3. Jenkins, *Convergence Culture: Where Old and New Media Collide*, p. 131.
4. Although retrospectively titled *Star Wars IV: A New Hope*, the chapter will mirror the video trailers and refer to this original film trilogy as *Star Wars*, *The Empire Strikes Back*, and *Return of the Jedi*. Following the modern trailer texts, the prequel trilogy will be referred to as *The Phantom Menace* (1999), *Attack of the Clones* (2002), and *Revenge of the Sith* (2005).
5. Advertisement for "20th Century–Fox Video: Star Wars," Video Review, September 1982. Reproduced at www.davisdvd.com/misc/starwars/ep4.htm, accessed January 9, 2007.
6. Voiceover, *Star Wars* video trailer, "CBS FOX Video Time In" trailer feature, *The Empire Strikes Back* video (1984).
7. Douglas Gomery, *Shared Pleasures: A History of Movie Presentation in the United States* (Madison, University of Wisconsin Press, 1992), p. 276; Mark Jancovich, Lucy Faire and Sarah Stubbins, *The Place of the Audience: Cultural Geographies of Film Consumption* (London: BFI, 2003), p. 193.
8. www.davisdvd.com/misc/starwars/ep_misc.htm, accessed January 9, 2007.
9. Advertisement for Portland-Video, *TV and Home Video* 2, 2 (February 1980): 52.
10. Gomery, *Shared Pleasures*, p. 282. The porn industry's early adoption of new dissemination technology has long fuelled the belief that the technology in question is guaranteed commercial success – the industry was an early adopter of home video, DVD and the Internet, and is making content available for mobile videophones.
11. Bart Mills, "Videograms," *TV and Home Video*, 2, 2 (February 1980): 51; "Video Reviews: Electric Blue 004," *TV and Home Video*, 3, 5 (May 1981): 45.
12. The decision to put trailers at the start of videocassettes mirrors a similar change in cinemas. After years of trailers appearing in the middle of a rolling cinema program, the growth of multiplex exhibition sites replaced the continual loop with the set program of advertisements, trailers and feature film that has remained dominant. It is uncertain whether video impacted on cinema, or vice versa.
13. Magnetic Video was the first home video company to license films from a major studio: 50 films from 20th Century–Fox in 1978. Fox bought the company in 1981, rebranding it

as Fox Video. CBS Video Enterprises had previously released output from CBS News, CBS Records and CBS television.

14. Voiceover, "CBS FOX Time In," *The Empire Strikes Back* video.

15. This aesthetic choice dates the video program, recalling graphic design motifs of the mid–1980s that were seen in locations as varied as the Duran Duran album cover *Rio*, and the *Max Headroom* TV show.

16. *The Right Stuff* video includes trailers for *Police Academy* (1984), *Of Unknown Origin* (1983) and *The Man with Two Brains* (1983); *Heartbreak Ridge* features short previews for *Mannequin* (1987), *Police Academy 4* (1987), *Little Shop of Horrors* (1986) and *Superman IV: The Quest for Peace* (1987).

17. Videos viewed: *Operation Petticoat* (The Video Collection, 1985); *She'll Be Wearing Pink Pyjamas* (Virgin Premiere Video, 1985) and *Mickey's Christmas Carol* (Buena Vista, 1983).

18. Gomery, *Shared Pleasures*, p. 287.

19. *Return of the Jedi* video (CBS FOX, 1989).

20. Andrew J. Kuehn, quoted on www.movietrailertrash.com/views/history.html (accessed April 14, 2005).

21. John Wyver, *The Moving Image: An International History of Film, Television and Video* (Oxford: BFI, 1989), pp. 277–278.

22. In order to approximate the original viewing experience, this trailer (and the *Alien/Die Hard* example) was watched in its intended 4:3 TV screen ratio.

23. Voiceover, "Star Wars Trilogy Widescreen Collection" video trailer, *Return of the Jedi* video.

24. There are two other instances where the full-screen image retreats into the center of screen, then reveals the missing visual information on either side: a lightsaber battle between Luke Skywalker and Darth Vader, and a point-of-view camera shot that twists and turns as it descends into the trench around the Death Star. Both demonstrate the lack of visual information available because the picture has been cropped.

25. Fox Video, "Widescreen Collection" booklet, contained within *Alien* "widescreen" video release, 1991, p. 7.

26. Fox Video, "Widescreen Collection" booklet, p. 7.

27. Fox Video, "Widescreen Collection" booklet, p. 4.

28. Voiceover, "Star Wars Trilogy Widescreen Collection" video trailer, *Return of the Jedi* video.

29. Anthony Goldschmidt, Intralink trailer company, www.movietrailertrash.com/views/history.html, accessed April 14, 2005.

30. Lizo Mzimba, "Force Fed," *Empire* 116 (February 1999): p. 44.

31. Star Wars fans desperate to watch (and re-watch) the new trailer allegedly increased the profits for those films by as much as 25 percent: Kendall Hamilton, Devin Gordon and Alisha Davis, "The Second Coming," *Newsweek* 132, 22 (November 30, 1998): 84.

32. As with all Hollywood "records" this has been beaten by subsequent projects such as *Lord of the Rings* and *Superman Returns* that have honed Internet promotional techniques to a fine art.

33. Sara Gwenllian Jones, "Web Wars: Resistance, Online Fandom and Studio Censorship," in *Quality Popular Television*, ed. Mark Jancovich and James Lyons, pp. 163–177 (London, BFI, 2003), p. 165.

34. Spoiler, noun: a remark which reveals important plot elements from books or movies, thus denying the reader (or the article) the proper suspense when reading the book or watching the movie. Definition from computing-dictionary.thefreedictionary.com/spoiler.

35. With no need to have the Internet advertising passed by the MPAA, the trailers can also stretch the boundaries of what to show: the "Change Your Life" trailer splices half-second images of Helena Bonham-Carter and Brad Pitt having sex into its montage, with Bonham-Carter's growing orgasmic moans forming the soundscape for the entire ad.

36. This direct address may also impact on the soundtrack in these spots, which features a disparate selection of noises and music cut and pasted together (a technique associated with music producers The Dust Brothers, who produced the film's soundtrack, and may have been involved with these trailers). Behind Norton's voice, the five online trailers mix an eclectic combination of hip hop, dramatic stabs, choral music, along with sound effects of sexual groaning, cartoon footsteps (familiar from Hanna Barbera's animation) and the bionic "noise" of the Six Million Dollar Man.

37. Anon, "Trailer Trash," *Sight & Sound* 10, 10 (October 2000): p. 9.
38. Yoda dialogue, *Star Wars: Episode II: Attack of the Clones*, "Mystery" teaser.
39. "Online Trailer: Frequently Asked Questions," www.starwars.com/site/news/2001/11/news20011106.html, accessed January 5, 2007.
40. "Lord Rings Up Internet Users," www.theonering.net (April 11, 2000), accessed August 24, 2006.
41. www.elizabethtown.com/home.html: the "Music," "Home Video," and "First Look" trailers were accessed and viewed on January 5–7, 2007.
42. Voiceover, *The Hitchhiker's Guide to the Galaxy* internet trailer.
43. Voiceover, *The Hitchhiker's Guide to the Galaxy* internet trailer.
44. Billy Wright (Orange Group Director of Content and Sponsorships): quoted in "Orange Mobile Phone Users Now Have The Power of the Force" Orange Press Release, October 1, 2004. Archived on www.starwars.com/episode-iii/release/promo/news20041001.html, accessed August 22, 2006.
45. The *Revenge of the Sith* trailer was downloaded from the Orange World portal and viewed on a Nokia 6630 videophone on January 10, 2007. Although regarded as free content, all trailer downloads available via Orange are subject to a data transfer charge.
46. As well as film-specific phone accessories like wallpaper, ringtones and trailers, Orange has the weekly "Orange Wednesday" two-for-one cinema ticket offer; sponsor the Orange British Academy of Film and Television Awards; and short "Orange Film Funding Board" comedy films run before film screenings to remind people to switch off their mobile phones.
47. Author interview with Simon Ashberry, Manager Orange Film Channel. See Appendix 4.
48. The ten trailers available for videophones were: *Bruce Almighty* (2003), *Calendar Girls* (2003), *Finding Nemo* (2003), *Johnny English* (2003), *Lord of the Rings: Return of the King* (2003), *Love Actually* (2003), *Matrix Reloaded* (2003), *Pirates of the Caribbean: The Curse of the Black Pearl* (2003), *Terminator 3: Rise of the Machines* (2003), and *X-Men 2* (2003).
49. Author interview with Simon Ashberry, Manager Orange Film Channel. See Appendix 4.
50. Author interview with Simon Ashberry, Manager Orange Film Channel. See Appendix 4.
51. Steve Jobs, quoted in Leander Kahney, "Apple Gives Video the iPod Touch," Wired News (October 12, 2005): available at www.wired.com/news/business/0,69193-0.html, accessed January 29, 2007.
52. www.apple.com/pr/library/2005/oct/12ipod.html, accessed January 9, 2007.
53. Both the *King Kong* and *Narnia* trailers were available as compressed zip files that could be downloaded and added to iTunes. *Kong* was available via www.apple.com in early November 2005 (ipastudio.com/forums/showthread.php/t/2360, accessed January 29, 2007). *Narnia* iPod content (including a trailer and short features) was released on November 30, 2005 (ipastudio.com/forums/showthread.php?t=2489 accessed January 29, 2007).
54. As well as the videophone's smaller screen resolution and pixel size, the playback format of the media file is a major issue for the quality of the image on phones and the Internet. While many mobiles use Mp4, Internet files are encoded for Quicktime or Windows Media — these offer better quality, but they require custom players that are not currently loaded onto mobile phones (due to the memory capacity of phone hardware). In terms of visual clarity, mobile phones also struggle to playback files that are encoded at a higher bit rate — which would include Quicktime or Windows Media.
55. www.lff.org.uk/content.php?CategoryID=797. The page also includes instructions for loading the trailers onto the iPod through iTunes.
56. Jenkins, Convergence Culture, p. 168.

Conclusion

1. Barbara Klinger, "Digressions at the Cinema: Reception and Mass Culture," *Cinema Journal* 28, 4 (Summer 1989): 9.
2. Universal vice-president Robert Cochrane, quoted in Janet Staiger, "Announcing Wares,

Winning Patrons, Voicing Ideals: Thinking About the History and Theory of Film Advertising," *Cinema Journal* 28, 3 (Spring 1990): 6.

3. Klinger, "Digressions at the Cinema: Reception and Mass Culture," pp. 3–19.

4. Thomas Elsaesser, "The New Film History," *Sight & Sound* 55, 4 (Autumn 1985): 247.

5. B. F. Taylor, *The British New Wave: A Certain Tendency?* p. 164.

6. Jonathan Munby, "From Gangsta to Gangster: The Hood Film's Criminal Allegiance with Hollywood," pp. 166–179; Sarah Street, "British Cinema, American Reception: *Black Narcissus* (1947) and the Legion of Decency," *The New Film History*, ed. Chapman, Glancy and Harper.

7. Richard Maltby, "'A Brief Romantic Interlude': Dick and Jane Go to 3? Seconds of the Classical Hollywood Cinema," in *Post-Theory: Reconstructing Film Studies*, ed. Bordwell and Carroll, pp. 434–459.

8. These trailers were first viewed at Tottenham Court Station. *Rocky Balboa* and *Ocean's 13* appear to be the first film trailers to make use of this technology. Other advertisers who have used the LCD screens include The Independent, Vodafone and Lucozade. These advertisements also used the multiple screens to portray different (related) visual messages, or animation that moved from screen to screen, keeping pace with the passenger. Information from www.grandvisual.com, accessed June 19, 2007.

9. Title cards, *Fantasia* and *Gone with the Wind* widescreen trailers.

10. "George Lucas to release the *Star Wars* movies in 3-D," www.movieweb.com/news/10/7210.php, accessed July 31, 2007.

11. Voiceover, *Star Wars* Trilogy Special Edition trailer.

12. *Brokeback to the Future* trailer, www.thetrailermash.com/brokeback-to-the-future-parody; *The Shining* romantic comedy trailer, www.thetrailermash.com/shining-romantic-comedy; Scary *Mary* trailer, www.thetrailermash.com/mary-poppins-horror/, accessed June 7, 2007.

13. Dialogue and voiceover, *Transporter 2* trailer.

14. Information from www.tzi.de/svp/index.html, accessed June 1, 2007.

15. "The One Abroad," www.starwars.com/episode-i/release/promo/f20000601/index.html, accessed August 7, 2007.

16. An "age gate" is an Internet system that requires the user to enter personal information (i.e., date of birth, zip code driver's license number). Access may also be restricted to certain hours in the evening and early morning. David M. Halbfinger, "Attention, Web Surfers: The Following Film Trailer May Be Racy or Graphic," *New York Times* (June 13, 2007): www.nytimes.com/2007/06/13/movies/13yell.html?ex=1339387200anden=5c292ac80cc2b0b2andei=5088andpartner=rssnytandemc=rss (accessed July 26, 2007); "BBC Statement: Trailer For *A Year with the Queen*," www.bbc.co.uk/pressoffice/pressreleases/stories/2007/07_july/12/apology.shtml, accessed July 20, 2007); "ESRB launching new game-trailer clampdown," *Gamespot UK News* (June 25, 2007): uk.gamespot.com/news/show_blog_entry.php?topic_id=25728372andpart=rssandsubj=6173105, accessed July 26, 2007.

17. Staiger, "Announcing Wares, Winning Patrons, Voicing Ideals: Thinking about the History and Theory of Film Advertising," p. 3.

Trailer-ography

1925
Circus Mania
Irish Luck
The Lost World
The Orphan of Paris

1926
The Ball of Fortune
Bluebeard's 7 Wives
Bride of the Storm

1927
Downhill
The Jazz Singer
Madame Pompadour

1928
Tropic Madness

1929
It's a Great Life
Noah's Ark

1930
Cape Forlorn
Journey's End
King of Jazz
Min and Bill

1931
The Bad Girl
Dracula

The Public Enemy
The Secret Witness
Top of the Bill

1932
Arrowsmith
Duck Soup
Frankenstein
I Am a Fugitive from a
  Chain Gang
Letty Lynton
One Hour with You
Night After Night
Scarface
Undercover Man

1933
42nd Street — Trailer A
42nd Street — Trailer B
Cavalcade
Dancing Lady
Footlight Parade
Gold Diggers of 1933
King Kong
Little Women
The Mummy
Radio Parade

1934
Chained
Death on the Diamond
The Man Who Knew Too
  Much

The Search for Beauty
The Thin Man

1935
Becky Sharp
Bonnie Scotland
Bride of Frankenstein
Captain Blood
Forever England
A Midsummer Nights
  Dream
Mutiny on the Bounty
Royal Cavalcade
The 39 Steps
Top Hat

1936
After the Thin Man
Camille
Dracula's Daughter
Fury
The Petrified Forest
San Francisco
Secret Agent
Wings of the Morning

1937
Bullets for Ballots
The Edge of the World
The Hurricane
In Old Chicago
The Lady Vanishes
Lost Horizons — teaser

A Star Is Born
Snow White & the Seven Dwarfs

1938

The Adventures of Robin Hood
Angels with Dirty Faces
Boys Town
The Divorce of Lady X
Happy Landing
Jezebel

1939

The Four Feathers
The Hunchback of Notre Dame
Intermezzo
Jamaica Inn
Mr. Smith Goes to Washington
Nurse Edith Cavell
The Roaring Twenties
Stagecoach

1940

City of Chance
Fantasia
The Fighting 69th
Foreign Correspondent
Girl in 313
Pinocchio
Rebecca
The Sea Hawk
The Thief of Baghdad

1941

A Woman's Face
Citizen Kane
Dive Bomber
Dumbo
49th Parallel
High Sierra
The Maltese Falcon
Mr. & Mrs. Smith
Sealed Lips
Suspicion
They Died with Their Boots On

1942

Across the Pacific
All Through the Night
Bambi
Casablanca
Fingers at the Window
Ghost of Frankenstein
The Glass Key
Grand Central Murder
Saboteur
This Gun for Hire
Yankee Doodle Dandy

1943

The Outlaw
Saludos Amigos
Shadow of a Doubt
Sherlock Holmes and the Secret Weapon (re-release)
Son of Dracula

1944

Double Indemnity
Gaslight
House of Frankenstein
To Have and Have Not
Henry V
Lifeboat
Ministry of Fear
National Velvet
Passage to Marseilles

1945

Adventure
Circumstantial Evidence
Conflict
Hangover Square
House of Dracula
Objective Burma!
The Picture of Dorian Gray
Spellbound
The Three Caballeros

1946

The Big Sleep
Deception
Dressed to Kill
It's a Wonderful Life
Make Mine Music
Notorious
The Postman Always Rings Twice
Strange Triangle
Terror by Night

1947

The Bishop's Wife
Blackmail
The Brasher Doubloon
Crossfire
Fun and Fancy Free
Hue & Cry
Lady in the Lake
Miracle on 34th Street
The Paradine Case
Ride the Pink Horse

1948

Abbott & Costello Meet Frankenstein
Act of Violence
Berlin Express
The Big Clock
Black Narcissus
The Cobra Strikes
Fort Apache
Key Largo
Kiss the Blood Off My Hands
Melody Time
The Pirate
Rope
Treasure of the Sierra Madre

1949

The Adventures of Ichabod and Mr. Toad
The Bribe
Kind Hearts and Coronets
Passport to Pimlico
The Third Man
Under Capricorn
White Heat

1950

All About Eve
Born Yesterday

Cinderella (Disney)
Destination Moon
Kim
Rocketship X-M
Stage Fright
Sunset Boulevard

1951

The African Queen
Alice in Wonderland
An American in Paris
The Day the Earth Stood
  Still
Detective Story
The Lavender Hill Mob
The Man in the White Suit
The Man from Planet X
On Dangerous Ground
Strangers on a Train
The Thing from Another
  World
When Worlds Collide

1952

Bwana Devil
High Noon
The Importance of Being
  Earnest
Ivanhoe
The Prisoner of Zenda
Singin' in the Rain
The Titfield Thunderbolt

1953

The Band Wagon
Beneath the 12-Mile Reef
The Big Heat
Calamity Jane
Carnival Story
Charge at Feather River
Devil's Canyon
Flight to Tangier
Fort Ti
From Here to Eternity
Gentlemen Prefer Blondes
The Glass Web
Gun Fury
Hannah Lee
Hondo
House of Wax

How to Marry a Million-
  aire — teaser
How to Marry a Million-
  aire (Italian)
How to Marry a Million-
  aire (German)
I Confess
Invaders from Mars
I, the Jury
It Came from Outer Space
Killers from Space
Louisiana Territory
Man in the Dark
The Master of Ballantrae
Mogambo
The Nebraskan
Peter Pan (Disney)
Project Moonbase
The Return of Captain
  Marvel (serial)
The Robe
Robot Monster
Roman Holiday
Sangaree
Second Chance
Shane
Split Second
The Stranger Wore a Gun
Those Redheads from Seat-
  tle
Wings of the Hawk

1954

The Barefoot Contessa
Beau Brummell
The Bounty Hunter
Brigadoon
Cat-Women of the Moon
The Command
Creature from the Black
  Lagoon
Dangerous Mission
Devil Girl from Mars
Dial M for Murder
The Diamond Wizard
Drums of Tahiti
The Egyptian
Escape from Fort Bravo
Executive Suite
Fantasia ("widescreen" re-
  release)

The Far Country
Female Jungle
The French Line
Gog
Gone with the Wind
  ("widescreen" re-release)
Gorilla at Large
Her Twelve Men
Jesse James Vs. the Daltons
Jivaro
Kiss Me Kate
Knights of the Round
  Table
The Last Time I Saw Paris
The Long, Long Trailer
The Mad Magician
The Maze
Miss Sadie Thompson
Money from Home
On the Waterfront
Phantom of the Rue
  Morgue
Private Hell 36
Rear Window
Rhapsody
River of No Return
Rose Marie
Seven Brides for Seven
  Brothers
Southwest Passage
A Star Is Born
Taza, Son of Cochise
Them!
Three Coins in the Foun-
  tain
Top Banana
20,000 Leagues Under the
  Sea
Valley of the Kings
Vera Cruz

1955

The Adventures of Quentin
  Durward
Bad Day at Black Rock
The Big Knife
The Blackboard Jungle
The Bridge on the River
  Kwai
The Cobweb
To Catch a Thief

Gentlemen Marry Brunettes
Gigantis the Fire Monster (Gojira no gyakushû)
Hit the Deck
I'll Cry Tomorrow
It's Always Fair Weather
The King's Thief
Kismet
Kiss Me Deadly
Lady and the Tramp
The Ladykillers
Love Me or Leave Me
Mister Roberts
Night of the Hunter
Oklahoma!
Picnic
Postmark for Danger, a.k.a. Portrait of Alison
The Quatermass Xperiment, a.k.a. Creeping Unknown
Rebel Without a Cause
Revenge of the Creature
Son of Sinbad
The Tender Trap
The Treasure of Pancho Villa
This Island Earth
To Hell and Back
The Trouble with Harry
Underwater!

1956

Around the World in 80 Days
The Bad Seed
Beyond a Reasonable Doubt
Bundle of Joy
The Court Jester
Earth vs. The Flying Saucers
The First Traveling Saleslady
Forbidden Planet
Giant
The Girl Can't Help It
The Great American Pastime
High Society — teaser
High Society — main trailer
Invasion of the Body Snatchers
The Killing
The Last Hunt
The Man Who Knew Too Much
The Opposite Sex
The Searchers
Somebody Up There Likes Me
The Swan
Tea & Sympathy
The Ten Commandments
These Wilder Years
tom thumb
War and Peace
The Wrong Man
X The Unknown

1957

The Abominable Snowman
Action of the Tiger
The Bad Seed
The Barretts of Wimpole Street
The Cosmic Monsters
Curse of Frankenstein
Designing Women
Don't Go Near the Water
Edge of the City
Hot Summer Night
The Invisible Boy
Jailhouse Rock
Les Girls
Lizzie
Man of a Thousand Faces
Monster from Green Hell
Pal Joey
Quatermass 2/Enemy from Space
Run of the Arrow
The Shiralee
Something of Value
To Catch a Thief
20 Million Miles to Earth
The Unholy Wife
Until They Sail
Will Success Spoil Rock Hunter?
The Wings of Eagles
Witness for the Prosecution

1958

Cat on a Hot Tin Roof
The Decks Ran Red
The Defiant Ones
Dracula/Horror of Dracula (U.S.)
Dragstrip Riot
Dunkirk
From the Earth to the Moon
Gigi
Man of the West
Mission to the Moon
Nowhere to Go
The Nun's Story
The Reluctant Debutante
Revenge of Frankenstein
Run Silent, Run Deep
Saddle the Wind
Some Came Running
South Pacific
Stage Struck
Touch of Evil
Verboten!
Vertigo (re-release)

1959

Anatomy of a Murder
Bell Book and Candle
Ben Hur
The Gazebo
The Giant Gila Monster
Green Mansions
The Hideous Sun Demon
Home from the Hill
The Horse Soldiers
The Hound of the Baskervilles
It Started with a Kiss
The Man Who Could Cheat Death
The Mummy
Never So Few
North by Northwest — main
North by Northwest — "Hitchcock Tours"

Trailer-ography

Nowhere to Go
Plan 9 from Outer Space
Rio Bravo
The Scapegoat
Sleeping Beauty
Solomon and Sheba
Some Like It Hot
The Woman Eater
The World, the Flesh and the Devil

1960

The Brides of Dracula
The Creature from the Haunted Sea
Exodus
Psycho
The Stranglers of Bombay
The Time Machine
The Two Faces of Dr. Jekyll

1961

Amazons of Rome
Breakfast at Tiffanys
The Curse of the Werewolf
The Day the Earth Caught Fire
King of Kings
One Hundred and One Dalmatians
Revolt of the Slaves

1962

Captain Clegg
Dr. No
How the West Was Won
The Manchurian Candidate
The Phantom of the Opera
Rear Window (re-release)
The Wonderful World of the Brothers Grimm

1963

The Birds
Cleopatra
The Damned
From Russia with Love
Irma La Douce

It's a Mad Mad Mad Mad World
Kiss of the Vampire
The Old Dark House
Samson and the Slave Queen
The Sword in the Stone
The Unearthly Stranger

1964

The Curse of the Mummy's Tomb
Dr. Strangelove
Evil of Frankenstein
Goldfinger
Goldfinger (TV)
The Gorgon
Hot Enough for June (TV)
Love in Las Vegas
Love in Las Vegas (TV)
Marnie
Nightmare
The Pink Panther
Revenge of the Gladiators
Sex and the Single Girl
A Shot in the Dark

1965

The Beach Girls and the Monster
Goldfinger/Dr. No (TV)
I, a Woman (Jag — en kvinna)
In Harm's Way
The Navy vs. the Night Monsters
The Robot vs. the Aztec Mummy
Spy in Your Eye
Thunderball
Thunderball (TV spots)
Women of the Prehistoric Planet

1966

Alfie (UK)
Alfie (U.S.)
Dracula: Prince of Darkness
Grand Prix

North by Northwest (re-release)
North by Northwest (re-release — TV)
Kiss the Girls and Make Them Die
The Last of the Secret Agents?
One Million Years B.C.
Plague of the Zombies
Rasputin
The Reptile
Thunderball/From Russia with Love (TV spots x 3)
Torn Curtain
Trunk to Cairo
The Witches/The Devil's Own (U.S.)

1967

Bonnie & Clyde
Born Losers
Camelot
Frankenstein Created Woman
The Good, the Bad & the Ugly
Helga
The Hellcats
Hells Angels on Wheels
The Jungle Book
The Mummy's Shroud
Quatermass and the Pit/ Five Million Years to Earth (U.S.)
Wild Rebels
You Only Live Twice

1968

Chitty Chitty Bang Bang
Chitty Chitty Bang Bang (French)
Chitty Chitty Bang Bang (TV)
College Girls
The Devil Rides Out
Dracula Has Risen from the Grave
Invitation to Ruin
Mission Mars

Planet of the Apes
2001: A Space Odyssey

1969

The Babysitter
Butch Cassidy and the Sundance Kid
Frankenstein Must Be Destroyed
Kenner
On Her Majesty's Secret Service
Topaz

1970

The Andromeda Strain
The Aristocats
A Clockwork Orange
The Curious Female
Horror of Frankenstein
Scars of Dracula
Taste the Blood of Dracula
THX 1138
tick ... tick ... tick ...
When Dinosaurs Ruled the Earth
When Dinosaurs Ruled the Earth — TV spot
When Women Had Tails
The Vampire Lovers

1971

Blood from the Mummy's Tomb
Creatures the World Forgot
Countess Dracula
Diamonds Are Forever
Diamonds Are Forever (TV)
Dr. Jekyll & Sister Hyde
Get Carter
The French Connection
Lust for a Vampire
Murders in the Rue Morgue
The Omega Man
Twins of Evil

1972

Dracula AD 1972
Everything You Always Wanted to Know About Sex but Were Afraid to Ask
Frenzy
The Godfather
The Last House on the Left
The Poseidon Adventure
Vampire Circus

1973

The Clones
The Golden Voyage of Sinbad
Live and Let Die
Robin Hood (Disney)
Savage!
Serpico
Soylent Green
The Wicker Man
The Wicker Man — TV

1974

Black Samson
Captain Kronos Vampire Hunter
Chinatown
The Conversation
Frankenstein and the Monster from Hell
The Godfather, Part II
The Legend of the 7 Golden Vampires
The Man with the Golden Gun
The Satanic Rites of Dracula
Savage Sisters
Sugar Hill
The Texas Chainsaw Massacre

1975

Carnal Madness/Delinquent Schoolgirls
The French Connection 2
One Flew Over the Cuckoo's Nest
Pick-up
Street Girls
Take a Hard Ride

1976

Carrie
Dixie Dynamite
Family Plot
Marathon Man
The Omen
The Pom Pom Girls
Rocky
Star Wars — teaser
To the Devil a Daughter

1977

Annie Hall
The Guy from Harlem
Mr. Billion
Rabid
The Rescuers
Rolling Thunder
The Spy Who Loved Me
Star Wars — main
Close Encounters of the Third Kind

1978

The Evil
Halloween
Superman
Stingray

1979

Alien — teaser
Alien — main trailer
The Amityville Horror
Burnout
The Dark
Dirt
The Empire Strikes Back — teaser
The Evictors
Moonraker
Rocky II
Skatetown U.S.A.
Star Trek: The Motion Picture teaser
Star Trek: The Motion Picture main
Van Nuys Blvd.

1980

Airplane
The Elephant Man

Trailer-ography

The Empire Strikes Back — main
Friday the 13th
Ordinary People
The Shining
Shogun Assassin
Superman II

1981

Clash of the Titans
Deadly Blessing
ET: The Extra Terrestrial
The Evil Dead
For Your Eyes Only
The Fox and the Hound
Friday the 13th Part 2
The Howling
Ms. 45
Raiders of the Lost Ark

1982

48 Hours
An Officer and a Gentleman
Conan the Barbarian
Fast Times at Ridgemont High
First Blood
Friday the 13th Part 3: 3-D
Ghandi
Poltergeist
Revenge of the Jedi — teaser
Rocky III
Star Trek II: The Wrath of Khan
Tron
The Verdict
The Wall

1983

A Christmas Story
Never Say Never Again
Octopussy
Return of the Jedi — main
The Right Stuff
Scarface
Superman III
War Games

1984

All the Right Moves (video)
Amadeus
Beverly Hills Cop
Cannonball Run (video)
Chariots of Fire (video)
Dune
Friday the 13th: The Final Chapter
Ghostbusters
Gremlins
Indiana Jones and the Temple of Doom
The Karate Kid
The Man with Two Brains (video)
The Natural
A Nightmare on Elm Street
Of Unknown Origin (video)
Once Upon a Time in America
Police Academy (video)
Purple Rain
Star Trek III: The Search for Spock
Star Wars (video)
The Terminator
To Be or Not to Be (video)

1985

Un Amour de Swann (video)
Back to the Future
The Black Cauldron
The Breakfast Club
Commando
Friday the 13th: A New Beginning
The Goonies
A Nightmare on Elm Street 2: Freddy's Revenge
Parker (video)
Rocky IV
A View to a Kill
Weird Science

1986

Aliens
Basil the Great Mouse Detective
A Better Tomorrow
Big Trouble in Little China
Friday the 13th: Jason Lives
Legend
Star Trek 4: The Voyage Home

1987

The Best of Times (video)
Evil Dead II
Fatal Attraction
Full Metal Jacket
Lethal Weapon (video)
Link (video)
Little Shop of Horrors (video)
The Living Daylights
The Lost Boys
Mannequin
Mannequin (video)
Mesmerise (video)
A Nightmare on Elm Street 3: Dream Warriors
Pirates (video)
Police Academy 4 (video)
Predator
Robocop — teaser
Robocop — main
The Running Man
Spaceballs
Superman IV: The Quest for Peace (video)
The Untouchables
Wall Street

1988

Beetlejuice
Die Hard
Friday the 13th VII: New Blood
Midnight Run
A Nightmare on Elm Street 4: The Dream Master
Oliver & Co.
Rain Man
Red Heat
Who Framed Roger Rabbit?
Willow

1989

The Abyss — teaser
The Abyss — main
Back to the Future II
Back to the Future III teaser
Back to the Future III main trailer
Batman
Casualties of War
Friday the 13th VIII: Jason Takes Manhattan
Ghostbusters II
Indiana Jones and the Last Crusade
License to Kill — teaser
License to Kill — main
The Little Mermaid
A Nightmare on Elm Street 5: The Dream Child
Star Trek V: The Final Frontier — teaser
Star Trek V: The Final Frontier — main
The War of the Roses
When Harry Met Sally...

1990

Days of Thunder
Die Hard 2: Die Harder
Edward Scissorhands
The Godfather, Part III
Home Alone
The Hunt for Red October
Misery
Presumed Innocent
Pretty Woman
The Rescuers Down Under
Rocky V
Total Recall
The Two Jakes

1991

Beauty and the Beast
Boyz in the Hood
Bugsy
Cape Fear
City Slickers
Freddy's Dead: The Final Nightmare
Happy Together
Home Alone (video)
Hot Shots
JFK
Life Stinks
The Long Walk Home (video)
Robin Hood: Prince of Thieves
Sleeping with the Enemy
Star Trek VI: The Undiscovered Country — teaser
Star Trek VI: The Undiscovered Country — main
Star Wars (widescreen video)
Star Wars — The Empire Strikes Back (widescreen video)
Star Wars — Return of the Jedi (widescreen video)
Sweet Talker (video)
Terminator 2: Judgment Day teaser
Terminator 2: Judgment Day trailer #1 — "This Time There Are Two"
Terminator 2: Judgment Day trailer #2 — "Same Make, New Mission"
Too Hot to Handle (video)

1992

Aladdin
Alien3 — trailer 1
Alien3 — trailer 2
Alien3 — trailer 3
Basic Instinct
Deadly Surveillance (video)
A Few Good Men
Homicide
Iron Maze (video)
The Last of the Mohicans
Let Him Have It
Neon City (video)
Patriot Games
The Player
Reservoir Dogs
Toys

1993

Army of Darkness
Carlito's Way
Cliffhanger
Falling Down
The Firm
The Fugitive
Jurassic Park
The Last Action Hero
Mrs. Doubtfire
The Pelican Brief
Sleepless in Seattle
Tombstone

1994

Ace Ventura: Pet Detective
Clear and Present Danger
Ed Wood
Forrest Gump
Interview with the Vampire
Leon
The Lion King
The Mask
Natural Born Killers
Pulp Fiction
The Shawshank Redemption
Speed
Stargate
Star Trek Generations
True Lies
Wes Craven's New Nightmare
Wyatt Earp

1995

The American President
Apollo 13
Babe
Bad Boys
Braveheart
China Moon (video)
Death and the Maiden
Die Hard with a Vengeance
Dirty Weekend (video)
Goldeneye
Heat
I.D.
Judge Dredd
Nell

Trailer-ography

Pocahontas
Separate Lives (video)
Se7en
Showgirls
Strange Days
To Die For
Toy Story — teaser
Toy Story — main
Trainspotting — teaser
Trainspotting — main
The Usual Suspects

1996

Bound
Broken Arrow
Eraser
From Dusk Till Dawn
The Hunchback of Notre Dame
Jerry Maguire
Independence Day — teaser
Independence Day — main
The Long Kiss Goodnight
Mission: Impossible
Mulholland Falls
Ransom
The Rock
Star Trek: First Contact — teaser
Star Trek: First Contact — main
Twister — teaser
Twister — main

1997

Air Force One
Alien Resurrection — teaser
Alien Resurrection — main trailer
Contact
The Devil's Advocate
Face/Off
The Fifth Element
Hercules
Jackie Brown
LA Confidential
A Life Less Ordinary
The Lost World: Jurassic Park
Men in Black — teaser

Men in Black — main
My Best Friend's Wedding
Starship Troopers
Titanic
Tomorrow Never Dies

1998

Antz
Armageddon
Blade
Dark City
Deep Impact
Godzilla
The Mask of Zorro
Meet Joe Black
Mulan
Pi
Pleasantville
Saving Private Ryan
Shakespeare in Love
The Siege
Star Trek: Insurrection — teaser
Star Trek: Insurrection — main
Star Wars: Episode 1 — The Phantom Menace — teaser
Very Bad Things
The X-Files
You've Got Mail

1999

American Beauty
Being John Malcovich
The Blair Witch Project — teaser 1
The Blair Witch Project — teaser 2
Eyes Wide Shut
Fight Club — teaser
Fight Club — main
Fight Club — "I Know You" (Internet spot #1)
Fight Club — "Deliver Me" (Internet spot #2)
Fight Club — "Change Your Life" (Internet spot #3)
Fight Club — "Football" (Internet spot #4)

Fight Club — "Mona Lisa/Rev" (Internet spot #5)
The Mummy
The Matrix
Notting Hill
Star Wars: Episode 1 — The Phantom Menace — main
Stepmom
Tarzan
There's Something About Mary
The World Is Not Enough
X-Men — teaser

2000

Almost Famous
Chicken Run — teaser
Chicken Run — main
The Emperor's New Groove
Erin Brockovich
Fantasia 2000
Ghost World
Gladiator — teaser
Gladiator — main
Gone in 60 Seconds
High Fidelity
The Perfect Storm — teaser
The Perfect Storm — main
Unbreakable
X-Men — main

2001

A.I. — trailer 1
A.I. — trailer 2
Amelie
Atlantis: The Lost Empire
Harry Potter and the Philosopher's Stone
Jurassic Park III
Lara Croft: Tomb Raider
Lord of the Rings: The Fellowship of the Ring
Monsters Inc. — teaser
Monsters Inc. — main
Moulin Rouge
The Mummy Returns
Pearl Harbor
Planet of the Apes
Shrek

Star Wars Ep. II — Attack of the Clones "Breathing"— teaser 1
Star Wars Ep. II — Attack of the Clones "Forbidden Love"— teaser 2
Star Wars Ep. II — Attack of the Clones "Mystery"— Internet teaser
Waking Life

2002
Comedian
Die Another Day
Die Another Day — TV
Lilo and Stitch
Lord of the Rings: The Two Towers — teaser
Lord of the Rings: The Two Towers — main
Spiderman — World Trade Center teaser
Spiderman — main trailer
Star Trek: Nemesis — teaser
Star Trek: Nemesis — main
Star Wars: Ep. II — Attack of the Clones "Clone Wars"— main
Treasure Planet

2003
Kill Bill, vol. 1
Lord of the Rings: The Return of the King
Lost in Translation
The Matrix Reloaded
The Matrix Revolutions
Minority Report — teaser

2004
Aliens vs. Predator
American Splendor
Brother Bear
The Day After Tomorrow — teaser
The Day After Tomorrow — main
Eternal Sunshine of the Spotless Mind
The Incredibles — teaser
The Incredibles — main
Kill Bill, vol. 2
Minority Report — trailer 1
Minority Report — trailer 2
Shaun of the Dead
Star Wars Ep. III: Revenge of the Sith — teaser

2005
Batman Begins — teaser
Batman Begins — main
Bubble
Chronicles of Narnia: The Lion, the Witch and the Wardrobe — teaser
Chronicles of Narnia: The Lion, the Witch and the Wardrobe — main
Chronicles of Narnia: The Lion, the Witch and the Wardrobe — iPod
Elizabethtown — internet "First Look"/"Music"/ "Home Video"
Elizabethtown — main
Fantastic Four — teaser
The Hitchhiker's Guide to the Galaxy — internet
The Hitchhiker's Guide to the Galaxy — teaser
The Hitchhiker's Guide to the Galaxy — main (UK)
The Hitchhiker's Guide to the Galaxy — main (U.S.)
King Kong — teaser
King Kong — main
King Kong — iPod
Serenity
Star Wars Ep. III: Revenge of the Sith — main
Star Wars Ep. III: Revenge of the Sith — TV spots #1 — #6
The Transporter 2
Wallace & Gromit: The Curse of the Were Rabbit — teaser
Wallace & Gromit: The Curse of the Were Rabbit — main
War of the Worlds — teaser
War of the Worlds — main

Bibliography

Adams, Val. "Commercials Are Challenged." *New York Times* (January 15, 1965), p. 87.
Albarino, R. "Buy Trailer, Get Video Re-edit Free." *Variety* 274, 5 (May 1, 1974): 8.
Allen, Robert C., and Douglas Gomery. *Film History: Theory and Practice*. New York: Alfred A. Knopf, 1985.
_____. "From Exhibition to Reception: Reflections on the Audience in Film History." In *Screen Histories: A Screen Reader*, edited by Annette Kuhn and Jackie Stacey, pp. 13–21. Oxford: Oxford University Press, 1998.
"American commentary," *Today's Cinema* 80, 6694 (February 11, 1953): 8.
Ames, Alan. "Utilizing Video." *New York Times* (September 16, 1951): 6X.
Anderson, Christopher. *Hollywood TV: The Studio System in the Fifties*. Austin: University of Texas Press, 1994.
_____, and Michael Curtin. "Writing Cultural History: The Challenge of Radio and Television." In *Media History: Theories-Methods-Analysis*, edited by Niels Brügger and Søren Kolstrup, pp. 15–32. Aahrus: Aarhus University Press, 2002.
Armes, Roy, ed. *Problems of Film History*. Barnet: Middlesex Polytechnic/BFI, 1981.
"Aromatic Movies." *British Kinematography* 36, 5 (May 1960): 138–140.
Balio, Tino, ed. *Hollywood in the Age of Television*. Boston: Unwin Hyman, 1990.
Banks, Miranda J. "Monumental Fictions: National Monument as a Science Fiction Space." *Journal of Popular Film and Television*, 30, 3 (Fall 2002): 136–145.
Barr, Charles. "CinemaScope: Before and After." In *Film Theory and Criticism*, edited by Gerald Mast and Marshall Cohen, pp. 139–163. Oxford: Oxford University Press, 1992, 4th edition.
Barrios, Richard. *A Song in the Dark: The Birth of the Musical Film*. New York; Oxford: Oxford University Press, 1995.
Bazin, André. "Will CinemaScope Save the Film Industry?" In *Bazin at Work*, edited by Bert Cardullo, pp. 77–92. London: Routledge, 1997.
"Behind the Scenes with a Trailer Producer." *The Cinema* 70, 5643 (May 5, 1948): 30.
Bell, Emily. "X Rated Box Office Hype." *The Observer* (February 21, 1993): 41.
Bell, Tim. "The Agency Viewpoint 3." In *British Television Advertising: The First Thirty Years*, edited by Brian Henry, pp. 437–453. London: Century Benham, 1986.
Belton, John. "CinemaScope: The Economics of Technology," *Velvet Light Trap* 21 (Summer 1985): 35–43.
_____. *Widescreen Cinema*. Cambridge, Mass.: Harvard University Press, 1992.
Bentley, Michael. "General Introduction: The Project of Historiography." In *Companion to Historiography*, edited by Michael Bentley, pp. xi–xvii. London: Routledge, 1997.

_____. *Modern Historiography: An Introduction*. London: Routledge, 2000.
_____, ed. *Companion to Historiography*. London: Routledge, 1997.
Bernstein, David. "The Television Commercial: An Essay." In *British Television Advertising: The First Thirty Years*, edited by Brian Henry, pp. 251–285. London: Century Benham, 1986.
"Big Teaser Boost for *Interpol*." *Today's Cinema* 88, 7758 (April 17, 1957): 10.
Blair, Iain. "Film Trailers: Attracting Audiences with Style." *On Location* (January 1983): 40–49.
Boddy, William. *Fifties Television: The Industry and its Critics*, Chicago: University of Illinois Press, 1993.
_____. "The Studios Move into Prime-Time: Hollywood and the Television Industry in the 1950s." *Cinema Journal* 24, 4 (Summer 1985): 23–37.
Bordwell, David. "Camera Movement: the Coming of Sound and the Classical Hollywood Style." In *The Hollywood Film Industry*, edited by Paul Kerr, pp. 148–153. London: Routledge and Kegan Paul, 1986.
_____. "The Studios Move into Prime-Time: Hollywood and the Television Industry in the 1950s." *Cinema Journal* 24, 4 (Summer 1985): 23–37.
_____, and Noel Carroll, eds. *Post-Theory: Reconstructing Film Studies*. Madison: University of Wisconsin Press, 1996.
Born Yesterday press book, BFI library microfiche.
Borneman, Ernest. "U.S. Versus Hollywood: The Case Study of an Antitrust Suit." In *The American Film Industry*, edited by Tino Balio, pp. 449–462. Madison: University of Wisconsin Press, 1985.
Branigan, Edward. "Color and Cinema: Problems in the Writing of History." In *The Hollywood Film Industry*, edited by Paul Kerr, pp. 120–147. London: Routledge and Kegan Paul, 1986.
Brennan, Richard. "Brian Trenchard Smith." *Cinema Papers* 24 (December 1979–January 1980): 598–603.
"Britain's First 3-D." *Hollywood Reporter* 126, 7 (September 15, 1953): 3.
"British premiere of *The Robe*." *Hollywood Reporter* 126, 22 (October 6, 1953): 2.
Brook, Simon. "The New Medium: Television Survey." *Daily Film Renter* (March 1, 1957): 8.
Buscombe, Ed. "All Bark and No Bite: The Film Industry's Response to Television." In *Popular Television in Britain: Studies in Cultural History*, edited by John Corner, pp. 197–209. London: BFI, 1991.
"*Bwana Devil* (3-D) for Rank Circuits." *Today's Cinema* 80, 6696 (February 13, 1953): 1, 10, 12.
Canby, Vincent. "Ads Will Stress Approved Films." *New York Times* (March 17, 1967): 34.
Chapman, James. "'This Ship Is England': History, Politics and National Identity in *Master and Commander: The Far Side of the World* (2003)." In *The New Film History*, edited by James Chapman, Mark Glancy and Sue Harper, pp. 55–68. Basingstoke: Palgrave Macmillan, 2007.
_____, Mark Glancy and Sue Harper, eds. *The New Film History*. Basingstoke: Palgrave Macmillan, 2007.
Charman, Bernard. "Commentary." *Daily Film Renter* 7166 (July 11, 1956): 2.
_____. "Commentary." *Daily Film Renter* 7175 (July 24, 1956): 2.
_____. "Commentary." *Daily Film Renter* 7193 (August 20, 1956): 2.
_____. "Commentary." *Daily Film Renter* 7720 (September 26, 1956): 2.
Chisholm, Brad. "Red, Blue, and Lots of Green: The Impact of Color Television on Feature Film Production." In *Hollywood in the Age of Television*, edited by Tino Balio, pp. 213–234. Boston: Unwin Hyam, 1990.
CinemaScope advertisement. *Today's Cinema* 80, 6933 (January 21, 1954): 4–5.
"CinemaScope, *Robe* Triumph." *Hollywood Reporter* 126, 9 (September 17, 1953): 1.

"CinemaScope Screens in 16 Different Sizes." *Hollywood Reporter* 126, 7 (September 15, 1953): 3.
"CinemaScope's Year." *Today's Cinema* 82, 6922 (January 6, 1954): 8.
"Clouds Thicken Over Film Makers Part in TV Programming." *Advertising Age* (October 31, 1955): 16.
Cohen, Jeffrey. "Trailer Trash: Hope For the Future: What Trailers Could (And Should) Be." *E Online* (June 28, 2000): www.eonline.com/Features/Specials/Trailertrash/000628.html.
———. "Trailer Trash: How They Do It: The Making of a Trailer." *E Online* (June 21, 2000): www.eonline.com/Features/Specials/Trailertrash/000621.html.
———. "Trailer Trash: Numbing Attractions: The Trouble with Trailers." *E Online* (June 14, 2000): www.eonline.com/Features/Specials/Trailertrash/000614.html.
Coleman, Ron. "Making $$$ in Filmmaking." *Filmmakers Newsletter* 11, 5 (March 1978): 38, 40–41.
Conant, Michael. *Antitrust in the Motion Picture Industry: Economic and Legal Analysis.* Berkeley: University of California Press, 1960.
Connor, Edward. "3-D on the Screen." *Films in Review* 17, 3 (March 1966): 159–174.
Cook, Pam. *Screening the Past: Memory and Nostalgia in Cinema.* Abingdon: Routledge, 2005.
Corliss, Richard. "Coming Attractions." *Film Comment* 33, 3 (May–June 1997): 14–23.
Crafton, Donald. "Enticing the Audience: Warner Bros. and Vitaphone." In *History of the American Cinema 4: The Talkies-American Cinema's Transition to Sound, 1926–1931*, edited by Tino Balio, pp. 120–126. New York: Charles Scribner's Sons Macmillan Library Reference USA, Simon & Schuster Macmillan, 1987.
———. "*The Jazz Singer*'s Reception in the Media and at the Box Office." In *Post-Theory: Reconstructing Film Studies*, edited by David Bordwell and Noel Carroll, pp. 460–480. Madison: University of Wisconsin Press, 1996.
Cricks, R. Howard. "Do We Want That Third Dimension?" *Picturegoer* 22, 854 (September 15, 1951): 15.
Cunningham, James C. "AromaRama Process Adds Odor to Films," *Film Daily* 116, 112 (December 10, 1959): 1, 7.
Dougherty, Phillip H. "First Bang of a Big Bang Bang." *New York Times* (April 30, 1968): 75.
D. R. "Something New in Exploitation." *Today's Cinema* 87, 7626 (October 9, 1956): 5.
Drewery, Brian. "Trailer for Sale or Rent." *Creation* (December 1999): 28–31.
Duncan, Jody. "A Look Back." *Cinefex* 80 (January 2000): 161.
Dunlap, Orrin E., Jr. "Television Show Reveals Current Stage of the Art." *New York Times* (February 21, 1937): 12.
D. W. C. "Renovating the Trailer." *New York Times* (May 10, 1936): 4.
Ede, Laurie. "Art in Context: British Film Design of the 1940s." In *The New Film History*, edited by James Chapman, Mark Glancy and Sue Harper, pp. 73–88. Basingstoke: Palgrave Macmillan, 2007.
"Editorial." *Motion Picture Herald* 185, 12 (22nd December 1951): 3.
Elsaesser, Thomas. "The New Film History." *Sight and Sound* 55, 4 (Autumn 1985): 246–251.
"ESRB launching new game-trailer clampdown," *Gamespot UK News* (June 25, 2007): uk.gamespot.com/news/show_blog_entry.php?topic_id=25728372&part=rss&subj=6173105.
"Esther Harris interview." The BECTU History Project, Tape 465 (January 18, 2000).
Eyman, Scott. *The Speed of Sound: Hollywood and the Talkie Revolution, 1926–1930.* New York: Simon & Schuster, 1997.
"Famous Players Issue Advance Film." *Moving Picture World* 29, 13 (September 30, 1916): 2094.

Francis, Barbara. "Movie Trailers: The Lure of the Filmstrip Tease." *Los Angeles Times Calendar* (October 7, 1979): 7.
Freer, Ian. "The 50 Greatest Movie Trailers of All Time." *Empire* (August 2003): 94–99.
Geffner, David. "Clip Art." *Filmmaker* 5, 3 (Spring 1997): 31–34.
Gibbs, John. *Mise-en-scène: Film Style and Interpretation*. London, New York: Wallflower Press, 2002.
Glancy, Mark. "*Blackmail* (1929), Hitchcock and Film Nationalism." In *The New Film History*, edited by James Chapman, Mark Glancy and Sue Harper, pp. 185–200. Basingstoke: Palgrave Macmillan, 2007.
Goldwyn, Samuel. "On Hollow: Producer Warns Against Ads That Mislead." *New York Times* (April 1, 1951): 100.
Gomery, Douglas. "The Coming of Sound: Technological Change in the American Film Industry." In *The American Film Industry*, edited by Tino Balio, pp. 229–251. Madison: University of Wisconsin Press, 1985.
———. *Shared Pleasures: A History of Movie Presentation in the United States*. Madison: University of Wisconsin Press, 1992.
———. "Writing the History of the American Film Industry: Warner Bros and Sound." In *Screen Histories: A Screen Reader*, edited by Annette Kuhn and Jackie Stacey, pp. 139–147. Oxford: Oxford University Press, 1998.
Goodman, Mort. "How Good Are TV Spots?" *The Journal of the Producers Guild of America* (June 1975): 19–20, 23.
Goodwin, Michael. "The Lost Films of Alfred Hitchcock." *New West* (April 1981): 84–87, 142.
Gould, Jack. "TV: *Mister Roberts* Rides Free; Sullivan Show is One Long Ad for Movie." *New York Times* (June 20, 1955): 41.
Gunn, James. "A Short History of the Space Program; or, A Funny Thing Happened on the Way to the Moon." *Vertrex* 2, 1 (April 1974).
Gunning, Tom. "The Cinema of Attractions: Early Film, Its Spectator and the Avant-Garde." *Wide Angle* 8, 3–4 (1986): 63–70.
———. "The Temporality of the Cinema of Attractions." *Velvet Light Trap* 32 (Fall 1993): 3–12.
Halbfinger, David M. "Attention, Web Surfers: The Following Film Trailer May Be Racy or Graphic." *New York Times* (June 13, 2007): www.nytimes.com/2007/06/13/movies/13yell.html?ex=1339387200&en=5c292ac80cc2b0b2&ei=5088&partner=rssnyt&emc=rss.
Hamilton, Kandall, Devin Gordon, and Alisha Davis. "The Second Coming." *Newsweek* 132, 22 (November 30, 1998): 84.
Handel, Leo A. *Hollywood Looks at Its Audience: A Report of Film Audience Research*. Urbana: University of Illinois Press, 1950.
Haralovich, Mary Beth. "Advertising Heterosexuality." *Screen* 23, 2 (July–August 1982): 50–60.
———. "Mandates of Good Taste: The Self-Regulation of Film Advertising in the Thirties." *Wide Angle* 6, 2 (1983): 50–57.
———, and Cathy Root Klaprat. "*Marked Woman* and *Jezebel*: The Spectator-in-the-Trailer." *Enclitic* (Fall 1981/Spring 1982): 66–74.
Harden, Fred. "Stereoscopic Film," *Cinema Papers* 43 (May/June 1983): 134–140.
Harper, Sue. "History and Representation: The Case of 1970s British Cinema." In *The New Film History*, edited by James Chapman, Mark Glancy and Sue Harper, pp. 27–40. Basingstoke: Palgrave Macmillan, 2007.
Harris, Esther. "The Production of Trailers." *British Kinematography* 23, 4 (October 1953): 98–103.
Hayes, R. M. *3-D Movies: A History and Filmography of Stereoscopic Cinema*. Jefferson, N.C.: McFarland, 1989.

Hayward, Susan, and Ginette Vincendeau, eds. *French Film: Texts and Contexts*. London: Routledge, 2000.
Hazelton, John. "For a Few Dollars More," *Screen International* (July 19, 1996): 10–11.
Hediger, Vinzenz. "The Art of Selling Things Twice. Trailers, Marketing and the Culture of Reconsumption." Presented at "Marketing the Movies," University of Warwick, February 24, 2007.
Heller, Steven. "Mr. Roughcut." *Eye* 32 (Summer 1999): 1.
Henderson, Jan Alan. "Lunar Ambition." *American Cinematographer* 81, 3 (March 2000): 108–112.
Hickman, Gail Morgan. *The Films of George Pal*. London: Thomas Yoseloff Ltd., 1979.
Hincha, Richard. "Selling CinemaScope: 1953–1956." *Velvet Light Trap* 21 (Summer 1985): 44–53.
Holmes, Su. *British TV & Film Culture in the 1950s: Coming to a TV Near You*. Bristol: Intellect, 2005.
Houston, Penelope, and John Gillett. "The Theory and Practice of Blockbusting." *Sight & Sound* 32 (Spring 1963): 68–74.
How to Marry A Millionaire advert. *Today's Cinema* 82, 6929 (January 15, 1954): 1.
Huntley, John. "'U' and cry — The Story of Denham's Trailer Department." *Film Industry* 2, 12 (June 1947): 8, 9 and 13.
Jacobs, Jason. *The Intimate Screen: Early British Television Drama*. Oxford: Clarendon Press, 2000
Jancovich, Mark, Lucy Faire, and Sarah Stubbins. *The Place of the Audience: Cultural Geographies of Film Consumption*. London, BFI, 2003.
Jenkins, Henry. *Convergence Culture: Where Old and New Media Collide*. New York: New York University Press, 2006.
Johnson, Patricia Lee. "Esther Harris: Doyenne of the Trailer Makers." *CinemaTV Today* 10015 (January 20, 1973): 7.
_____. *Textual Poachers: Television Fans and Participatory Culture*. New York: Routledge, 1992.
Johnston, Keith. *Becoming Attractions: The History and Theory of Film Trailers, 1916–1939*. Unpublished M.A. dissertation, University of Kent, 2004.
Johnston, Sheila. "It's the Way You Sell 'Em." *The Independent* (April 12, 1991): 17.
Jones, Sara Gwenllian. "Web Wars: Resistance, Online Fandom and Studio Censorship." In *Quality Popular Television*, edited by Mark Jancovich and James Lyons, pp. 163–177. London, BFI, 2003.
Jones, Sinead. "Trailer Trial." *Film Directions* 6, 23 (Summer 1984): 46.
Kahney, Leander. "Apple Gives Video the iPod Touch." *Wired News* (October 12, 2005): www.wired.com/news/business/0,69193-0.html.
Kerbel, Michael. "3-D or not 3-D." *Film Comment* 16, 6 (November–December 1980): 11–20.
Kernan, Lisa. *Coming Attractions: Reading American Movie Trailers*. Austin: University of Texas Press, 2004.
Kerzoncuf, Alain, and Nándor Bokor. "Alfred Hitchcock's Trailers." *Senses of Cinema* 35 (April–June 2005): www.sensesofcinema.com/contents/05/35/hitchcocks_trailers.html.
King, Geoff. *Spectacular Narratives: Hollywood in the Age of the Blockbuster*. London: I. B. Tauris, 2000.
Kirihara, Donald. "Reconstructing Japanese Film." In *Post-Theory: Reconstructing Film Studies*, edited by David Bordwell and Noel Carroll, pp. 501–519. Madison: University of Wisconsin Press, 1996.
Kismet press book, MGM 1955.
Klinger, Barbara. "Digressions at the Cinema: Reception and Mass Culture." *Cinema Journal* 28, 4 (Summer 1989): 3–19.

———. "Film History Terminable and Interminable: Recovering the Past in Reception Studies." *Screen* 38, 2 (Summer 1997): 107–128.
Kneale, Nigel. "Not Quite So Intimate." *Sight & Sound* 28, 2 (Spring 1959): 86.
Kuhn, Annette. *An Everyday Magic: Cinema and Cultural Memory.* London, I. B. Tauris, 2002.
———, and Jackie Stacey, eds. *Screen Histories: A Screen Reader.* Oxford: Oxford University Press, 1998.
Lasky, Jesse. "The Producer Makes A Plan." In *We Make the Movies,* edited by Nancy Naumberg, pp. 1–15. London: Faber & Faber, 1938.
Lazarus, Paul N. "National Screen Service Corporation." In *The Movie Business: American Film Industry Practice,* edited by William A. Bluem and Jason E. Squire, pp. 234–236. New York: Hastings House, 1972.
———. "The Wet Finger Method for Evaluating Film Success." *The Journal of the Producers Guild of America* (September 1969): 31–33.
Lee, Beaupré. "How to Distribute a Film." In *The Hollywood Film Industry,* edited by Paul Kerr, pp. 185–203. London: BFI, Routledge, 1986.
Lees, David. *The Movie Business.* New York: Random House, 1981.
———, and Stan Berkowitz. The True Story Behind These Coming Attractions." *Los Angeles* (January 1979): 94–99.
"Lewis, Howard T. *The Motion Picture Industry.* New York: D. Van Nostrand Company, 1933.
"Loews Goes Big Screen O'Seas." *Hollywood Reporter* 125, 49 (September 2, 1953): 1.
Lughi, Paolo. "When Saying Is Getting Somebody to Do Something: Manipulations and Speech Acts in Verbal Language of the Trailer." *Semiotic Enquiry/Recherches Semiotiques* 4, 3–4: 356–371.
MacDonald, Fred J. *One Nation Under Television: The Rise and Decline of Network TV.* Chicago: Nelson-Hall, 1990.
Maltby, Richard. "'A Brief Romantic Interlude': Dick and Jane Go to 3 1/2 Seconds of the Classical Hollywood Cinema." In *Post-Theory: Reconstructing Film Studies,* edited by David Bordwell and Noel Carroll, pp. 434–459. Madison: University of Wisconsin Press, 1996.
———. "Why Boys Go Wrong: Gangsters, Hoodlums and the Natural History of Delinquent Careers." In *Mob Cultures: Hidden Histories of the American Gangster Film,* edited by Lee Grievson, Esther Sonnet and Peter Stanfield, pp. 41–66. New Brunswick, N.J.: Rutgers University Press, 2005.
Manovich, Lev. *The Language of New Media.* Cambridge, Mass.: MIT Press, 2001.
Marling, Karel Ann. *As Seen On TV: The Visual Culture of Everyday Life in the 1950s.* Cambridge, Mass.: Harvard University Press, 1994.
Matthews, Virginia. "Mini Epics of the Big Screen." *The Guardian* (October 27, 1986): 11.
Mauceri, James. "AromaRama (Pic That Smells) Wafts in, Dec." *Film Daily* 116, 82 (October 27, 1959): 1, 5.
"Maurice Binder Obituary." *The Times* (April 18, 1991): 20.
Maxford, Howard. *The George Lucas Companion.* London: B. T. Batsford, 1999.
McElwee, James P. "The Trailer." *Films in Review* 39, 10 (October 1988): 472–479.
McGee, Mark Thomas. *Beyond Ballyhoo: Motion Picture Promotion and Gimmicks.* Jefferson, N.C.: McFarland, 1989.
Medhurst, Andy. "The Big Tease." *Sight & Sound* 8, 7 (July 1998): 24–26.
Meech, Peter. "Watch This Space: The On-Air Marketing Communications of UK Television." *The International Journal of Advertising* 18, 3 (1999): 291–304.
"Metro's Countrywide Contest Ties with *Kismet* Gen. Rel." *Today's Cinema* 88, 7732 (March 12, 1957): 5.
"MGM to Show 3-D Film at Empire." *Today's Cinema* 80, 6696 (February 13, 1953): 1, 10 and 12.

Millar, Mark S. "Helping Exhibitors: Pressbooks at Warner Bros. in the Late 1930s." *Film History* 6, 2 (Summer 1994): 188–196.
Mills, Bart. "Video Reviews: *Electric Blue 004*." *TV and Home Video* 3, 5 (May 1981): 45.
_____. "Videograms." *TV and Home Video* 2, 2 (February 1980): 51.
Milne, Tom. *Time Out Film Guide*. London: Penguin, 1993, 3rd edition.
Mitchell, Rick. "The Tragedy of 3-D Cinema." *Film History* 16, 3 (2004): 208–215.
"Movie Makers Named in Antitrust Suit." *New York Times* (April 29, 1952): 33.
Mueller, Roxanne. "Bigger Than Life: Episodes in the Erratic Life of 3-D Technology." *American Classic Screen* 5, 6 (November/December 1981): 26–29.
Munby, Jonathan. "From Gangsta to Gangster: The Hood Film's Criminal Allegiance with Hollywood." In *The New Film History*, edited by James Chapman, Mark Glancy and Sue Harper, pp. 166–179. Basingstoke: Palgrave Macmillan, 2007.
Munz, Peter. "The Historical Narrative." In *Companion to Historiography*, edited by Michael Bentley, pp. 851–872. London: Routledge, 1997.
"Myerberg's Test Footage." *Hollywood Reporter* 126, 8 (September 16, 1953): 2.
Mzimba, Lizo. "Force Fed." *Empire* 116 (February 1999): 44.
Neale, Steve. *Cinema and Technology: Image, Sound, Colour*. London: MacMillan Education Ltd., 1985.
Netzley, Patricia D. *The Encyclopedia of Movie Special Effects*. Phoenix: Oryx Press, 2000.
Noble, Peter. *The British Film and Television Yearbook 1955–1956*. London: Gordon White, 1956.
_____. *The British Film and Television Yearbook 1975–1976*. London: King Publications, 1976.
Observer. "Up and Down the Street," *Today's Cinema* 77, 6356 (October 11, 1951): 4.
_____. "Up and Down the Street." *Today's Cinema* (January 30, 1956).
_____. "Up and Down the Street." *Today's Cinema* 87, 7611 (September 19, 1956): 5.
Ogle, Thomas. "Technological and Aesthetics Influences Upon the Development of Deep Focus Cinematography in the United States." *Screen* 13, 1 (Spring 1972): 45–72.
Oliver, Mary Beth, and Sriram Kalyanaraman. "Appropriate for All Viewing Audiences? An Examination of Violent and Sexual Portrayals in Movie Previews Featured on Video Rentals." *Journal of Broadcasting & Electronic Media* 46, 2 (2002): 283–299.
Onosko, T. "'53: The New Era. A Brief History of the Three-Dimensional Film." *Velvet Light Trap* 11 (Winter 1974): 12–16.
Oxenhorn, P. "Trailers Are Compact, Complex and Costly." *Making Films in New York*, 8, 36 (October 7, 1974).
Parisi, Paula. *Titanic and the Making of James Cameron*. London: Orion, 1998.
Parsons, P. A. "A History of Motion Picture Advertising." *Moving Picture World* 85, 4 (March 4, 1927): 301–311.
Persons, Dan. "Retrospect: *2001: A Space Odyssey*." *Cinefantastique* 25, 3 (June 1994): 32.
Prokop, Tim. "Launching *Apollo 13*." *Cinefex* 63 (September 1995): 60.
Quigley, Martin, Jr. "NSS: The Prize Baby Remembers." *Motion Picture Herald* (November 7, 1959): 16–17.
_____. "The NSS Story of Service." *Motion Picture Herald* (March 14, 1959): 18–21.
"Return to Basic Showmanship Is Needed — Al Duff." *Today's Cinema* 87, 7611 (September 19, 1956): 8.
Richards, Jeffrey. "The Politics of the Swashbuckler." In *The New Film History*, edited by James Chapman, Mark Glancy and Sue Harper, pp. 119–136. Basingstoke: Palgrave Macmillan, 2007.
_____. "Rethinking British Cinema." In *British Cinema: Past and Present*, edited by Justine Ashby and Andrew Higson, pp. 21–34. London: Routledge, 2000.
Richmond, Theo. "Esther Harris: Titillator." *The Guardian* (May 3, 1970): 11.
Rickman, Gregg. "Introduction." In *The Science Fiction Film Reader*, edited by Gregg Rickman, pp. xii–xxxii. New York: Limelight, 2004.
Rigney, George. "Sound for 3-D." *American Cinematographer* 65, 7 (July 1984): 101–103.

Sammons, Eddie. *The World of 3-D Movies*. New York: Delphi, 1992.
Schatz, Thomas. "The New Hollywood." In *Film Theory Goes to the Movies*, edited by Jim Collins, Hilary Radner and Ava Preacher Collins, pp. 8–36. New York: Routledge, 1993.
Schlax, Julie. "Movie Marketing March." *Forbes* 147, 4 (February 18, 1991): 95.
Sendall, Bernard. *Independent Television in Britain: Volume 1: Origin and Foundation 1946–1962*. London: Macmillan, 1982.
_____. *Independent Television in Britain: Volume 2: Expansion and Change, 1958–1968*. London: Macmillan, 1982.
Sennett, Ted. "'Coming Attractions' Must Be a Good Movie, It's Playing at All the Local Theatres." *Variety* (January 3, 1968): 39.
Shannon, John. "Panic on Liberty Island." *Cinefex* 52 (November 1992): 79–80.
Shay, Don. "Effects Scene: 64th Academy Awards." *Cinefex* 50 (May 1992): 12.
_____, and Jody Duncan. "*2001*: A Time Capsule." *Cinefex* 85 (April 2001): 105.
Shone, Tom. *Blockbuster, or How Hollywood Learned to Stop Worrying and Love the Summer*. London: Simon & Schuster, 2004.
Silverman, Jason. "Meet Avi Arad, the Man Who Launched the Superhero Craze." *Wired*, www.wired.com/entertainment/hollywood/news/2007/05/spider_aviard?currentPage=2.
Singleton, Ralph. *Filmmaker's Dictionary*. Beverly Hills: Lone Eagle, 1986.
Slide, Anthony. *The American Film Industry: A Historical Dictionary*. New York: Greenwood Press, 1986.
"'Smell-O-Vision." *British Kinematography* 36, 3 (March 1960): 59.
"Smiley TV Ad." *Kinematograph Weekly* (August 2, 1956): 5.
Sobchack, Vivian. *Screening Space*. New York: Ungar, 1988.
"Specialized Techniques in Trailer Production." *The Cinema* 51, 4034 (October 5, 1938): 11.
Spellerberg, James. "CinemaScope and Ideology." *Velvet Light Trap* 21 (Summer 1985): 26–34.
Spiegel, Gabrielle M. *The Past as Text: The Theory and Practice of Medieval Historiography*. Baltimore and London: John Hopkins Press, 1997.
_____. *Romancing the Past: The Rise of Vernacular Prose Historiography in Thirteenth-Century France*. Berkeley: University of California Press, 1993.
Spielvogel, Carl. "C.U. Rejects Plug." *New York Times* (January 17, 1958): 38.
SPL. "Robert Faber: The Trailer Maker." *The Cinemaphile* (April 1976): 4, 10.
Staiger, Janet. "Announcing Wares, Winning Patrons, Voicing Ideals: Thinking about the History and Theory of Film Advertising." *Cinema Journal* 29, 3 (Spring 1990): 3–31.
_____. *Interpreting Films: Studies in the Historical Reception of American Cinema*. Princeton, N.J.: Princeton University Press, 1992.
Stanfield, Peter. "Walking the Streets: Black Gangsters and the 'Abandoned City' in the 1970s Blaxploitation Cycle." In *Mob Cultures: Hidden Histories of the American Gangster Film*, edited by Lee Grievson, Esther Sonnet and Peter Stanfield, pp. 281–300. New Brunswick, N.J.: Rutgers University Press, 2005.
"Star Names Still the Top Draw." *Today's Cinema* 87, 7631 (October 17, 1956): 3.
"Starburst History of 3-D. Part One: The Best ... The Making of *House of Wax*." *Starburst* 64 (December 1983): 12–13.
"Starburst History of 3-D. Part Two: The Rest ... *It Came from Outer Space* to *Revenge of the Creature*." *Starburst* 64 (December 1983): 19–25.
Starks, Michael. "The Rebirth of 3-D." *American Cinematographer* 63, 10 (October 1982): 987–993.
Stokes, Mervyn. "*Gone with the Wind* (1939) and the Lost Cause: A Critical View." In *The New Film History*, edited by James Chapman, Mark Glancy and Sue Harper, pp. 201–214. Basingstoke: Palgrave Macmillan, 2007.
Street, Sarah. *Black Narcissus*. London: I. B. Tauris, 2005.
_____. "British Cinema, American Reception: *Black Narcissus* (1947) and the Legion of

Decency." In *The New Film History*, edited by James Chapman, Mark Glancy and Sue Harper, pp. 201–214. Basingstoke: Palgrave Macmillan, 2007.
Taylor, B. F. *The British New Wave: A Certain Tendency?* Manchester: Manchester University Press, 2006.
"Theatre Publicity Using 3-D." *Today's Cinema* 80, 6704 (February 25, 1953): 1, 15.
"Third Renter Uses Plug TV for Film." *Today's Cinema* 87, 7577 (August 1, 1956): 3.
Thomas, Kevin. "Movie Trailers Have Long Run." *Los Angeles Times* (October 25, 1966): 10.
Thompson, Herbert. "Trailer Stupidity." *Film Weekly* 18, 453 (June 19, 1937): 7, 9 and 14.
Thompson, Kristin, and David Bordwell. *Film History: An Introduction*. New York, McGraw-Hill, 1994.
"3-D Films Planned." *Today's Cinema* 80, 6666 (January 2, 1953): 1.
"3-D Newsreels on the Way." *Today's Cinema* 80, 6697 (February 16, 1953): 1.
"3-D Puppetry in Screen Advertising." *Today's Cinema* 82, 6939 (January 29, 1954): 5.
"335 Radio Spots on *Marry*." *Hollywood Reporter* 126, 40 (October 30, 1953): 4.
Tosh, John. *The Pursuit of History: Aims, Methods and New Directions in the Study of Modern History*. Harlow, Longman, 2000, 3rd edition.
"Trailer Trash." *Sight & Sound* 10, 10 (October 2000): 9.
Traubner, Richard. "Retrospectives in Berlin." *Films in Review* 31, 7 (August/September 1980): 419–422.
Turan, Kenneth. "The Lure of Trailers." *American Film* 8, 1 (October 1982): 50–55.
"20th's 3-D Inferno 2-D Only in Britain." *Hollywood Reporter* 126, 22 (October 6, 1953): 1.
"Two-Way TV Plug." *Today's Cinema* 87, 7657 (November 22, 1956): 5.
"Unforgiven or Unrepentant?" *The Economist* 327 (April 2, 1993): 97.
Vaines, Colin. "Forthcoming Attractions...." *Screen International* 250 (July 19, 1980): 11.
Vaz, Mark Cotta, and Patricia Rose Duignan. *Industrial Light & Magic: Into the Digital Realm*. London: Virgin Publishing, 1996.
"Warners Goes CinemaScope." *Hollywood Reporter* 126, 35 (October 23, 1953): 1.
Weaver, William R. "Arch Oboler Will Make 3-Dimension Picture." *Motion Picture Herald* 186, 6 (February 9, 1952): 35.
Wierzbicki, James. "Weird Vibrations: How the Theremin Gave Musical Voice to Hollywood's Extraterrestrial 'Others.'" *Journal of Popular Film and Television* 30, 3 (Fall 2002): 125–135.
Wilkerson, W. R. "Trade Views." *Hollywood Reporter* 126, 7 (September 15, 1953): 1.
Williams, Alan D. "Convergence Techniques for 3-D Filming — Part 1." *American Cinematographer* 65, 3 (March 1984): 91–99.
_____. "Convergence Techniques for 3-D Filming — Part 2." *American Cinematographer* 65, 4 (April 1984): 99–103.
Williams, Stephanie. "The Attack of the 2-Minute Movie." *TV Guide* (August 16, 1996): 38–40.
Wings of the Hawk advert. *Hollywood Reporter* 125, 48 (September 1, 1953): 12.
Wyver, John. *The Moving Image: An International History of Film, Television and Video*. Oxford: BFI, 1989.
Zanger, Anat. "Next on Your Screen: The Double Identity of the Trailer." *Semiotica* 120, 1/2 (1998): 207–230.
"*Zukor* trailer in Paravision." *Today's Cinema* 80, 6709 (March 4, 1953): 26.

Online Resources

BBC Press Release on Queen Trailer: www.bbc.co.uk/pressoffice/pressreleases/stories/2007/07_july/12/apology.shtml
Bremen Semantic Video Pattern Project: www.tzi.de/svp/index.html

A Brief Trailer History: www.movietrailertrash.com/views/history.html
Cinerama Premiere Book: www.redballoon.net/~snorwood/book/index.html
Elizabethtown Official Site: www.elizabethtown.com
"First Pictures Nazi Rocket Bomb in U.S.": www.archive.org/details/1946-05-13_1st_Pictures_Nazi_Rocket_Bomb_in_US
London Underground "Video Posters": www.grandvisual.com
Lord of the Rings Fan Site: www.theonering.net
Star Wars Official Site: www.starwars.com
Star Wars Video Advertising: www.davisdvd.com/misc/starwars/ep4.htm
Trailer Mash Site: www.thetrailermash.com
ViewMaster Information: www.rollanet.org/~vbeydler/van/vmcolect.htm

DVD Resources

Coming Attractions: The History of the Movie Trailer (Kaleidoscope Creative Group, 2005).
Disney's Complete Classics Collection (Buena Vista, 2006).
Festival of 3-D Movie Trailers (SabuCat Productions, 2003).
42nd Street Forever: Volume 1 (Synapse Films, 2005).
42nd Street Forever: Volume 2: The Deuce (Synapse Films, 2006).
The Horror of Hammer (Umbrella Entertainment).
Pulp Cinema (All Day Entertainment, 2001).

Index

Numbers in ***bold italics*** indicate pages with photographs.

Abbott and Costello Go to Mars television trailers 74, 76
Abicair, Shirley 70–72
absent trailers 32, 37, 39, 42, 63–65
The Abyss 116; trailer 119
Academy Awards 98, 185n21, 185n22
Academy of Motion Picture Arts and Sciences (AMPAS) 98
The Ace of Space ***45***
active audience 39, 44, 181–182n22
Adams, Julie 72
Al Jolson in the Plantation Act 19
Alfie trailer 1
Alien: trailer 109, 111, 114, 117; widescreen video trailer 132, 135
Alien: Resurrection trailer 118
The All American television trailer 74
All I Desire television trailer 73
All the Right Moves video trailer 129–130
Allen, Robert 5–6, 8, 9, 11, 13
Allyson, June 56
American Gigolo (video release) 128
American International Pictures (AIP) 87
The American President trailer 121
Ames, Alan 66, 68–70, 72, 73
Anderson, Christopher 61–62
The Andromeda Strain 107
Anscocolour 16
Anthony and Cleopatra 167
Apollo 13 trailer 115, 118–119, 121, 154
Apple 141, 144, 146
Are You Being Served? 167
Armageddon trailer 118, 123
Ashberry, Simon 174–177
Associated Rediffusion 69

Associated Television (ATV) 69, 70
At the Earth's Core 167
audience immersion 27–28, 30–38, 44
audiences 3, 7, 9, 31, 120, 124, 127–128, 136, 144, 154; and control 124, 127, 131, 137, 143, 149, 151, 158; *see also* fan trailers; fandom; female audiences; interactivity
Away All Boats television trailers 69, 72, 81–82,

Bacall, Lauren ***54***, 54, 55
Back to the Future 126
Banks, Miranda J. 92
Barr, Charles 29
Barrett, Lionel 70
The Barretts of Wimpole Street trailer 57
Barrymore, Lionel 20
Battle Beyond the Stars trailer 109
Battle of the Bulge 170
Battleship Galactica 109
Bazin, André 29
Becky Sharp trailer 1, 31
Bedtime for Bonzo television trailer 67, 69, 79, 89, 138
behind the scenes footage 141, 142–143, 147, 151
Bell, Tim 69, 71
Belton, John 18, 29, 78, 79
Ben Hur 119, 170
Beneath the 12 Mile Reef trailer 27, 30, 170
The Benny Goodman Story television trailer 69, 72
Beowulf 3-D trailer 157
Bergman, Ingrid 6

Bernstein, David 69, 71
Betamax 127
The Big Sleep trailer 1
Binder, Maurice 165
The Black Hole 114
Black Narcissus 10
The Black Shield of Falworth television trailer 77, 78, 80
Black Widow television trailer 77–78, 81, 89
Blackmail 10
Bloom, Orlando 142
The Blue Lamp 7
Bogart, Humphrey 1, *2*, 6, 27
Bor, Mike 1–2
Bordwell, David 6, 91–92
Born Yesterday television trailers 66–69, 72, 73, 74, 75, 78, 79, 81, 84, 89, 154
Born Yesterday trailer 66
Boy on a Dolphin 170
Braveheart 139
Breen, Joseph 6
Bride of the Storm trailer 19
British Board of Film Classification (BBFC) 1–2, 165
British Broadcasting Corporation (BBC) 67, 69, 161
British Film Institute 9
British New Wave 8
Brokeback Mountain 150, 158
Brokeback to the Future (trailer parody) 150–151, 158
Brooks, Mel 129–130
Bubble trailer 24
Burton, Richard 52
Buscombe, Ed 61
Butch Cassidy and the Sundance Kid 131
Bwana Devil 42–43, 98

The Cannonball Run 131; video trailer 129–130, 131
Captain Lightfoot television trailer 78, 79, 138
Carlson, Richard 38, 39–41, **40**, 58
Carrey, Jim 21
Carroll, Noel 6
Casablanca 6, 155; trailer 51
Cat Women of the Moon trailer 48
CBS FOX video 129, 131, 132
CBS Video Enterprises 129
Chapman, James 10
Chariots of Fire video trailer 129–130
Charisse, Cyd 14, 16, 17
Chitty Chitty Bang Bang teaser trailer 88
Chretien, Henri 52
The Chronicles of Narnia: The Lion, the Witch and the Wardrobe 144; iPod trailer 147–148
Cinerama 22, 28, 30, 31–38, 41, 44, 49, 50, 51, 58, 92, 107–108, 124, 134, 157, 168–170; program 36, 169; projection issues 36, 168
CinemaScope 22, 27–31, 32, 38, 41, 46, 49–57, **55**, 58, 59, 60, 61, 63, 64, 66, 70, 74, 77–80, 89, 98, 103, 105, 124, **133**, 134, 150, 155, 157, 161, 166, 170, 180n35
CinemaScope 55 57
cinema slides 21, 70
Citizen Kane trailer 151
Clooney, George 156
Close Encounters of the Third Kind 92; trailer 109, 111, 114
Cochrane, Robert 153
Collins, Joan 56
color film production 1, 13, 16, 18, 21, 31, 65, 74, 101, 103, 121, 164, 180n35
Columbia 52, 67, 68, 73, 171, 172
Coming Attractions: The History of the Movie Trailer 18, 180n36
computer animation 110–111, 113–114, 129
computer generated imagery (CGI) 93, 114, 115–123, 129–130, 136, 139–140, 141–142, 148, 158
consumer culture 28
Costello, Dolores 19, 20
Cousteau, Jacques 30
Crafton, Donald 6, 11, 13
Crash Dive 99
Crawford, Broderick 66
Creative Partnerships 165
Creature from the Black Lagoon trailer 46; television trailer 76, 79
Crowe, Cameron 142
Current Release 62

Dahl, Arlene 47–48, **48**, 56
The Dark Knight 161
Davis, Bette 4, 27
Day of the Jackal 167
The Day the Earth Caught Fire television trailers 81–85, **83–84**, 87, 88, 89, 93, 120, 142
The Day the Earth Stood Still trailer 101, 104
Death on the Nile 167
Demetrius and the Gladiators 105
Destination Moon trailer 23, 93, **94**, 94–**97**, 100, 101, 103, 105, 106, 107, 109, 118, 119, 122
Devlin, Dean 117
Dial M for Murder trailer 46
Die Hard widescreen video trailer 132, 135
Disney Home Video 131

Disney Studio 30, 52, 62, 73, 147
Disneyland (television program) 62
dissolves 12, 166
Dr. Strangelove, or How I Learned to Stop Worrying and Love the Bomb trailers 81, 86–88, 89
Don Juan 19
Downhill trailer 19
Dracula trailer 1
Drums of Tahiti trailer 46
Duff, Al 82
Dune 116
Dunst, Kirsten 142
DVD 23–24, 123, 127, 135, 140, 142, 143–144, 153, 160–161

Earth vs. the Flying Saucers trailer 93, 94, 95, 98, **99**, **100**, 100–105, **102**, 111, 117, 122
Earthquake 119
Eastmancolor 16, 103
Ede, Laurie 10
Electric Blue 004 video 128–129
Elizabethtown online trailers 142, 151
Elsaesser, Thomas 5, 11, 154
Emmerich, Roland 117
The Empire Strikes Back 140; trailer 106, 112–113, 119, 128; video release 127, 129
Entertainment Software Ratings Board (ESRC) 161
E.T. The Extra Terrestrial 114
Ewell, Tom 57

Fall of the Rome Empire 166
fan trailers 126, 139–140, 158
fandom 125–126, 137–143, 150, 152, 158, 161
Fantasia SuperScope trailer 158
feature excerpts 62, 66, 69, 72, 73, 74–80, 82, 89, 136, 140
female audiences 98
female body in trailers 1, 38, 46–48, 56–57, 154
female sexuality in trailers 30, 38, 85, 154
Ferro, Pablo 87–88, 166
Fight Club Internet trailers 138–139, 140, 141, 144; lack of censorship 188n35
Flash Gordon 114, 167
Footloose 132
Forbidden Planet trailer 93, 95, 98, 103–105, 107, 108, 122
Force 10 from Navarone 167
Forrest Gump trailer 115, 120
The Four Musketeers 167
Francis, Anne 104–105
Frankenstein trailer 1
The French Line trailer 46

Friday the 13th Part III 49
The Frogmen television trailer 73

gender representation in trailers 14, 16–17, 30, 47–48, 154
General Screen Enterprises 165
genre (in trailers) 1, 3, 4, 12, 13, 21, 24, 36, 39, 46, 52, 57, 59, 76–77, 88, 104, 105, 107, 112, 113, 116, 118, 119, 122, 127, 128, 131, 142, 154, 155, 159, 161; *see also* science fiction trailers
George Lucas Presents "Singin' in the Rain" 150
Ghandi 167
Ghostbusters 114; link with music videos 132
The Giant Gila Monster trailer 106
Gibbs, John 7–8, 11, 13
Gladiator 93; trailer 120
Glancy, Mark 10
Godzilla trailer 121
Goldfinger trailers 87
Gomery, Douglas 5–6, 8, 9, 11, 127
Gone with the Wind 10, 119; "widescreen" trailer 157–158
Gorham, Maurice 67
Gorilla at Large trailer 48
Grable, Betty **54**, 54
Grand Prix trailer 32, 36–37, 170
graphic wipes (in trailers) 12, 16, 21, 27, 69, 155
Gray, Dolores 56
The Great American Past-time trailer 57
The Great Rupert 97, 185n17
Greystoke 167
The Guinea Pig 7
Guns of Navarone 166

Hallelujah Trail 170
Hammer Horror trailer collection 161
Happy Feet 3-D trailer 157
Haralovich, Mary Beth 4, 8, 14
Harper, Sue 10, 14
Harris, Esther 163, 165
Harry Potter and the Order of the Phoenix 157
Harryhausen, Ray **99**, 103
Hays, Will 19
Hayworth, Rita 48
Heartbreak Ridge video release 131
Hediger, Vinzenz 179n4, 180n35
Help! 166
Higson, Andrew 8
Hitchcock, Alfred 167
The Hitchhiker's Guide to the Galaxy online trailer 142–143, 149, 160

Holden, William 66
Holliday, Judy 66
Hollywood Flashes 73
Hollywood star system 1, 3
Holmes, Su 61, 62–63
Hondo trailer 46
Hopkins, Miriam 31
House of Wax trailer 44, 47, 49
How the West Was Won trailer 32–36, 58, 59, 93, 120, 154, 168–170
How to Marry a Millionaire 78, 89; trailer 49–56, **50**, **55**, 58, 59
Hurst, Veronica 41

I Wanted Wings 99
illustrated radio 65, 66, 70
IMAX 3-D 157
The Incredible World of James Bond (Trailers) 128
The Incredibles 174
Independence Day 93; trailer 94, 115, 116–118, 120, 121, 122, 123, 187n52
Industrial Light and Magic (ILM) 107, 109, 112, 114
interactivity 126, 137, 139–140, 149–151
internet 2, 3, 9, 21, 23, 24, 120, 123, 124, 125–126, 136–143, 145–146, 149–151, 160–161; production diaries 141–142; trailers 136–143, 145–146, 149, 157 (*see also* fan trailers)
Internet Movie Database (imdb) 159, 161
intimacy in television trailers 66, 82, 86; in video trailers 127
Invaders from Mars 100, 105
Invasion of the Body Snatchers trailer 105–106
iPhone 150
iPod 24, 123, 124, 125, 143–149, 150–152, 153, 156, 161; trailers 132, 146–149, 151
It Came from Outer Space trailer 38, 39–41, **40**, **42**, **43**, 46, 49, 58, 59; inter-titles 39, 41–42, 182n29
It Started with a Kiss trailer 57
It's a Mad Mad Mad Mad World 170

Jackson, Peter 141–142
Jacobs, Jason 63–64, 90
Jacqueline television trailer 69–73, 79, 80, 81, 89
Jancovich, Mark 127
Jaws 3-D 49
The Jazz Singer 6, 15; trailer 18–20, **19**, 27, 31, 47, 155, 157
Jenkins, Henry 125–126, 151
Jeopardy television trailers 72, 74

Jesse James vs. the Daltons trailer 46
Jessel, George 20
Jezebel trailer 4
Jivaro trailer 46
Jobs, Steve 147
Johnston, Erskine 79, 138
Jolson, Al 15, 19, 20, 31
Judd, Edward 83, 84
Jurassic Park 92; trailer 116, 117

Kaleidoscope 132
Kelly, Gene 13–16, 154
Kernan, Lisa 4, 8, 18, 23, 61
Key Largo trailer 55
Kilbride, Percy 67–68, 138
King, Geoff 92
King Kong trailer 94, 95, 116
King Kong (2005 remake) 142; iPod trailer 144, 147
Kiss Me Kate trailer 46
Klaprat, Cathy Root 4–5, 8
Klinger, Barbara 3, 12, 120, 153, 154
Kneale, Nigel 65, 66
Knights of the Round Table trailer 54, 134
Kubrick, Stanley 86–88, 166, 167
Kuehn, Andrew J. 132, 180n36

Lady and the Tramp 62
The Ladykillers 7
Lamas, Fernando 47–48, **48**
laserdisc 127, 135
Lawrence of Arabia 59, 170
Lazarus, Paul N. 121–122, 171–173
letterboxing 77, 139, 145–146, 147, 150; *see also* pan and scan
Lewis, Howard T. 1
London International Film Festival 147
London Underground video posters 153, 156–158
The Longest Day 131
The Lord of the Rings trilogy 125, 141, 147, 151; online trailer 141–142, 147–148
The Lost World trailer 94, 95, 116
Lucas, George 106, 126, 136, 139, 160
Lucasfilm 136, 141, 158, 175

Magnetic Video 129, 187–188n13
The Making of Star Wars video 128
The Maltese Falcon trailer 1, **2**
Maltby, Robert 6, 8, 155
The Man in the Grey Flannel Suit television trailer 69
Marie Antoinette 144; iPod trailer 148–149, 154
Marked Woman trailer 4

Marling, Karel Ann 62
Mary Poppins 158
M*A*S*H 131
Master and Commander: The Far Side of the World 10
master of ceremonies trailer 20, 39–40, 45, 67
The Matrix 160
The Maze trailer 41, 44–45, 49, 154
McAvoy, Mary 20
McKern, Leo 83, 184n
Medhurst, Andy 1
Meet Joe Black 136
Meet the Robinsons 3-D trailer 157
Men in Black trailer 118, 123
Menace II Society 10
Metro-Goldwyn-Mayer (MGM) 13–16, 33, 36, 45, 52, 103–104, 168, 170
Miljan, John 18–20, **19**, 155
mise-en-scène analysis 7–8, 10, 11, 13, 16, 114, 155
Miss Sadie Thompson trailer 48
mobile media players 23, 126, 149
mobile phones 23, 123, 126, 143- 151, 157
Monroe, Marilyn 54–56, **54**, **55**, 154
Monster from Green Hell trailer 106
montage editing 29, 82, 85, 86, 108; in internet trailers 132, 137, 138, 142–143, 150, 151, 158, 159
motion control 109–112, 119, 186n34
Motion Picture Association of America (MPAA) 161
Movietone newsreels 96
MTV 132
The Mummy trailer 1
Munby, Jonathan 10, 155
Munro, Janet 83, 84
music videos 129, 132, 142, 147, 148–149, 151
My Fair Lady 131
MySpace 137, 150

National Broadcasting Company (NBC) 67, 89
National Screen Service 45, 70, 163–167, 171–173
Neale, Steve 21, 91
negative perception of trailers 1–2
New Film History (Elsaesser) 5
The New Film History 8–11, 155
New Line Cinema 141
newsreel footage in trailers **94**, 94–96, 101–102, 105
Nielson, Leslie 104–105
Noah's Ark trailer 49, 94, 119

Norton, Edward 138–139
Novello, Ivor 19

Ocean's 13 trailer 156, 157
O'Connor, Donald 13–16
An Officer and a Gentleman video trailer 128
The Omega Man 107
The Opposite Sex trailer 56
optical printing 18
Orange 144–146, 174–177, 189n46
Orphan of Paris trailer 70

Pacino, Al 156
Pal, George 94, 96–97, 99, 100, 106, 107, 114, 117, 119, 123, 185n17
pan and scan 63, 77–79, 89, 130, 133, 135, 150; *see also* letterboxing
Panavision 32, 57, 58, 170
Paramount 20, 105, 110, 185n17
Paramount Decree 15, 28
Peck, Gregory 35
The Perfect Storm trailer 115, 120–121, 123
Perkins, V.F. 8
Peter Pan 62
Peterson, Colin 70–71
The Petrified Forest trailer 1
The Phantom of the Opera trailer 109
Phillips, Julia 110
Phillips, Michael 110
Picture Parade 62, 63
Picture Production Company 165
Pidgeon, Walter 104
Pillow Talk television trailer 87
Pirates of the Caribbean 59
Pitt, Brad 138–139
Pleasantville trailer 121, 187n58
pornography trailers 126, 128–129, 187n10
poster advertising 3, 46–47, 117, 118, 120, 121, 154, 165, 171–172
press books 3, 10, 29, 118
Production Code Administration (PCA) 6, 155
Psycho trailer 1
The Public Enemy trailer 151

Quicktime 126, 140–141, 146
Quiz Show trailer 1

radio production practices 64, 72
Raft, George 27
Raiders of the Lost Ark 114
Rank Organisation 70, 165
Real Player 8 141
Rebel Without a Cause 29
reception studies 3, 7, 9, 12, 153, 161

Reed, Donna 72
Return of the Jedi 136, 140; 1989 video release 131–132
Revenge of the Creature 46
Reynolds, Debbie 13–14, 16–17
Richards, Jeffrey 6–7, 8, 10, 11
The Right Stuff video release 131; trailer 187n56
River of No Return 29
Robbins, Herman 171
Robby the Robot 104–105, 154
The Robe 105; trailer 52–53, 98
Robin Hood 131
Rocky Balboa trailer 157
Rush, Barbara 40–41
Russell, Jane 46–47, 48
Ryan's Daughter 10

San Diego Comic Con 142
Sangaree trailer 47–48, **48**, 49, 154
Scary Mary trailer parody 158
Scott, Randolph 48
science fiction trailers 91–123, 127–128, 131
Screen Gems 67, 68
Screen Opticals 163, 165
Selznick, David O. 62
sepia tinted-film in television trailers 66, 68
711 Ocean Drive television trailer 73
Seven Wonders of the World trailer 33–34, 37, 51, 169
Seymour, Bill 163–167
Shatner, William 110
Sheridan, Ann 56
The Shining 158
Shrek 174
The Siege 136
Sign of the Pagan television trailer 78
Simmons, Jean 52
Singin' in the Rain trailer 12–17, 154
The Singing Fool trailer 20
Sittig, John 34, 51, 168–170
Sleeping Beauty 131
Smiley television trailer 70–72, **71**, 81, 89, 154
Sobchack, Vivian 92, 102
Soderbergh, Steven 24
The Sound of Music 131
South Pacific 170
Soylent Green 107
Spartacus television trailers 81, 85–86, 87, 88, 89, 142
special effects 21, 22, 91–123, **102**, 126, 130, 136, 139–140, 141, 144, 155, 185n20, 186n39; and production schedules 105, 106, 110–112, 114, 115, 119, 122

Spielberg, Steven 110
spoilers 137, 143; definition 188n34
Staiger, Janet 3, 161
Stanwyck, Barbara 72
star images in trailers 1, **2**, 3–4, 9, 12–13, 14, 17–18, 19, 20–21, 24, 31, 35, 36, 39, 46, 52, 53, 54–57, 59, 67, 72, 88, 99, 104, 110, 154, 155, 156, 159; technology as star 27–28, 30–59, 124; special effects star 94, 96–97, 107, 110–111, 114, 115, 117, 123, 136, 144, 185n10
Star Trek: The Motion Picture trailers 106, 108–109, 110–112, 114, 115, 122
Star Trek II: The Wrath of Khan trailer 106, 112–114, 116
Star Wars 92, 93, 106–109, 112, 114, 119, 125–126, 131, 140, 142, 143, 147; trailer 23, 59, 106–109, 110, 111, 112, 115, 117, 122, 186n35; in 3-D 158; video trailer 127–130, 144; *see also The Empire Strikes Back; Return of the Jedi*
Star Wars Episode 1: The Phantom Menace trailer 118, 136; DVD release 140; Internet release 136–138, 141, 142
Star Wars Episode 2: Attack of the Clones Internet trailer 140–141, 149; fan trailer 139–140, 150
Star Wars Episode 3: Revenge of the Sith teaser trailer 144–145, 154; mobile phone trailer 144–146, 148, 149, 174–176
Star Wars Trilogy widescreen trailer 132–134, 135, 145, 150, 188n24
Starship Troopers trailer 118
stereophonic sound 22, 52, 58, 60, 64, 74, 133, 170
Stereophonic Sound and Picture Test 52
Stewart, Jimmy 21, 35
Stokes, Mervyn 10
The Stranger Wore a Gun trailer 48
Street, Sarah 10, 155
Sullivan, Barry 72
Sullivan, Ed 69
Superman Returns 142, 157; on videophones 176
SuperPanavision 36
SuperScope 158
synchronized sound 18–21, 31, 155

Taylor, B.F. 7–8, 11, 13, 154
Taza, Son of Cochise trailer 46
Technicolor 1, 13, 14, 16, 17, 22, 31, **45**, 76, 95, 99, 164
Technirama 170
television 15, 16, 21, 22, 24, 28, 59, 60–90, 92, 98, 101, 107, 120, 121, 124, 130, 132,

134, 143–144, 147, 149, 151, 153, 154, 155, 157, 161, 166; commercials 67, 69, 74; technology 65, 66–68, 74; trailers 60–90, 91, 113, 117, 118, 120, 121, 127, 130, 138, 142
The Ten Commandments 119; trailer 1
The Terminator 115
Terminator 2: Judgment Day trailer 23, 115–116, 118, 121
The Thief of Baghdad 99
The Thing 114
The Thing from Another World 100, 109
Thirty Seconds Over Tokyo 99
This Is Cinerama 31, 32, 36, 37, 50, 169
Thomas, Lowell 31
Thompson, Kristin 91–92
Those Redheads from Seattle trailer 48
Three Coins in the Fountain trailer 51, 54, 170
3-D 22, 24, 28, 30–31, 32, 38–49, **40, 42, 43**, 50, 52, 56, 57, 58, 59, 60, 61, 63, 64, 66, 74–77, 78, 79, 89, 91, 98, 157–158, 161; inter-titles 39, 41–42, **43**, 182*n*29; projection 42–43, 158
Thunderball trailers 87
The Time Machine trailer 106
Titanic 59, 92; trailer 120, 122
To Be or Not to Be video trailer 129–130
Toast of the Town 69
Todd-AO 57, 58, 170
Top Gun 114; link with music videos 132; 1987 video release of 131
The Towering Inferno 119
trailers: demographic targeting in 88; gallery (or "trailer park") 129–131, 135; inter-titles 12, 13, 18, 21, 27, 41–42, **43**, 53–54, 58, 73, 83, **84**, 136, 167, 182*n*29, 182*n*35; mobility 124–152; parodies 150–151, 158; soundtrack 12, 13, 17, 18–21, 47, 52, 65, 68, 70, 71–72, 74, 76, 79, 81, 82, 87, 89, 96, 113, 115, 118–119, 128, 129, 130, 131–132, 134, 138, 142–143, 156, 188*n*36; importance in videophone and iPod trailers 144–145, 147, 148, 151 (*see also* voiceover [female], voiceover [male]); temporality 4–5, 23–24, 124, 125, 127, 135, 157–158
Transporter 2 159–160
travelogue imagery 32–37, 50–51, 53, 57, 59
Trevor, Claire 48
Tron 116
The True Story of Jesse James 29
Trumbull, Douglas 110, 114
TV ... Wide Vision and Stereophonic Sound trailer 60, 64, 89

20th Century–Fox 10, 20, 27, 30, 50, 52, 53, 57, 58, 70, 77, 78, 112, 116, 117, 171
20th Century–Fox Video 129, 134
20,000 Leagues Under the Sea 30, 62
2001: A Space Odyssey 92, 110; trailer 36, **37**, 107–108, **108**, 170

unified analysis 11–17, 19–22, 24–25, 28, 30–59, 60–90, 91–123, 125–152, 154, 156, 160, 161
United Artists 52, 171
Universal 1, 45, 60, 73, 81–82, 85, 96, 119
University of Bremen Semantic Video Pattern (SVP) project 158–160

VHS 127
video 23–24, 123, 124–137, 143, 149, 153, 164; billboards 156–158, 190*n*8
The Video Collection 131
Videodisc 127
video games: consoles 23, 153, 161; trailers 161
video graphics 129–130
video trailers 124, 127–136, 137, 164; intimacy 127; placement 187*n*12
Video 2000 127
videophones 124, 132, 143–146, 147, 149–151, 155, 156, 161, 174; limitations of screen 144–145, 189*n*54
Viewmaster(r) 45
Vista Vision 57, 58
visual spectacle 12, 21, 22, 23, 32, 53–57, 86, 91–123, **108**, 125, 128, 131, 132, 138, 159–160; lack of spectacle in videophone trailers 144–145
Vitaphone 18–20, **19**, 22, 31
voiceovers: female 47–48, 71–72, 87; male 1, 52, 66, 69, 72, 76, 82, 87, 96, 110, 115, 129, 134
V2 rockets 96, 97, 98, 101, 186*n*23

Wallis, Hal 6
War of the Worlds trailer 105, 106, 107
Warner Bros. 5, 9, 19–20, 52, 62, 160, 171, 172, 176
Warner Bros. Presents 62
Warner Home Video 131
websites 120, 123, 125, 137–143, 147
Welles, Orson 110
When Worlds Collide trailer 105, 107, 119
widescreen 18, 21, 22, 24, 27–38, 49–59, 60, 62–63, 64, 74, 77–80, 86, 91, 101, 124, 126, 127, 132–135, 136, 139, 145, 147, 149, 150, 166, 175, 181*n*5; *see also* Cin-

erama; CinemaScope; Panavision; Todd-AO
widescreen excerpts on television 62, 75, 77–80
widescreen video 126, 127, 132–135
Williams, John 131, 133
Wings of the Hawk television trailers 75, 79, 89; demographic targeting in 84–85

The Wonderful World of the Brothers Grimm trailer 32, 34, 35, 168–169

YouTube 137, 146, 150, 161, 177

Zanuck, Daryl 52, 53, 55
Zulu 166

www.ingramcontent.com/pod-product-compliance
Lightning Source LLC
Chambersburg PA
CBHW020859020526
44116CB00029B/710